JUST BEFORE DARK

JUST BEFORE DARK

COLLECTED NONFICTION BY

JIM HARRISON

HOUGHTON MIFFLIN / SEYMOUR LAWRENCE

BOSTON · NEW YORK · LONDON

PUBLISHED BY ARRANGEMENT
WITH CLARK CITY PRESS.

LIBRARY OF CONGRESS CATALOGING-IN-PUBLICATION DATA
Harrison, Jim, date.
[Selections. 1992]
Just before dark : collected nonfiction / by Jim Harrison.
p.   cm.
ISBN 0-395-61329-9
I. Title.
PS3558.A67A6 1992
814'.54 — dc20   91−33168
                                                      CIP

PRINTED IN THE UNITED STATES OF AMERICA

MP 10 9 8 7 6 5 4 3 2 1

To Steve, Jamie, and Will

The worst of all things is not to live in a physical world.
WALLACE STEVENS

CONTENTS

Introduction

There is something quite comic involved in the process of editing, to wit, the notion that a successful self-editor should end up with nothing at all. Everything written in the past should be discarded in favor of the free flow of what is at hand. Life, anyway, is an immutable disappearing act. Pitch the manuscript and catch a plane. That sort of thing.

But then cautionary good sense tells us that to publish is to rid ourselves of a burden and offer it to someone else, pleasant or not. In this case the burden began as seven hundred pages which was reduced to half of that. The effort was not to sanitize the past but to present experiences that were more fully realized in the writing. The only piece about which my mixed feelings still run deep is called "A Natural History of Some Poems" in the "Literary Matters" section. I view this as juvenilia, of interest only to assistant professors, should my work prove durable. My choice of a publisher far from the centers of ambition was based on wishing to avoid the enervating hoopla that tends to accompany the publication of books in New York.

It had occurred to me early, by the mid-sixties in fact, that I was temperamentally unsuited for teaching, the usual career of a literary writer. I hadn't thought it through at the time but the real reason for the brevity of my teaching career was that the universities I admired were so far from the woods and water I had emotionally depended on since my youth. To earn a living for my family I began an essentially quadra-schizoid existence, continuing to write the poems I had begun with and adding all matter of journalism, novels, and screenplays.

When a writer lifts his obsessed and frazzled head from the work there is frequently what Walker Percy called "the reentry problem." Literary history abounds with cases of multi-addiction and personal mayhem of the most childish sort. To put it modestly, I have not been consistently innovative in avoiding the usual problems, but have tried to counter them with equal obsessions for the natural world, fishing, hunting, the study of Native Americans, cooking, the practice of Zen, not as a religion but as an attitude. "To study the self is to forget the self and become one with ten thousand things," said Dogen.

When you lift your head from the work you want to return to earth, simply enough. Just recently I visited the Animas Mountains in New Mexico where I explored the Gray Ranch, a five-hundred-square-mile spread acquired last year by the Nature Conservancy. In my journal I wrote: "Before making camp on Double Adobe Creek I headed up a feeder creek, the dense riparian thicket of a long, narrow canyon. I felt a wonderfully mindless eagerness toward exploring the new territory, a palpable return to the curiosity of childhood when the responses to the natural world are visceral. The pulse races at an unrecognized welter of tracks (javelina), then softens, determining where mule deer and a single, large bobcat stopped to drink. Walking at twilight owns the same eeriness of dawn. The world belongs again to its former prime tenants, the creatures, and within the dimming light and crisp shadows you return to your own creature life that is so easily and ordinarily discarded. I have always loved best this time just before dark when the antennae stretch far and caressingly from the body. I heard the flap of a raven's wings before I saw it, and exchanged a series of greetings before heading back."

Of course today's serenity easily slips into tomorrow's nonsense. To become prematurely autumnal is to lose the writer's most cherished possession—the negative capability that keeps the work's heart pumping. Perhaps, as someone said, there are no truths, only stories. I began as a young poet, standing on the roof looking at the moon and stars, smelling and listening to the swamp out back, dreaming the world. As a middle-aged poet, an identity that seems undisturbed, I have seen much of the world and am trying to dream myself back to where I already am. Midway between these two points I wrote a series of poems that took the form of letters addressed to Yesenin, a long-dead Russian poet I admired. This one in particular shows some of the character of the journey of the book that follows:

from LETTERS TO YESENIN, NO. 22

These last few notes to you have been a bit somber like biographies
of artists written by joyless people so that the whole book is
a record of agony at thirty rather than thirty-three and a third.
You know the sound—Keeeaaattts wuzzzz verrrry unhapppppppy abouttt
dyinnnng. So here are some of those off the wall extravagancies.
Dawn in Ecuador with mariachi music, dawn at Ngorongoro with elephant
far below in the crater swagging through the marsh grass, dawn in
Moscow and snowing with gold minarets shouting that you have at last
reached Asia, dawn in Addis Ababa with a muslim waver in the cool
air smelling of ginger and a lion roaring on the lawn, dawn in
bleery Paris with a roll tasting like zinc and a girl in a cellophane
blouse staring at you with four miraculous eyes, dawn in Normandy
with a conceivable princess breathing in the next room and horses
wandering across the moat beneath my window, dawn in Montana with
herons calling from the swamp, dawn in Key West wondering if it was
a woman or tarpon that left your bed before cockcrow, dawn at home
when your eyes are molten and the ghost of your dog chases the fox
across the pasture, dawn on the Escanaba with trout dimpling the
mist and the water with a dulcet roar, dawn in London when the party
girl leaves your taxi to go home to Shakespeare, dawn in Leningrad
with the last linden leaves falling and you knocking at the door
for a drunken talk but I am asleep. Not to speak of the endless and
nearly unconscious water walks after midnight when even the stars
might descend another foot to get closer to earth. Heat. The wetness
of air. Couplings. Even the mosquitoes are lovely and seem to imitate
miniature birds. And a lion's cough is followed rhythmically by a
hyena's laugh to prove that nature loves symmetry. The black girl
leaves the grand hotel for her implausibly shabby home. The poet
had dropped five sorts of drugs in his belly swill of alcohol and
has imagined his deathless lines commemorating your last Leningrad night.

Livingston, Montana
February 15, 1991

FOOD

Eat or die.

Mikhail Lermontov

Sporting Food

Small portions are for small and inactive people. When it was all the rage, I was soundly criticized for saying that *cuisine minceur* was the moral equivalent of the fox-trot. Life is too short for me to approach a meal with the mincing steps of a Japanese prostitute. The craving is for the genuine rather than the esoteric. It is far better to avoid expense-account restaurants than to carp about them. Who wants to be a John Simon of the credit-card feedbag? I'm afraid that eating in restaurants reflects our experiences with movies, art galleries, novels, music: that is, experiences that inspire mild amusement but mostly a feeling of stupidity and shame. Better to cook for yourself.

I eye the miniature Lake Superior brook trout I have grilled over an oak fire, the sliced tomatoes, fresh corn, and wild leeks vinaigrette, and think back to a winter day when it was a few degrees above zero and I was out on the ice of Bay de Noc near Escanaba in the Upper Peninsula of Michigan, beyond the last of the fish shanties. It doesn't matter how far but rather how long it took to get there—an hour out and an hour back to my hotel, the House of Ludington. Unfortunately, I was caught in a whiteout, a sudden snow squall out of the northwest, and I couldn't see anything but my hands and cross-country skis, a short, broad type called Bushwhackers, which allow you to avoid the banality of trails. I turned myself around and tried to retrace my path, but it had quickly become covered with the fresh snow. I had to stand there and wait it out because the evening before a tanker and a Coast Guard icebreaker had come into the harbor, which meant there was a long path of open water or some very thin ice out there in the utter whiteness. I would most certainly die if I fell in, and that would mean, among other things, that I would miss a good dinner, and that's what I was doing out here in the first place—earning, or deserving, dinner.

I became very cold in the half an hour or so that it took for the air to clear.

I thought about food and listened to the plane high above, which was circling and presumably looking for the airport. With the first brief glimpse of shore in the swirling snow, I creaked into action, and each shoosh of ski spoke to me: Oysters, snails, maybe a lobster or the *Kasseler Rippchen*, the braised lamb shanks, a simple porterhouse or Delmonico, with a bottle or two of the Firestone Merlot or the Freemark Abbey Cabernet I had for lunch . . .

The idea is to eat well and not die from it—for the simple reason that that would be the end of my eating. I have to keep my cholesterol count down. There is abundant dreariness in even the smallest health detail. Skip butter and desserts, and toss all the obvious fat to the bird dogs. But as for the dinner that was earned by the brush with death, it was honest rather than great. As with Chinese food, any Teutonic food, in this case smoked pork loin, seems to prevent the drinking of good wine. In general, I don't care for German wines for the same reason I don't like the smell down at the Speedy Car Wash, but perhaps both are acquired tastes. The fact is, the meal required a couple of Heileman's Exports, even Budweisers, but that occurred to me only later.

Until recently, my home base in Leelanau County, in northern Michigan, was over sixty miles from the nearest first-rate restaurant, twice the range of the despised and outmoded atomic cannon. This calls for resourcefulness in the kitchen, or what the Tenzo in a Zen monastery would call "skillful means." I keep an inventory taped to the refrigerator of my current frozen possibilities: local barnyard capons; the latest shipment of prime veal from Summerfield Farms, which includes sweetbreads, shanks for *osso bucco*, liver, chops, kidneys; and a little seafood from Charles Morgan in Destin, Florida—triggerfish, a few small red snappers, conch for chowder and fritters. There are two shelves of favorites—rabbit, grouse, woodcock, snipe, venison, dove, chukar, duck, quail—and containers of fish fumet, various glacés, and stocks, including one made from sixteen woodcock that deserves its own armed guard. I also traded my alfalfa crop for a whole steer, which is stored at my secretary's home because of lack of space.

In other words, it is important not to be caught short. It is my private opinion that many of our failures in politics, art, and domestic life come from our failure to eat vividly, though for the time being I will lighten up on this pet theory. It is also one of the writer's neuroses not to want to repeat himself—I recently combed a five-hundred-page galley proof of a novel, terrified that I may have used a specific adjective twice—and this urge toward variety in food can be enervating. If you want to be loved by your family and friends, it is important not to drive them crazy.

The flip side of the Health Bore is, after all, the Food Bully. Several years ago, when my oldest daughter visited from New York City, I overplanned and finally drove her to tears and illness by Christmas morning (grilled woodcock and truffled eggs). At the time, she was working at Dean & Deluca, so a seven-day feast was scarcely necessary. (New Yorkers, who are anyway a thankless lot, have no idea of the tummy thrills and quaking knees an outlander feels when walking into Dean & Deluca, Balducci's, Zabar's, Manganaro's, Lobel's, Schaller & Weber, etc.) I respected my daughter's tears, albeit tardily, having been brought to a similar condition by Orson Welles over a number of successive meals at Ma Maison, the last of which he "designed" and called me at dawn with the tentative menu as if he had just written the Ninth Symphony. We ate a half-pound of beluga with a bottle of Stolichnaya, a salmon in sorrel sauce, sweetbreads *en croûte*, and a miniature leg of lamb (the whole thing) with five wines, desserts, cheeses, ports. I stumbled to the toilet and rested my head in a greasy faint against the tiled walls. Welles told me to avoid hat-check girls, since they always prefer musicians. That piece of wisdom was all that Warner Brothers got for picking up the tab.

Later, John Huston told me he and Welles were always trying to stick each other with the tab and once faked simultaneous heart attacks at a restaurant in Paris. In many respects, Orson Welles was the successor to the Great Curnonsky, Prince of Gourmands. This thought occurred to me as I braced my boots against the rocker panel to haul the great director from his limousine.

When my oldest daughter, who had since moved to Montana (where the only sauce is a good appetite), came home to plan her wedding, her mother cautioned the Food Bully, threatening the usual fire extinguisher full of lithium which we keep in the kitchen for such purposes. While dozing, I heard my daughter go downstairs to check out the diminishing wine cellar. (I can't hear an alarm clock, but I can hear this.) Certain bottles had been preserved for a few guests the evening before the wedding: a '49 Latour, a '61 Lafite, a '47 Meursault (turned, but the disappointment was festive), a '69

Yquem, and a couple of '68 Heitz Martha's Vineyards for a kicker. It was a little bizarre to consider that these bottles are worth more than I made the year my daughter was born.

That first late evening, we fed her a winter vegetable soup with plenty of beef shanks and bone marrow. By the next evening, she was soothed enough for quail stuffed with lightly braised sweetbreads, followed by some gorgeous roasted wood ducks. This meal was a tad heavy, so we spent the next afternoon making some not-exactly-airy cannelloni from scratch. Later, I pieced up two rabbits and put them in a marinade of ample amounts of Tabasco and a quart of buttermilk, using the rabbit scraps to make half a cup of stock. The recipe is an altered version of a James Villas recipe for chicken (attribution is important in cooking).

The next evening, we floured and fried the rabbit, serving it with a sauce of the marinade, stock, and the copious brown bits from the skillet. I like the dish best with simple mashed potatoes and succotash made from frozen tiny limas and corn from the garden. The rabbit gave me a thickish feeling, so the next day I broiled two small red snappers with a biting Thai hot-and-sour sauce, which left me refreshingly hungry by midnight. My wife had preserved some lemon, so I went to the cellar for a capon as she planned a Paula Wolfert North African dish. Wolfert and Villas are food people whom you tend to "believe" rather than simply admire. In this same noble lineage is the recent *Honey from a Weed* by Patience Gray (Harper & Row), a fabulous cookbook. Gray's a wandering Bruce Chatwin of food.

Naturally, I had been floundering through the deep snow an hour or two a day with my bird dogs in order to deserve such meals. But enough was enough. I hadn't exactly been saving up for the big one. A cautionary note here, something Jack Nicholson said to me more than a decade ago after I had overfed a group in his home: "Only in the Midwest is overeating still considered an act of heroism." Still, I find it important to go on with eating, not forgetting the great Lermontov's dictum: eat or die.

So I eye the brook trout again and consider my options. It is almost the fall bird season, when the true outer limits of my compulsion are tested. Perhaps when winter comes I will resume running at night, all night long across frozen lakes, trying to avoid the holes left by the ice fishermen.

1988

Meals of Peace and Restoration

I believe it was the late John Wayne who said, "It pushes a man to the wall if he stands there in the buff and looks straight down and can't even see his own weenie." I *think* it was John Wayne who said that. However, I'm a poet and a novelist, not a John Wayne authority, and so what if I'm a tad burly? In my childhood we prayed every evening for the starving children in Europe, causing a primitive fear of hunger. There are also the scars from my youthful New York City art wars, when I thought I was Arthur Rimbaud and the average dumpster ate better than I did. And then there is the notion of the French surrealist poet Alfred Jarry: "I eat, or someone will eat in my place." In any case, I have decided it is time to escape the sodden mysteries of personality and try to help other folks. Not that I really wish to become the Baba Ram Jim of food advice, but something calls me to offer a handful of garlic along the way.

Times have changed. We have seen the passing of the blackjack and the accordion. Few of us sing alone on our porches on summer evenings, watching the sexual dance of fireflies in the burdocks beside the barn. The buzz of the airport metal detector is more familiar than the sound of the whippoorwill or coyote. The world gets to you with its big, heavy, sharp-toed boot. We are either "getting ready" or "getting over." Our essential and hereditary wildness slips, crippled, into the past. The jackhammer poised daily at our temples is not fictive, nor is the fact that all the ceilings have lowered, and the cold ozone that leaks under the door is merely a signal that the old life is over. There is a Native American prophecy that the end is near when trees die from their tops down (acid rain).

To be frank, this is not the time for the "less is more" school when it comes to eating. The world as we know it has always been ending, every day of our lives. Good food and good cooking are a struggle for the appropriate and, as such, a response to the total environment. Anyone who has spent an afternoon in New York has seen the sullen and distraught faces of those who have eaten julienned jicama with raspberry vinaigrette and a glass of European water for lunch.

But let's not dwell on the negative, the wine of illusion. You begin with simple truths in food: for instance, peeling sweetbreads is not really exercise. When you're trimming a two-pound porterhouse, don't make those false, hyperkinetic motions favored by countermen in delicatessens. Either trim it or skip trimming. Eat the delicious fat and take a ten-mile walk. Reach into your memory and look for what has restored you, what helps you recover from the sheer hellishness of life, what food actually regenerates your system, not so you can leap tall buildings but so you can turn off the alarm clock with vigor. Chances are you will come up with something Latin—I mean food that is quite different from our own in areas of fruit growth, food from a place where garlic and flowers abound, where there are blue water and hot sun. At the bottom of dampish arroyos are giant butterflies and moths, extravagantly plumed birds that feed on the remains of lightning and sunbeams, the unique maggots that feed only on the spleens of road kill. Farther up the cliffs, where the cacti are sparser, rattlers sun themselves. At first you are uncomfortable, then disarmed by the way the snakes contract over hot coals. They are particularly good with the salsa that goes by the brand name Pace.

Last March I was hiking out of the Seri Indian country, south of Caborca along the Sea of Cortés, with Douglas Peacock, the fabled grizzly-bear expert. We were both out of sorts: he, because he can't seem to make a living; I, because my sinus pain was so extreme that I had to bash my head against the car door and specific boulders we passed. Luckily, we were able to dig a full bushel of clams at a secret estuary and make a hearty chowder with a pound of chilies and garlic, which started me on the road to recovery. Broiled tripe from an unborn calf helped, as did giant Guaymas shrimp. After this infusion of health I was able to dance five hours with a maiden who resembled a beige bowling ball. She was, in fact, shaped rather like me. In the morning my clothes were crisp from exertion; my head, bell clear. The world seemed new again—like a warm rain after a movie.

One late-November night, on the Navajo reservation in Arizona, I was camping out with two old men who I was reasonably sure were witches, although kind witches. I was researching a film on the life of Edward Curtis and that morning had received word that the studio had fired me again. But that night there was a big moon through the intermittent snow, and above the fire a *posole* was cooking, with its dark freight of several different chiles, a head of garlic, sun-dried hominy, and the neck, ribs, and shanks of a young goat. After eating the *posole*, we hiked in the moonlight, and one of the old men showed me his raven and coyote imitations, jumping in bounds the length of which would have shamed Carl Lewis.

Posole is a generic dish, and I've eaten dozens of versions and made an equal number of my own. The best are to be found in Mexico. *Menudo* is a similar dish and a fabulous restorative, the main ingredient being tripe. I would offer specific recipes, but you should immediately buy *Authentic Mexican* by Rick and Deann Bayless, published by William Morrow. And if you are in Chicago, you can literally eat your way through the book at their splendid restaurant, Frontera Grill. I've made a good start on the project.

Curiously, though, *menudo* has specific effects around which you can design a day. Picture yourself waking on Sunday morning with a terminal hangover and perhaps a nosebleed, though the latter has fallen from favor. You have a late-afternoon assignation with a fashion model you don't want to disappoint with shakes and vomiting rather than love. Just eat a couple of bowls of *menudo* sprinkled with chopped cilantro and scallions, wild Sonoran *chiltepines*, and a squeeze of lemon. The results are guaranteed by the tripe cartel, which has not yet been a victim of arbitrage.

Last fall I felt intense sympathy for a friend, Guy de la Valdène, who was arriving in Michigan for bird season after a circuitous road trip through Missouri, Iowa, and Minnesota. If you've ever passed through them, you doubtless know that these are not food states. On the phone I could tell that Valdène's spirit was utterly broken, so three days before his arrival I began making Paula Wolfert's *salmis de cuisses de canard*, from her *Cooking of South-West France*. Since there were to be two of us, I increased the recipe, using nineteen duck legs and thighs, a couple of heads of garlic, two pounds of lean salt pork (homemade by my butcher), a half-cup of Armagnac, a bottle of Echêzeaux, and so on. (Wolfert's new effort, *World of Food*, can also be read as an edible novel.) During the three days of preparation, it occurred to me how Ronald Reagan was outsmarted by François Mitterrand a few years back. Reagan purportedly concentrates on a diet of lean fish, turkey breast, raw zucchini, and jelly beans, while Mitterrand snacks on caviar, truffles, foie gras, and jellied calves' feet and drinks fine bordeaux and burgundy (rather than Reagan's habitual Riunite on the rocks with seltzer). At least George Bush eats pork rinds—a step in the right direction. Anyway, I helped my friend directly to the table, and within twenty-four hours we had finished the dish, his health completely restored.

Not to belabor the peasant motif, a week later Valdène ordered two pounds of beluga malassol from Caviarteria in New York, which we ate in a single sitting with my wife and daughter. I reminded myself not to do this too often, since the next morning my goutish left big toe tingled, making bird hunting awkward.

It's interesting to see, in the manner of a pharmacist, how particularized the food nostrum can be: for clinical depression you must go to Rio to a *churrascaria* and eat a roast sliced from the hump of a zebu bull; also try the *feijoada*—a stew of black beans with a dozen different smoked meats, including ears, tails, and snouts. For late-night misty boredom, go to an Italian restaurant and demand the violent pasta dish known as *puttanesca*, favored by the whores of Rome. After voting, eat collard greens to purge yourself of free-floating disgust. And when trapped by a March blizzard, make venison *carbonnade*, using a stock of shin bones and the last of the doves. If it is May and I wish to feel light and spiritual, I make a simple sauté of nuggets of sweetbreads, fresh morels, and wild leeks, the only dish, so far as I know, that I have created.

I recently went to Chicago to see the Gauguin retrospective at the Art Institute. The show was so overwhelming that I actually wept, jolted into the notion that art does a better job for the soul than food for the body. I remembered reading, though, that Gauguin himself, when a little low and cranky, liked to have a goblet of rum followed by breadfruit, a fresh steamed fish with ginger, and perhaps a roast piglet. No mention was made of dessert. During my art-dazed walk back to the hotel, I slipped into the Convito Italiano for a bite—a simple carpaccio and a hit of grappa. Finally, after a long nap with South Seas dreams, I went up to Café Provençal for a grand feast. So it goes.

1989

Hunger, Real and Unreal

Did you ever notice how we never allow ourselves to be actually hungry?" said Russell Chatham, a burly painter of some note. We were eating a prehunt breakfast, parked beside Oleson's buffalo paddock outside Traverse City, Michigan. All of the little boy buffalo, ignorant of gender, were chasing one another around, hell-bent on sex, their red wangers bobbing in the air. "Those guys are a tad confused," Chatham added, eyeing the corked bottle of wine, at which we both coughed, thinking that ten in the morning isn't too early for a sip of red wine with a sandwich. Way up here in the northland there's a fine Italian delicatessen, Folgarelli's, and Chatham was having a hot Italian sausage with marinara sauce and melted mozzarella, while my choice was a simple prosciutto, mortadella, Genoa salami, and provolone on an Italian roll.

Throughout the day we mulled over the not-exactly-metaphysical question of why we never, for more than a moment, allowed ourselves to be hungry. Could this possibly be why we were both seriously overweight? But only a fool jumps to negative conclusions about food, especially before dinner. *Cuisine minceur* notwithstanding, the quality of food diminishes sharply in proportion to negative thinking about ingredients and, simply put, the amount to be prepared. There is no substitute for Badia A Coltibuono olive oil. Period. Or the use of salt pork in the cooking of southwest France. Three ounces of chablis are far less interesting and beneficial than a magnum of bordeaux. I have mentioned before that we are in the middle of yet another of the recurrent sweeps across our nation of the "less is more" bullies. When any of these people arrive in my yard, I toss a head of iceberg lettuce and some dog biscuits off the porch.

Despite these apparent truths, almost biblical in veracity, and bearing some of the grandeur of our Constitution, I recently learned that hunger is the actual sensation of the body burning its own fat. This is not a very appetizing idea but is, nonetheless, a positive experience when the body wears too much fat. I learned this when I spent two weeks at the Rancho La Puerta health spa in Tecate, Mexico, in order to quit smoking.

Almost incidentally I lost seventeen pounds. This appears impossible, but some of it was "easy" weight from a feast (the usual wonderful squid, chicken, tuna, carpaccio, lamb, etc.) at Rondo's in Los Angeles the evening before my incarceration. I also worked out six to eight hours a day: I took a solo four-hour mountain hike each morning to look for birds and follow the tracks of coyote, bobcat, and puma, and I did up to three hours of exercise in the gym.

Now this was an unconscionable and pathetic amount of exertion, but necessary to avoid cigarettes. I plummeted into a depression in which the first of my ideals to fly away into the mountains was literature. The Rancho's menu was vegetarian with fish twice a week. Chef Ramon Flores took this limited cuisine as far as it can be taken, but not quite far enough for the grief of a man who had temporarily lost his calling. One late morning after an exhausting hike, I began to tremble uncontrollably, a state I recognized as protein starvation. A tumbler of Herradura tequila was a temporary measure until I gathered the strength to call a cab and head into town for a slab of swordfish with garlic sauce and a full order of *carne asada*.

Quite naturally, as Americans we all loathe decadence, though our notions of decadence change from time to time. Around the turn of the century, a man's girth was a fair estimate of his prosperity and moral worth, and the thin, sallow look, so much the rage at present, was considered fair evidence of low birth and probable criminal intent. (Curiously enough, of the countless times I've been swindled in Hollywood, the guilty parties have always been thin.) Men nowadays will not settle for a Paul Newman washboard stomach but want an entire washboard body, even though none of them remembers an actual washboard in his past.

Let's all stop a moment in our busy day and return to some eternal verities. It's quite a mystery, albeit largely unacknowledged, to be alive, and, quite simply, in order to remain alive you must keep eating. My notion, scarcely original, is that if you eat badly you are very probably living badly. You tend to eat badly when you become inattentive to all but the immediate economic necessities, real or imagined, and food becomes an abstraction; you merely "fill up" in the manner that you fill a car with gasoline, no matter that some fey grease slinger has put raspberry puree on your pen-raised venison. You are still a nitwit bent over a trough.

At the Rancho one day at lunch I told some plumpish but kindly ladies what I thought was a charming story of simple food. One August, years ago, I was wandering around the spacious property of a château up in Normandy, trying to work up a proper appetite for lunch. The land doubled as a horse farm, and a vicious brood mare had tried to bite me, an act I rewarded with a stone sharply thrown against her ass. Two old men I hadn't seen laughed beneath a tree. I walked over and sat with them around a small fire. They were gardeners and it was their lunch hour, and on a flat stone they had made a small circle of hot coals. They had cored a half-dozen big red tomatoes, stuffed them with softened cloves of garlic, and added a sprig of thyme, a basil leaf, and a couple of tablespoons of soft cheese. They roasted the tomatoes until they softened and the cheese melted. I ate one with a chunk of bread and healthy-sized swigs from a jug of red wine. When we finished eating, and since this was Normandy, we had a sip or two of calvados from a flask. A simple snack but indescribably delicious.

I waited only a moment for the ladies' reaction. *Cheese*, two of them hissed, *cheese*, as if I had puked on their sprouts, and *wine*! The upshot was that cheese is loaded with cholesterol and wine has an adverse effect on blood sugar. I allowed myself to fog over as one does while reading bad reviews of one's own work.

That evening, Gael Greene, also a Rancho guest, spoke of the travails of being a food critic, making me ache for the usual foie gras and truffles. Later I told her that I used to carry a notebook and dictaphone into restaurants, assuring myself of a good meal as a bogus food critic. I never actually said I was a critic, only that I couldn't talk about it. I reflected, too, on the idea of food snobbism: my friends in Paris are cynical about the idea of a good meal in New York, and in New York the idea of eating in Chicago is somewhat laughable, and so on through Los Angeles and San Francisco in every direction. I enjoy telling them that in recent years my best meal was at the Ali-Oli in San Juan, Puerto Rico. True.

At dawn the next morning I decided to spend the day in the mountains. I figured that Aldous Huxley, one of my boyhood heroes, who used to hang out at the Rancho, would have done the same thing. I took my binoculars, an orange, a hard-boiled egg, and a one-ounce bottle of Tabasco for the egg.

Four hours into the mountains I ate the egg and the orange. I was seated downwind from a bobcat cave, hoping for a sighting but knowing it was doubtful until just before dark. The cave had a dank, overpowering feline odor similar, I imagined, to that of the basement of a thousand-year-old Chinese whorehouse (the visionary propensities of hunger!).

Then out of the chaparral appeared a tough, ragged-looking Mexican who asked me if I had anything to eat. I said no, wishing I had saved the orange. He smiled, bowed, and continued scampering up Mt. Cuchama, presumably toward the United States and the pursuit of happiness, including something to eat. He had chosen the most difficult route imaginable, and I followed his progress with the binoculars, deciding that not one of the Rancho's fitness buffs, including the instructors, could have managed the mountain at that speed.

I didn't feel the couch liberal's guilt over not having saved the orange for him, just plain old Midwestern Christian guilt. In my deranged state I thought that maybe the guy was Jesus, and I had denied him the orange! Then I lapsed into memories of things I had eaten when I was actually hungry, such as the fried trout I used to eat at streamside with bread and salt. I remembered, during my wandering-starving-artist years in the late 1950s, spending subway fare for a thirty-five-cent Italian-sausage sandwich and walking seventy blocks to work the next morning, eating free leftovers given to me by Babe and Louis at the Kettle of Fish bar, buying twenty-five-cent onion sandwiches on rye bread at McSorley's. I had wonderful meals while working as a poetic busboy at the Prince Brothers Spaghetti House in Boston; I often devoured two fried eggs at a diner after Storyville, the best jazz club ever, closed at dawn. In the San Francisco area there were two-for-a-nickel oranges, the oddly delicious macaroni salad at the Coexistence Bagel Shop for a quarter, the splurge of an enormous fifty-cent bowl of pork and noodles in Chinatown. And let's not forget the desperation of eating ten-cent cafeteria bread and catsup in Salt Lake City or the grapefruit given me by an old woman in the roadside dust near Fallon, Nevada.

When I arrived home from one of these trips, mostly brown skin and bones, my father said, "If you had stayed away longer, you wouldn't weigh nothing at all. It's plain to see it will be some time, if ever, before you know what you are doing, James." Then he fired up the grill, and we went into his enormous garden and picked all manner of fresh vegetables. He broiled some chickens with lemon, garlic, and butter. That's what I remembered on the way down the mountain.

1989

Then and Now

I have a good memory, though *good* is somewhat questionable, since there is a tendency to over-remember life rather than to look for new life to be lived. "Late in the Great Depression, on the first day of spring in 1938, in fact, I gazed from the cradle as my parents ate smoked pork chops and the last of the home-cured sauerkraut, which was particularly redolent from six months in the crock, whose stone surface I often licked for salt while crawling around the floor, looking up at the underside of the world, the small strawberry birthmark on the back of my lovely aunt's thigh just below the apparent bird's nest wrapped in white cotton. I rejected baby food with sobs and howls, preferring whole venison hearts, herring, pike, perch eggs, the souse that Grandmother boiled down from an enormous pig's head on the wood stove."

That sort of thing. "I still remember the mosquito-bite scab on the dirty left knee of the little girl who put out my eye with a broken bottle on a cinder heap at the edge of the woods in 1945. We were playing doctor. The Tigers were in third place, and Hal Newhouser was going to pitch that day. On the way to the doctor, our car smelled because I had left a bluegill in the trunk behind the tire but was afraid to admit it. When I was in the hospital, my parents brought me herring, the odor of which repelled the nurse. I thought I'd look like the little pig that lost its eye to a rusty nail protruding from a pen board. The second board from the bottom on the north side. For several painful months, the blind eye shone like a red sun in my head."

Again, that sort of thing. Luckily, we eat in the present tense, else we might travel further into madness. That goes for fishing, too. When you combine fishing, eating, and a little drinking, you are riding the cusp of sanity as you did, quite happily, the schoolyard swing or that rope at the swimming hole that arced you out over a deep hole of cold, clear water, where you dropped down on startled brown trout whose fingerlings were

speared by the kingfisher perched on the elm's bald branch. Jerry Round
jumped from the bridge top and died, driving his head into his body. Naturally, I thought of turtles which Vince Towne purged in a washtub before
he ate them. He told us that fried turtle would make our peckers grow big,
a comment about which we had mixed feelings.

Fishing and eating, not without a few drinks at day's end. Hundreds of
years ago, a *roshi* admonished his students not to prate about Zen to fishermen, farmers, and woodchoppers, since they probably already knew the
story. Because I live up in Michigan and don't much like ice fishing, I've
been going to the lower Florida Keys for a little winter fishing since 1968.
With ice fishing, you dress up bulky like an astronaut and stare through a
round black hole you've spudded in the ice. The "spud" is the tip-off that
you're in the wrong place—it is an enormous forty-pound chisel. The sandwiches we brought along used to freeze in our pockets, and one day the
wine froze at twenty below zero.

The question at hand is, "Are the Keys the same or as good as in the old
days?" This is an especially stupid question that I have been asked countless
times by dozens of people. My answer, "yes and no," is usually unsatisfac-
tory except to the timid, so I add a little gingerbread, to wit, isn't the past
the silliest of tautologies? Have you forgotten Mircea Eliade's blessed "con-
crete plane of immediate reality"? Didn't René Char tell us not to live on
regret like a wounded finch?

Where have any of us ever been that some nitwit doesn't tell us that we
should have been there before? They are only pissing on a fireplug to establish territory in the face of recent arrivals. In Aspen, at the Hotel Jerome,
you will always meet a stockbroker with an overbite much envied in London who is eager to establish that he was there first. I've developed a good
tactic: wherever you are, say that you were born and raised there, but infinitely prefer living in Detroit.

The fishing in the Keys is about the same, but the food is better. There
are more fishing guides, but the water is scarcely cluttered. I wouldn't return again in March, when college students on spring break flood the town
of Key West. They invariably march around in groups, puking drunk, reminding me of the Nazi youth that cursed the world. They are all apparently the soul children of Ronald Reagan and should be packed off to Day-
tona Beach before they further destroy the community. If you like this sort

of thing, you can save a lot of money by hanging out in a college community after a football game.

Far from this caveat is the notion that much of the food used to be quite awful except for what was served at Rene's, down on Duval, or in the better Cuban restaurants such as El Cacique. Now you can eat better in Key West than in any town I can think of in America fifteen or twenty times its size. Of course, there was a period in the early seventies when you might fly-fish for tarpon on three hits of windowpane acid backed up by a megaphone bomber of Colombian buds that required nine papers and an hour to roll. You weren't exactly ready for fine food when you got off the boat. What you had in mind has still not been determined.

There is something in the character of flats-fishing in the tropics that diminishes the appetite: a mixture of sun, heat, fatigue. You are fly-fishing in the shallow water of a river that is fifty miles wide, and casting only to visible fish. The energy expended in the relentless staring into water is exhausting. You are utterly immersed in the act and dare not let a single extraneous thought enter your mind or you'll miss the fish. It was upsetting this year to find that I have become much better at fly-fishing now that my drinking has vastly moderated. A hangover, simply enough, internalizes the quality of attentiveness, and you're looking inside at your myriad fuckups rather than outside at fish.

Not that I couldn't eat adequately, only that I'm usually a multiple-entrée type of guy, and I came to know the certain sadness of watching my wife, two daughters, and son-in-law eat more than I did. The tradition of piggery carries on, I thought. Chef Norman Van Aken's Mira is a grand place, with a first-rate wine list devised by Proal Perry. You should buy Van Aken's book, *Feast of Sunlight*, published by Ballantine. For day-to-day excellence we chose Antonia's, eating rather elaborate meals there three times in two weeks, though you can order simply from the appetizers and list of pastas (including stone-crab claws and mussels in a cream sauce on homemade linguine). Frankly, I find no fault with Antonia's. In a dozen visits I've never met the chef, Phillip Smith, nor the owner, and not a single visit was an expense-account item. There were no disappointments, and the serving staff is deft and unobtrusive.

We also frequented Louie's Backyard, whose upstairs café is informal and beautifully decorated. One day, chef Bill Prahl will become as inventive as

Van Aken. The menu could be called "nouvelle Cuban," and Prahl's squid rings with citrus aioli are exquisite, as are the Havana pork roast and the shellfish *zarzuela*. Downstairs the atmosphere is more formal but the food, prepared by Doug Shook under the direction of co-owner Phil Tenney, fine indeed. I prefer this area for lunch when the fried-chicken salad is available, along with onion rings made from marinated Spanish red onions. One day a shellfish gumbo beat senseless anything Louisiana ever offered me. A short drive up the Keys to Cudjoe to Rick Lutz's Cousin Joe's will give you a taste of what the area used to be like, only the food is much better.

Back in Key West I can also recommend Café des Artistes (unbelievable desserts), Dim Sum, the Crêperie, and Kyushu. For a relief from the pricey and somewhat formal, we returned frequently to the Full Moon Saloon for the hottest chicken wings imaginable, grouper and conch sandwiches, conch chowder, and conch fritters, as well as more elaborate meals, all turned out by chef Tom Sawyer. (I keep mentioning chefs for the same reason you tell folks who wrote the book.) I eat breakfast at Dennis Pharmacy on Simonton because it doesn't limit you to the nutritional vacuum of bacon and eggs, offering a number of Spanish soups, including red bean, and pigs' feet. For sandwiches for the boat, go to Uncle Garlin's Food Store out on Flagler, where the meatloaf is better than Mom's.

Curiously, I didn't gain an ounce in two weeks. At least I don't think I did. I defy the mechanistic world of scales, banks, lawyers, dentists, and I wouldn't balance a checking account at gunpoint. My aide-de-camp handles all of this except the dentist. A scale is meaningless when some days you feel light and some days you feel heavy. I have chosen the weight of 135 pounds as appropriate and have stuck to it. You might ask the local farmers who see me running in the dawn mists well ahead of my panting bird dogs. Once, at the Denver airport, a bald girl in an orange dress told me that I could be what I wanted, so it's 135, period.

Back to the old days, the late sixties and early seventies. I don't miss all of the stuff that made me feel bad, and gentrification, wherever it takes place, tends to wipe out all but a charade of the indigenous culture. It can still be there, but you have to look for it.

I miss the fighting roosters crowing at dawn, but not the cocaine jag that enabled me to hear them. I miss feeling the thrill of the possible future so adumbrated by despair and empty pockets, the night thick with the scent of garbage and flowers, the fecund, low-tide odor of our beginning.

Now I go there just for the fishing and, secondarily, the eating. My family likes it, and it's doubtful I'd chance a trip without them. There are the ghosts of those I cared for who did not survive the behavior the rest of us survived. But it is the water, the life we can only visit and barely comprehend, the thousand life forms of the flats, imperceptible unless you care to learn, a saline *mysterium*. This year there were two beached, rotting sperm whales on the flats facing Snipe Key, their skins too tough for the seabirds to feed on. I wondered where those whales were born, where they traveled on this bloody journey, what they felt when they died together far from their natural home, all of it quite beyond the range of my speculation or imaginings, the vast, brownish, sun-blasted hulks resting on the lovely flats. Some locals had cut out their valuable teeth with chain saws, but this fact seemed singularly puny, however coarse, compared with the inviolable beauty of the seascape, the whales resting not in peace but, as all of us will, in inevitable resignation.

1989

Consciousness Dining

An artist (a generic term covering poet, composer, painter, sculptor, perhaps novelist) consciously or unconsciously takes a vow of obedience to awareness. In order not to be lost in the whirl of time, either past or present, the artist must look at all things with the energy and clarity of a hyperthyroid Buddha.

Frankly, this awareness is not always fun, a fact that explains certain consciousness-reducing vices. In some locales it is even less fun than in others. Just recently I drove south from my wilderness cabin in Michigan's Upper Peninsula to my farm, where I packed for a trip to Los Angeles. We all know that air travel is currently a big step down from what Greyhound travel was in the days of yore. And in the past year or so, the food has further degenerated in the first-class cabin of my favorite airline, American. Now a bottle of Tabasco lasts only three trips, whereas in the old days it lasted a dozen. I have filed an application to be towed by future planes in a gunnysack full of fish guts, which will improve the trip.

I am mindful that what initially takes a novelist to L.A. is greed and, often enough to be worth mentioning, a fascination with movies. My arrival is always buffered by my getting naked into bed in a darkened hotel room, no matter what time of day, and listening to Mexican music on the radio. This is a little trick you all might try. I stay either at the Westwood Marquis, because you can walk in the UCLA Botanical Gardens and also because it is a fine hotel, or at the Shangri-La out in Santa Monica which offers, right out the window, the nonclaustrophobic feature of the Pacific Ocean, or the "Big P," as it is known locally.

Hollywood is not a kind and gentle place, but it's where my work takes me. On the first day of a recent meeting, we worked fourteen hours, a reminder that the place doesn't necessarily dollar up on the side of frivolity. This schedule continued for several days, until I felt like one of the well-known, three peeled throats of Cerberus, exhausted, fluttery, my imagination a mud puddle rather than a mighty river. To put it simply, I wasn't getting enough to eat. My partners (Harrison Ford and Douglas Wick) own the sharpish features of the underfed, features that any phrenologist will tell you reflect an interest in money and power rather than in the fruits of the imagination.

Anyway, in the middle of a serious point, I slipped into an out-of-body experience and was swept away to New York City, tracking myself as I left the therapist's office where I am treated for the usual obsessive-compulsive disorders. My first stop was the Ideal Lunch & Bar on Eighty-sixth Street, for a quick boiled pig hock, then on to the Papaya King hotdog stand on the corner of Eighty-sixth and Third for a quick frank with sauerkraut and mustard, down Third to Ray's for a slice of pizza with eggplant, then over to JG Melon for a simple rare burger and a double V.O. When I came to, I discovered that I had been talking with incisive brilliance and the meeting was over, which proves that even ghost food is better than none. Unfortunately, I don't have any of the notes.

The point is that there's no snack food in L.A. on the order of New York's. I ate very good dinners at Dan Tana's and at Osteria Orsini, where my table was presided over by the best waiter on the West Coast, the fabled Igor. The last night I agreed hesitantly to Chaya's, doubtful that a restaurant that "hot" could also be good. The meal was splendid, again highlighting the fact that I have never had an accurate intuition (raw-tuna salad, a pasta with peerless squid and slivered jalapeños, a small grilled chicken with a side of garlic the equal of any I've ever had, *pommes frites*, and a whole bottle of Château Montelena just for me).

Despite this grand send-off, I arrived home in a palsied state—tremors of exhaustion, near tears, that sort of thing. My wife noted a burnt-rubber scent coming out of my ears, firm evidence of my brain's drag racing with itself in film country. To set the brakes I wandered for hours in the woods, looking for morels, but it had been a dry, bitterly cold spring, and the mushrooms were scarce. At one point I walked three hours to find four morels. I did, however, gather enough to cook our annual spring rite, a simple sauté of the mushrooms, wild leeks, and sweetbreads. Regardless of this tonic for the body, I fired off inconsolably angry letters to no one in particular and lightly spanked the bird dogs for minor infractions, until I gave up on domestic life and packed north to the cabin, with three cartons of books on Native Americans and John Thorne's *Simple Cooking*. Native Americans are an obsession of mine, totally unshared by New York and Los Angeles for the average reason of moral vacuum. Native Americans are like good poetry, and it is particularly banal that we are dying from the lack of what both tell us.

A number of years ago, I had the notion that I wished to write a poem as immediately fascinating as a recipe or a dirty picture. Fat chance. Art is in no position to duke it out with our baser appetites, appetites that are the cornerstones of our individual pyramids; art is only the pointed, three-cornered capstone, signaling finally what we had in mind. Meanwhile, down at the bottom, it is clear that instincts toward sex and food must be aesthetically satisfied, or the pyramid is the usual garbage heap. It is also clear, in a historical perspective, that our current, most active generation— those between twenty and forty—is placing a giant fiber-laden, aerobic turd of greed on the history of the republic.

John Thorne is not to be confused with Nicholas Thorne, the dark genius of contemporary classical music. John Thorne's unqualified genius is for food, and I suspect that he will justly inherit the mantle from M.F.K. Fisher as our best food writer. Others, Paula Wolfert, for instance, have a much more startling flair, and I suspect that since I am an outright pig I'd choose her table over Thorne's. But for day-in, day-out innovative brilliance and lucid prose, Thorne is my favorite. For nine years he has been writing a newsletter called *Simple Cooking* (available from the author at Box 58, Castine, Maine 04421), and this year he published with Penguin a cookbook of the same name. Perhaps living at the northeasternmost tip of America keeps Thorne unencumbered with the faddish, those tiny points of dullish light that signal some new craze like homemade tomato soup. In both the newsletter and the book, he writes of food as varied as red beans and rice, versions of corn bread, roasted red pepper and mushroom *tian*, bread and olives, *focàccia*, varieties of chowder, olive oils, nun's farts (*pet de nonne*—a type of fritter), *boeuf à la ficelle*, collards, pork, and apple pie.

Thorne's Yankee modesty shields innovation from pretension. He doesn't show off, and all of his energies go toward food that resonates, that is genuine and memorable. His ego is quite barren and the attributions generous—it is an oddity of the genre that most cookbooks pretend they are the only ones in existence. Thorne even writes a convincing essay on why he isn't a good cook. He admits that he loves fried-chicken-skin sandwiches—a truly nasty idea, but to admit that you would eat them is admirable. On a long, warm flight up from New Orleans, he imagined that the two pounds of *boudin* in his suitcase were spoiling, so he ate them all on arrival, the sort of timeless wisdom to which I can respond.

So I was rereading all of Thorne and experimenting with his recipes rather than beginning the revision of the screenplay (*revision* being a euphemism for doing the whole thing over without saving a word of the first draft). Simply enough, hunger had overly cleansed our doors of perception, and we had come up with a better idea. After a few days at my cabin, I found that the food reading and long hikes had restored my appetite for life the way Henry Miller used to do when I was a young bohemian.

Curiously, in both writing and cooking you're a dead duck if you don't love the process. When you short-circuit or jump start the process in either, you end up with an imitation of your own or someone else's best effects. You will get away with it a few times, but the germs of shame will be there, and inevitably you will end up serving your dinner guests or your reading public mere filigree, plywood gingerbread, M.F.A. musings, housebroken honeycomb, in short, the thief of fire as a college cheerleader.

Back to the obedience to awareness: still within the aftereffects of L.A. burnout, I nearly stepped on a nest of grouse chicks and forgot that Buddha's birthday was falling on the same day as the full moon. When will this happen again? I forgot to leach the eggplant and the parmigiana was mushy! So were the cannellini beans I cooked too hard, neglecting to add the *pancètta* rind! Son of a bitch, but I was delaminating!

I decided to start over as a regular guy, an ordinary fellow. For dinner I'd cook a Thorne version of fish chowder. Dad used to say that fish was brain food. Since I was busy with the screenplay, I put out an illegal setline in the river next to the cabin, already cheating on the process. I tended to ignore the writing, rechecking the setline every fifteen minutes or so, the first I had used since my youth. In fact, I became childish, imagining that the salt pork, potatoes, onion, and cream were lying in wait for the fish.

Finally, late in the afternoon, the line was headed upstream rather than downstream where I had tossed it. I began to draw it in, then discovered that though indeed I had a fish on, the fish had wrapped the line around some sunken alder branches. I scrambled back up the bank and put on my waders.

Unfortunately, when I stepped in the river, the water came a full foot above my waders, and the current swept my feet out from under me. I howled in shock—there was still some snow in the woods, and the water was very cold—and hauled myself out on a log. Now I was, frankly, pissed off. I grabbed the line and jerked mightily, launching both broken branch and fish into the air, where the fish parted from the hook. I lunged back into the river, grabbing at the stunned fish. She glanced at me a moment, recovered her senses, and sped off. For some reason I'm sure it was a female.

I changed clothes and headed to town for some beverages, remembering a line from Stephen Mitchell's fine translation of the *Tao te Ching*:

> *I am different from ordinary people.*
> *I drink from the Great Mother's breasts.*

1989

The Tugboats of Costa Rica

Many of us like to think we own some unappreciated talent, modestly concealed and perhaps lacking the urgency to rise toward the light. Youngsters playing catch on the lawn make elaborate movements, hoping that the passing green 1949 De Soto contains a pro scout who might take notice of them, even at this early age. It is said that Henry Kravis, the fabled Wall Street predator, can pick up a coin without bending over.

While I have the gravest doubts about the durability of any of my writing, few can beat me at the graceful dance of knife, fork, and spoon across the plate or the capacity to make a pickle last as long as a sandwich. I have thought of rigging tiny lights to my eating utensils and getting myself filmed while eating in the near dark: imagine, if you will, the dancelike swirl of these points of light. Just last evening in my cabin, the performance took place over a humble, reduced-calorie Tuscan stew (very lean Muscovy duck, *pancétta*, white beans, copious garlic, fresh sage, and thyme). Since I was alone in the twilight, the applause rang a bit hollow.

To be sure, our limitations strangle us, letting us know who we are. On a semireligious level, normally we have a secret animal we favor, but this is dangerous territory. Never tell a government official your secret animal, since it will one day be used against you. On a more mundane plateau, if you were a boat, what kind of boat would you be? You must be honest, since I can't interrogate you, what with each of us being alone. No dream boats, grand sloops, ghostly galleons, if you please. As for me, and I'm doing the writing here, I have long confessed to being a tugboat: slow, rather stubby, persistent, functional, an estuarine creature that avoids open water.

This is all prefatory to my irritation on being asked if I was a good fly-fisherman. I had just returned from a trip to Costa Rica with the painter Russell Chatham and the sportsman Guy de la Valdène, where we were fly-fishing for billfish up in Guanacaste Province on the Pacific. A little of my testiness might have been caused by garden-variety dysentery and a skin rash that turned my entire torso into a pizza. The consolation is that dysentery is a grand leap forward on a brand-new diet, though Chatham noted that the connection between his dysentery and diet was like pitching a shuffleboard puck off a cruise ship. I shall never forget his pathetic yelp in the night as he pooped his bed during a feverish dream. My skin rash, incidentally, left doctors helpless, but I cured it myself with a slush devised out of baking soda and Epsom salts, patent pending. Chatham and I questioned why de la Valdène remained disease-free, but then it occurred to us that he no longer eats his way through a menu merely out of curiosity. We wished him an attractive middle age at La Cascada, outside San José, a fabulous place with good wine and a boggling array of fresh seafood and beef. For some reason, Costa Rican beef is exquisitely flavorful, though very lean. It tastes like the best beef of your childhood, before the advent of short-cut packing, feed lots, chemicals, and no aging.

But to address my irritation about whether I'm good at fly-fishing: why bother if you haven't taken the time to learn to make the throw? Beyond that point, any spirit of competition in hunting or fishing dishonors the prey. It means that you are either unaware of, or have no feeling toward, your fellow creatures. Fishing tournaments seem a little like playing tennis with living balls, say, neatly bound bluebirds. Competition also engenders anger, and there's little point in being out in the forest, in a river, or on the ocean if you're going to be pissed off.

It just occurs to me that I shouldn't tell you where we went fishing in Costa Rica. There's no travel writer's obligation here. Find your own place. The location isn't lacking in business, and I'd hate to return and find the place mobbed. Anyhow, there are certain disadvantages: the charter plane from San José had no working gauges, and the land beneath the plane, a lovely green hell, lacked landing strips. Just hills and gorges. There were scorpions on the path from the marina and restaurant to the hotel, shaking their malevolent asses at sea-weary drunks. We did miss the bandied-about march of tarantulas. Our presiding captain had a softball-size, pitch-black sore on his arm from a "little spider" he rolled over on in his sleep. Our wonderful captain of the last day, a surgeon who took early retirement from the frenzy of the States, said that the occasional missing arms and feet in

surrounding villages were from the fer-de-lance, an aggressive viper. To me
this added to the fabulous beauty of the place, the green mountains meeting
the blue sea, the deserted beaches, the hundred-acre schools of spotted dolphin, the 353 green parrots sitting in a shoreline tree above an immense
green marine iguana sunning on a rock. The location is doubtless safer than
crossing Lexington on Seventy-second or turning left on Laurel Canyon off
Sunset Boulevard.

Modest dangers make you attentive, while extreme danger can explode
your equilibrium, sometimes permanently, as we see in certain Vietnam
veterans. When your engines quit far out at sea, you become a great deal
more conscious of the immensity of the ocean. But then you have a ship-
to-shore radio, though this is scarcely foolproof. One afternoon we moni-
tored a Mayday from another charter boat. It had broken a shaft, lost a pro-
peller, and couldn't offer a navigational fix for rescue craft! Moreover, the
current was drifting the boat toward Nicaraguan waters. Our Spanish captain assured us that the latter wasn't significant, since the two countries
aren't hostile. Looking north across the expanse of water, I found it difficult
to feel the threat of this country, which, as William Greider pointed out,
owns only two workable elevators. Perhaps the Russian atomic subs cruis-
ing the Jersey waters are more important. Perhaps the Nicaraguan threat
was a red herring to cover up the massive savings-and-loan swindle, the
HUD pillaging, the Pentagon procurement scandal, the eight solid years of
ignoring the environment.

The purpose of my trip, however, was to fly-fish for billfish, which
might be called stunt fishing. I had done it a decade before in Ecuador,
where the current run of striped marlin had proved unmanageable. In Costa
Rica we hooked some Pacific sailfish, and for an hour I fought one that was
over 150 pounds. The excitement is intense when fish are rising to the baits,
which are large rubber squid. You tease the fish with the squid, and when
the fish are properly turned on you stop the boat and fly cast. It sounds quite
ordinary, but several times the fish in question were blue and black marlin
weighing in excess of five hundred pounds, bigger around than an oil barrel
and over ten feet long. The blue marlin in particular seems perpetually angry. I watched from the flying bridge as an enormous blue slashed at the
baits, half out of the water, then took de la Valdène's streamer fly, thrashing
his head and breaking the line. Marlin flash iridescent blue and green when

they attack a bait, startlingly beautiful against the darker water. Our surgeon-captain told me he had seen spotted dolphin bump marlin away from baited hooks.

Curiously, our most pathetic meal on the coast was also our best. Hubert and Agnes, the proprietors of the Amberes Restaurant, had made a stew out of the fresh local catch and shellfish. It was pathetic because Agnes was doctoring Chatham's dysentery and allowed him only plain rice with a ginger ale on the side. He glowered, beet red from the sun and fever and in pain from boating a fish while aching with a bad back, fighting the sailfish, hunched over like a nautical Quasimodo. I expressed my sympathy by losing a lot of money at the casino.

1989

Midrange Road Kill

For a reason that must be specific, albeit untraceable, no phrase causes me more mental discomfort than "sudden weight loss." This condition, of course, presages dozens of fatal diseases that can pluck us off the earth as if there had never been any gravity, or gravy, for that matter. A psychoanalyst has helped me locate the nexus of this terror but not the particularities of the childhood trauma hidden in the mists of stateside World War II. The central images, doubtless from *LIFE* magazine, are of the great vegetarians, Hitler and Tojo, who wished to chop off our country's head. From Buchenwald to Bataan, these two managed to make millions of souls permanently thin and to rape the consciousness of a round, brown, country child. When I close my eyes, my mind can still reel off the photos of the carnage of starvation, as if my brain were a slide show manned by a speed freak. In those years we were advised daily at dinner to finish our plates because the children in Europe had nothing to eat—a warp of logic typical in parent-child control.

The child is father to the man, as Wordsworth would have it, so the time and energy I've spent avoiding sudden weight loss come as no surprise. At no time is this effort more energetic and heroic than when my system is verging on a depression. Now, I've had five identifiable whoppers in my life (none in eight years), and once you get past the early stages you should literally turn yourself in for whatever professional help you can find or afford, because you can't truncate the process by yourself, and simply living through it makes you vulnerable to suicide. (The most elegant and intense record of an encounter with the disease was written by William Styron and appeared in the December 1989 *Vanity Fair*.) Beyond the early phase, the pathology of the disease establishes itself as icy, sodden, and remote; Inertia herself becomes queen of the endless days and nights. The anguish is so palpable that an actual fractured skull would be a sweet relief, and there is a relentless temptation to kiss the Back Wall.

However, resourcefulness and attention to early warning signs can put you in what fighter pilots call an "avoidance posture," though sometimes the causes of depression are so connected to the roots of life that any precaution resembles the psychobabble of self-improvement schemes.

When entering a depression, you become a consensus human, a herd creature going through the motions that the wolves, the interior predators, can spot a mile away. You go through the motions of consensus: eating food from consensus cookbooks and restaurants; imbibing consensus perceptions, beliefs, and knowledge from consensus newspapers and magazines, feeling consensus feelings offered by consensus television, music, and drama, and reading poetry, fiction, and nonfiction from consensus publishers. You have become the perfect midrange road kill. You are suffocating in lint. The nervous laughter that greeted Divine's eating dog shit in *Pink Flamingos* was caused by the shock of recognition.

You shouldn't read another word if you think you're going to get some free advice. Over the years my advice has been a contributing factor in at least a half-dozen suicides. Seriously. Now I am limiting my wisdom to food and, occasionally, the connection between food, sex, and depression, in hopes of saving millions of lives.

There is a poignant anecdote here under the category of the wisdom of the weird. In the late seventies I visited a friend on a movie set in a canyon near Trancas, in western Malibu. The movie being shot was a soft-core porn/nature feature called *The Legend of the Mynah Bird* which eventually did well in Ireland and western Australia. My friend the director was coked up and kept sending the naked starlet up a steep arroyo at a dead run, through eleven takes, until a break was called because she had developed exertion blotches. Her boyfriend had been on a rice rampage, his eyes crusty in the corners from vitamin-A deprivation. He was selling Humboldt County weed and a homemade Kama Sutra lotion that smelled like fish oil and badly burned onions. He pointed at his girlfriend, whose blotches I was watching disappear, and said, "For every top there is a bottom. She must eat. She must make love." It occurred to me later that he was also hustling the lady, but the wide blue Pacific to the west beckoned. In short, I had to get out of there, and I filed the information under the wisdom of California.

Despite our cultural snobbism, we are all not unlike our lady of the disappearing blotches, though she was far more attractive than most of us. Eat and love, to be sure, but you'd better eat first. And if you are verging on depression and you wish your loins to stir mightily, be careful about what you eat. Don't, for instance, head into a big platter of *choucroute garnie*, a heap of wurst, bacon, pig hocks, and sauerkraut, since this meal will make you feel blimpy and murderous. You are suited only for a fistfight or a Big Ten pep rally, or maybe for driving your car into a fire hydrant or an abortion center, but not for a lifting of spirits and the sacred act of love. I'm not talking about the garden-variety smut machinations pushed on us by the media, but the collision of Heathcliff and Catherine on the moors, Zhivago and Lara in the frozen attic, or even Ava Gardner and a bullfighter.

The initial suggestions are obvious: tripe in any form, oysters raw or roasted with shallots, butter, and cayenne, sweetbreads in any form, the New Iberian rendition of "dirty rice" with an adequate amount of gizzard, squid in any form except the Japanese which is too self-conscious and can cause performance difficulties. An ample mixed grill is a mistake unless you are Sean Connery or Winston Churchill, though grilled kidneys or *rognons de veau à la moutarde* are fine.

Far be it from me to say that women are the more glandular sex, but for some reason the cookbooks written by women are a better direction for those in this condition: Paula Wolfert, Diana Kennedy, Patience Gray, Mireille Johnston, Elizabeth David, Alice Waters, and Marcella Hazan come to mind. For instance, Hazan's *bollito misto* with *picante* sauce will enrage your privates, while the fabled *feijoada* of Brazil will put you to sleep unless you dance until dawn. Don't roast a whole lamb punctured with a hundred cloves of garlic, rubbed with olive oil and stuffed with a thatch of fresh thyme over a wood fire, because it is too dramatic. A simple marinated rabbit grilled over the same fire with veal sausage, however, will destroy sexual torpor. The fat lady in the rum ads will stir your weenie after this meal.

Less than a decade ago, in the middle of January, I was in bad shape. Professional help had been rejected, but my wife had alerted a country friend. When he arrived, I was standing out in our pasture; a white hat of snow had gathered on my head. He waved an enormous bird in front of my face, and, though I had tunnel vision, it was clearly recognizable as a wild turkey, the finest table bird on earth. We walked gravely toward the house, plucking the bird as we made our way through the snowdrifts. He said he had hit the bird accidentally with his car, but when we finished plucking, I saw the neat dark hole of a .22 bullet. He had broken the law for his friend! (These birds are ineffably better in the north, where they feed on acorns.) We roasted the beauty, and by the time it was done, I could see the entire kitchen and my beloved family and friends. We drank my last two magnums of Margaux, remnants of the vile but prosperous times that had sent me into the pasture.

I am not sure I awoke the next morning as a bearded gobbler, but I was on the road back.

1990

The Panic Hole

I am on the road for reasons unshared by Jack Kerouac and Charles Kuralt, Charlie Starkweather and William Least Heat Moon. A movie, *Revenge*, that I had had a modest part in by writing the novella and a few drafts of the script, was on the eve of coming out, and I felt raw, exhausted, and, worst of all, vulnerable. What is thought of as success meant only that absolute strangers bothered you in restaurants or on the street in resort towns. Success tends to make you think backward, where you rehearse the steps that brought you the check, an event that caused good feelings at the time. People use cocaine to feel successful, which means there are dubious aspects to the emotion. Anyway, I was feeling put-upon, a close second to self-pity as a destructive state. On the way home from the bar, I suddenly wanted to drive a Butternut Bread truck and eat a hasty meal of fish sticks and coleslaw before going bowling.

So I got out of town. One of my favorite authors, the great Gerald Vizenor, said that "the present is a wild season, not a ruse." As you get older, it occurs to you that "the present" is in increasingly short supply. The virtue of spending a couple of weeks stuck in a dentist's chair is less apparent than it used to be. The notion of "taking your medicine" like a sick dog poised before the phone is morose and Calvinistic when all you have to do is disappear. "Vamoose. Sayonara, motherfucker," as we used to say in high school. Man is not an answering machine.

Vizenor developed a saving idea called a panic hole in his novel *The Trickster of Liberty*. *Panic hole* is defined as a place where you go physically or mentally or both when the life is being squeezed out of you or when you think it is, which is the same thing. A panic hole is a place where you flee to get back the present as a wild season rather than a ruse. For the time being, my panic hole is an enormous, red Toyota Land Cruiser. A mile from my home, which has a bull's-eye painted on its roof, I felt a whole lot better, the oppressiveness slipping out the window and discoloring the 185 inches of snow we had received thus far.

For reasons that are obscure, perhaps genetic, I headed even farther north than my own frozen landscape. White snow and black trees are soothing and more anguish-absorbent than the obvious tropics, where the foreign heat bubbles your skin and brain. The tropics tend to distract you rather than empty you out. In the north it can be a really big day when you see three crows. And there are times when three crows more than equal a girl in a bikini, the Gulf Stream, and conch fritters.

Curiously, my first stop was Escanaba, at the House of Ludington, where I began this column two years ago. It was then that I announced my belief that small portions are for small and inactive people and that *cuisine minceur* was the moral equivalent of the fox-trot. Life was too short for me to approach with the mincing steps of a Japanese prostitute. My idea was to eat well and not die from it—for the simple reason that that would be the end of my eating.

I succeeded in not thinking about the time in between by using a few mail-order secrets on how to give up your name. After twelve hours of sleep, I took a long dawn walk far out on the ice, where I glassed three ravens feeding on a fish. What luck! I lay on the ice to make myself less obtrusive and listened to the vast nothingness of Lake Michigan. The landscape was empty except for the lump of me and three ravens watching one another across a hundred yards of blinding white.

This sort of epiphany goads the appetite savaged by sixteen months of work. Other than during bird season I had become so picky that I had lost a few pounds. At the hotel's Sunday brunch, I got a "tsk-tsk" from the waitress when I failed to polish off the plate of fruit and basket of breads, the platter of eggs, bacon, ham, real beef hash, and chicken livers, which was followed by an assortment of desserts, including a whipped-cream-stuffed pastry swan. My error was in reading during the meal—Bernard Heinrich's *Ravens in Winter*, from which I learned that in the late forties in Illinois 100,000 crows were destroyed in a single night by hand grenades. This was the American version of Cortés burning the aviaries of Montezuma, and it put me off my feed.

My spirits were revived at the Chippewa midwinter powwow that afternoon. On entering, I watched a very old man dancing in a full bearskin cape, his skull encased in the bear's head. He gracefully shook his war club at the gymnasium ceiling. A little later, fifty young girls in native costume did the crow dance so convincingly that I shivered, then, not surprisingly, wept. One day out and I was getting a long way from show business.

The next morning before I left, I called the Swedish Pantry to check out its soups. "We always have the same soups," I was told, the phone voice informed with what passes for mystery among the Swedes. It was, however, the best pea soup I had ever eaten, and, accompanied by *limpa* bread and a side of herring, it was a fine load of fuel for the drive to Appleton, Wisconsin, where I visited my daughter at her college. That evening a peculiar thing happened at a restaurant with the equally peculiar name of Hobnobbin'. The gizmo used to clamp an escargot backfired and shot the snail directly into my chest, spraying its freight of garlic-laden butter all over my expensive suede sport coat. For some reason, I thought this was very funny. I had a fine chat with my daughter and went on to eat an enormous slab of heart-smart rare roast beef, something that I rarely order but found utterly delicious in this restaurant.

There were moments of backsliding in the Midway Motor Lodge in La Crosse, Wisconsin, quarters I shared with a group called the Young Farmers and another named the Tri-County Breeders (presumably of cattle). A phone call, naturally, told me that the fish-wrap technocrats of the movie arts didn't care for *Revenge*. Sad that they'll never realize their fond dreams of being slammed in the butt by Don Johnson's speedboat, I thought, and went for a long walk during which I saw three bald eagles feeding on dead shad on the partially frozen Mississippi River. This was not a "sign" of anything except that three bald eagles were hungry.

That evening I dined on pork and beef ribs at Piggy's in downtown La Crosse on the river, a restaurant that had recently won the National Pork Producers Restaurant of the Year Award, no mean feat. The ribs were well cooked and the locally brewed Heileman's Export was delicious, though I am not a beer drinker. Piggy's should add a hot sauce as an alternative to its regular offering. My dinner was disturbed by the gradual evolution of an idea, the pinpointing of a grave threat to America. I slept on the idea, deeming it not yet ready for the man on the street.

The next morning, at the beginning of my long drive to Lincoln, Nebraska, I could not contain myself and delivered a speech through the windshield to the subzero landscape: "Who *are* these WASP eco-yuppies? They are afraid of blacks and ignore them. They think Native Americans are hopelessly messy. They scorn all cowboys, hate ranchers, loathe hunters, fishermen, and trappers (I agree on this one), won't eat beef or pork or drink hard liquor. These folks are thinking about their life-styles and missing the point: the bitterest of struggles against business, industry, and government, which are using the environment, as always, as a cheap toilet. The struggle is against a nation that will always spit in its grandchildren's faces for immediate profit. As Vizenor would say, 'Their Mother Earth is a blond.' "

In Lincoln I checked into the Cornhusker Hotel, another of my panic holes. They know what they're doing at the Cornhusker, and they mean to be normal, with food and service nearly the equivalent of those in a deluxe hotel in New York for less than one-third the price. But then one of the main reasons I like Lincoln is that it is not Manhattan. On your first visit you will sense a haunting boredom that, on following trips, you will recognize as Life herself without rabid hype. In Lincoln I eat relentlessly at the Bistro, where there is a surcharge of thirty-five cents if you want a Caesar salad rather than a tossed salad. At lunch I have red beans and rice the equal of any of the dozen versions I've had in New Orleans. At dinner I enjoy the spinach gnocchi and Italian sausage. One night for dinner, John Carter, a folklorist and historian, took me to the Steakhouse, where we had a delicate appetizer of several pounds of fried chicken gizzards followed by wonderful porterhouses and Geyser Peak Cabernet. During the day I looked at nineteenth-century photographs at the Nebraska State Historical Society.

After four days at the Cornhusker, I've become prelapsarian Adam and am ready for a slow drive home by the identical route. I want to see the same landscape from the opposite direction. And at dawn I do the same thing I've done for years, a not-so-banal trick I learned from the Navajo. You bow deeply to the six directions. That way you know where you are on earth— at least for the time being. Much earlier in this century, an Austrian journalist, Karl Kraus, pointed out that if you actually perceived the true reality behind the news, you would run, screaming, into the streets. I have run screaming into the streets dozens of times but have always managed to return home for dinner—and usually an hour early so that I can help in the preparation.

A few weeks ago, while preparing roast quail stuffed with leeks and sweetbreads (served on a polenta pancake with a heavily truffled woodcock sauce), I realized that it was far too late for me to cooperate politically or artistically with a modern sensibility that so apparently demands the cutest forms of science fiction for its soul food. After dinner, I floundered in the drifts, looking at the full moon up through the blizzard. The moon had somehow ignored the destruction of the middle class, the most recent fall of Europe, the Trump split, and the release of dozens of movies and books. It was the same moon I had rowed toward in a wooden boat as a child, my dog and a pet crow in the backseat. This winter moon was a cold but splendid comfort.

1990

Piggies Come to Market

Betimes, when I awake at dawn or a few hours thereafter, I must remind myself that I am not a coal miner or even the farm laborer I was in my youth. I no longer work twelve hours a day to take home fifteen bucks. What happened to my battered tin lunch bucket, where I stored my dreams of New York City and the beautiful girls who looked as if they changed their underwear every single day? What does it mean that this year I will make forty times what my dad did his best year? He doesn't mind up in heaven, but for some reason I do.

In such somber moods I glance in the mirror and don't see Mother Teresa. In such moods I am infected by the disease of social conscience brought about by my youthful forays into civil rights and the reading of Eugene Debs, Thorstein Veblen, Frantz Fanon, and others. Nowadays a social conscience is a disease you can purportedly cure by sending off a check for the rain forest.

Don't for an instant believe that I'm going to chug along on this banal train of thought, certainly a nexus of regret many of us are familiar with, particularly those who never expected to be successful in financial terms. There is also a specific danger in manufacturing, like William Buckley, a social and philosophical system to justify your prosperity. Life gets used up damned fast by the exhaustion of peripheries. Besides, I have proved repeatedly that I have no gifts for rational discourse, no gifts outside the immediate confines of the imagination. A number of years ago, at a rancorous public meeting, I said, "In the wrong hands even a container of yogurt can be a fatal weapon." Perhaps it was an acid flashback.

It was only last evening, while I was working on a screenplay with, of all things, the Academy Awards on the tube in the background, that I identified the malaise. It was the painful rejuvenescence of March, the brutality of a northern spring, when the songbird that was celebrating sixty degrees one day flops in its death throes at ten below under a cedar tree the next morning. This year a group of mallards had their feet frozen to a pond's surface, and now a bald eagle busies himself swooping in and tearing off their heads. Rages and pleasures mix themselves in this spring stew. Last week, a dear friend in a tequila rage shot himself in the parking lot of a bar. My beloved and saintly glutton of a Labrador must have her ulcerated left eye removed. Now we will be blind on the same side. Perhaps while we are hunting next fall, if she makes it, we will run into the same tree in the woods. When I was a boy, my left side was always bruised.

Of course, an older fool should be able to counter the emotional claymores brought about by the change of seasons and the pummeling of fortune's spiky wheel. The first move is to question whether certain of my grand assumptions about life have turned cheesy. Perhaps it is time to take down the motto from Deshimaru that is pinned to the wall above my desk: "You must concentrate upon and consecrate yourself wholly to each day, as though a fire were raging in your hair." Perhaps this coda I so devoutly try to follow is allowing insufficient oxygen? This Oriental ruthlessness may be inappropriate unless you work for Sony, which in fact I do, via Columbia Pictures, come to think of it.

Naturally, this foment has had a negative effect on my cooking. A few weeks ago, passing through my grocer's, I bought a packet of dehydrated French's pork gravy. The label noted that this gravy was award-winning. Since I have never won an award, who am I to question this gravy? Tom Wolfe probably won an award for *Campfire of the Vanities*, so he doesn't have to try this gravy. I can't recommend it, even with the addition of garlic. My wife, Linda, watched quizzically from the far side of the kitchen.

No lessons were learned. Two days later, I felt another rage for normalcy and bought two cans of Hormel chili (one with beans, one pure "meat") and a copy of *People* magazine. After this luncheon mud bath I actually burst into tears, then walked exactly eleven miles to purge the whole experience. That evening, after a classic French-roasted capon, I trashed my notes (seriously) for a somewhat scholarly essay I had intended to write, to be called "Brain Vomiters: The Twilight of the American Novel."

Things were plainly getting out of hand. One warm morning, before it snowed again, I yelled at the birds in the barnyard because they were too noisy. I stopped cooking altogether. Linda tempted me with fine new dishes made according to the recently published *Monet's Table*. They were splendid, but I could not eat the accustomed quantity, and I began to shed ounces. Then pounds dropped off. Contrary to most folks, I have to eat *real* big to stay big. The most destructive force in my life tends to be the unwritten poem, but despite my best efforts I was stropheless, except for my first epitaph: All Piggies Must, Finally, Come to Market.

There was the possibility that I had been sucker-punched by a dangerous fad last year. In an effort to shape up for bird season, I had begun to eat a nasty, fibrous cereal for breakfast. It was something to be endured, like a theater line. Not that I wanted bacon and eggs, another nasty fad that had its inception in the dizzy thinking that followed shortly after World War I. But in my heart I knew I'd rather eat the cow than the oats the cow eats.

This notion prompted a rage at the nitwits on the National Beef Council and their sniveling ads. Why don't they say you can have your beef if you give up all that fat-laden junk food, tasteless domestic cheeses, and ersatz French desserts? A T-bone has to be better for you than the $28 sea-urchin custard that is all the current rage in Gotham. Mind you, I have eaten versions of this dish in Paris and its alter ego, Los Angeles, and wouldn't feed it to Donald Trump, Tom Wolfe, or Hitler's daughter, Gretchen, who may also work for Sony.

Naturally, I rushed out and bought a largish Delmonico for brunch, but a watery pink fluid came out at first cut. What the fuck! I ate it anyway and dreamed of the fine steaks I used to eat in New York at Bruno's, Pen & Pencil, the Palm, and Gallagher's, or the sirloin at Elaine's before which you eat mussels and then spinach as a side to the meat. Florentine wines are better with steak than those of Bordeaux or Burgundy.

Beef is pleasure food, and we deserve pleasure because we live nasty, brutish lives. In ten days, I'll be in Valentine, Nebraska, where I'll eat a thirty-two-ounce aged porterhouse with two bottles of cabernet because there's no Barolo in Valentine. The following morning I will take a four-hour walk in the unfathomably beautiful Sandhills and count meadowlarks. I predict that my cholesterol count will not rise above its current 147, the same number of meadowlarks I'll see.

My disease of consciousness was somewhat alleviated by a week's trip with my wife and youngest daughter to Boca Grande, on the west coast of Florida. Boca Grande is lovely, safe, and sedate, and no one there is likely to slip you a manuscript or borrow money. I went sailing and bird-watching with my old friend Tom McGuane, who is a part-time resident (so much for our shared reputation as rounders).

Oddly, we saw only three birds on the wilderness island of Cayo Costa. How could this be, we wondered, the unused binoculars flapping on our chests. Then we noticed there were a lot of birds walking around on the ground just like us. We presumed they were feeding. On close inspection some of the birds were brown, and so were others. They were clearly, we decided, critic birds.

On the way home there was another pratfall after a pleasantly lavish night in Chicago at a hotel called 21 East, recently changed to Le Meridien. The dining room is among the three or four great restaurants in that city. Unfortunately, the next morning, after riding to O'Hare in one of the hotel's fleet of 750 BMWs, I watched a family of six poor folk there to pick up Grandma (I was listening). I was eating an expensive breakfast hot dog, which they decided against for financial reasons. I computed that hot dogs and soft drinks for this family of six would come to just over twenty-seven bucks. Anytime a hot dog approaches an hour at minimum-wage work, the state is in peril. My scalp prickled in shame for my sad country, its veins swollen with the pus of greed and dark scorn for the poor.

I also wondered about the eight hundred bucks I had spent in the last twenty-four hours. I could barely finish my hot dog but did, because I was thinking how in the past nine years the Republicans, with the dithering cooperation of the shamelessly class-conscious media, had isolated the bottom one-third of our population as social mutants. Frankly, this is unchristian, and these assholes better pay for it in hell, since they are doing quite comfortably on earth.

Back to the Academy Awards and the shrill evidence of an extreme black phobia in Beverly Hills. Spike Lee and Ed Zwick don't drive Miss Daisy. Afterward, I watched an intriguing video, rented at a convenience store, called *Cheerleader Camp*, starring Lucinda Dickey. These gals looked real good until they started killing one another. Blood is antierotic except in a steak. I was reminded of Eric von Stroheim's description of his life as "a symphony of disappointments." I was also reminded of hot dogs and the question, How can a modestly prosperous writer cast his spiritual lot with the social mutants?

In a few days I am beginning an irrational ten-thousand-mile car trip. I am going to look at a secret half-man and half-wolf petroglyph in Utah. After all, Thoreau said it is in "wildness" (not wilderness) that we find our preservation.

1990

The Fast

"Above all, do not lose your desire to walk: every day I walk myself into a state of well-being and walk away from every illness; I have walked myself into my best thoughts, and I know of no thought so burdensome that one cannot walk away from it . . . but by sitting still, and the more one sits still, the closer one comes to feeling ill. . . . Thus if one just keeps on walking, everything will be all right."
            —SÖREN KIERKEGAARD

Throughout the long night I ate nothing. The fast had begun early the evening before, after a bowl of Brazilian salt-cod chowder with a wedge of corn bread and a large glass of cold water. The meal was a bit simpleminded for so auspicious an event, auspicious at least to me, and I was the one going without food—not you, gentle reader, with your vibrant nightmares of self-indulgence.

But why was I fasting alone in my cabin, thirty-seven degrees in early July with a fifty-knot gale blowing north-northwest off Lake Superior? What's the point of fasting when no one is there to admire you—the same problem, in fact, in being a spy when you can't tell anyone you're a spy? Many years ago in Key West, when I was a private detective, I'd have a few drinks in a saloon and admit to strangers that I was a private detective, which somewhat decreased my effectiveness. Word gets around via the coconut telegraph in that city.

Frankly, I was fasting for wisdom. A career change was imminent, and I was in transition. (In case you don't know, and you probably don't, in traditional cultures one fasts for wisdom at such junctures.) During the past week I had walked seven miles a day in the undistinguished, slovenly wilderness of the Upper Peninsula. It was only wilderness by default, because no one could make another buck out of the depleted land, the enormous white-pine stumps forming their own ghost forest.

That morning I had mentally taken myself out of contention for the presidency of Harvard. There were no sandhill cranes in Cambridge, and they were my current obsession, along with other birds, bears, coyotes, and wolves, all quite scarce in the Boston area. Harvard would have to get along without my leadership as it entered the next millennium with its casual, aristocratic pout. My obvious sacrifice was the stewed tripe at Locke-Ober's, the flavors married dizzily to a bottle or two of La Tache, certainly a power lunch, especially if taken solo.

The hungry night found me caught in the lateral career change from writer to amateur naturalist. Life is short, and money buys so little. I felt depleted beyond reason, burned out to the point that I could actually hear the unearthly screams of the butchered piglet within me, and no animal's cries were more anguished in my forty-year-old barnyard memories. I could not balance the idea that, while the exposed heart is richest in feeling, there is a point at which it never recovers. The merest news item of another child beaten to death would occasion tears. And the princelings of the evil empire in Washington, D.C., had burned five hundred billion flags in the savings-and-loan swindle, leaving not a sou to help the social mutants, the poor and homeless, the Chicanos, blacks, and Native Americans. These princelings were the same shitbirds of greed cutting down six-hundred-year-old trees on public land while reassuring us that they were replanting, so if we could hang in there for six hundred years the forest would again have grand trees. The only soothing fantasy was that a million-strong lynch mob would invade Washington to terminate a political life that had become a paradigm of child pornography.

Of course, this sort of maudlin bullshit, the furious introspection we are prey to when society runs amok, covered a deeper unrest that I had revealed to myself in a naive sentence in a novel, to the effect that we are all, in totality, what we wish to be, barring unfortunate circumstances. And I no longer wanted to be a writer; I wanted to become an amateur naturalist.

The dominant question on the eve of this rebirthing was, What does an amateur naturalist eat? For starters, nothing; hence the fast. Writing is such a sedentary profession that I had become a tad burly, and to whirl through the forest with my single eye cocked on the flora and fauna, I needed to be light of foot. But then there were the contrasting styles of two friends who are naturalists, Peter Matthiessen and Doug Peacock. Matthiessen is rail lean from such small numbers as walking across East Africa and hauling fifty-pound bags of rice over nineteen-thousand-foot passes on the Tibetan Plateau of Nepal. In *The Snow Leopard*, he unfortunately neglects to mention what spices and condiments were used to prepare this rice. Peacock is decidedly chunky but owns a pair of legs somewhere between Arnold Schwarzenegger's and Herschel Walker's, the result of twenty years of tracking grizzlies and marching endlessly through the desert, the working theory being, When you are out of sorts, walk a hundred miles.

On a recent trek into Utah to look for petroglyphs, Peacock and I had, I thought, eaten rather poorly, concentrating on a big bag of *tsamba* that Yvon Chouinard, the famed mountaineer, had prepared for us. *Tsamba*, Tibetan in origin, is a mixture of grains tasting like the mixed sweepings off a granary floor, despite the addition of hot peppers. Tsamba swells up in your gut and displaces any interest in women, whiskey, cigarettes, or foie gras. Tsamba quickly turned me into a rambling eco-dope in the vast canyon lands of Utah.

It was barely dark at eleven outside my cabin on the Upper Peninsula when I went out to the pump house and turned off the generator. I remembered that a sage had said, "There must be freedom before there can be freedom," and scooted back to the cabin, hearing a pack of coyotes in chase under the howling wind. The meaning of the sage was clear enough: I had been wandering around the woods ever since my left eye was severely injured at age seven. All I had been doing recently was taking it to its proper limits and becoming more technically attentive to what I saw. I had already discovered that if you're not in a sex or food trance when you walk, you see the cranes before their enraged flush and note the change of pace in the bear tracks after it has caught your scent. You see that birds squeeze their eyes shut when they lay eggs and that the raven that answered you fifty-seven times was saying nothing in particular.

It was a very long night without my usual trip to the Dunes Saloon for a few nightcaps, without the assortment of snacks that aid sleep. Might I offer myself a sprig of parsley in my cheek? No, the parsley, like marijuana, could lead to further crime. How about a large glass of red wine, which, after all, was technically fruit juice? Nope. The coyotes passed within a few feet of the window, closing in on their midnight snack, a snowshoe rabbit. The beasts were eating, but not me; but then, raw rabbit lacked appeal.

Total sobriety and an empty stomach made for a restless, dream-filled sleep. I tended the votive fire relentlessly, so that the flames would acquire the correct shape. In a weak moment, I allowed myself to relive a great meal I had recently had at Lutèce (*soupe de poisson, poussin en croûte*) after which I got to shake hands with the great Andre Soltner himself, an event that beat any experience in show biz except for a dinner years ago with Federico Fellini, Marcello Mastroianni, Alberto Sordi, Giulietta Masina, and Anouk Aimée. You know, those folks. At about 4 A.M., the vision arrived with the force of a cattle prod or lightning down the chimney. The wind had subsided, and I was standing naked out on the picnic table, eyeing the three-quarter moon and trying to howl up a fresh batch of coyotes. I received a single, somewhat retarded response from down in the river delta near a den I had previously located. They were evidently done hunting for the night. I was actually hoping for a wolf, but I hadn't heard one in nearly four years, though the day before I had found a set of tracks in the drying mud of a pond's edge.

It was with this memory that the vision struck. Just before I had found the set of tracks, when I was well back from the pond, I had glassed a Hudsonian godwit, a rare shorebird. I then realized that with a few notable exceptions, such as the Hudsonian godwit and the ruddy turnstone, the birds of North America needed renaming.

I shuddered at the enormity of the project. Most writers know only four birds—hawk, gull, crow, robin—and I was looking at more than 600 species that required fresh names. I thought I'd better get started promptly, in order to finish before I kicked the bucket and my soul was hurled into the usual black hole in the cosmos. I went back into the cabin, dressed warmly, and headed east, fording a thigh-deep creek and passing a location I think of as the Place of the Bears. The area smelled dense and rank, and I imagined for a moment that I was in the locker room of the Soviet ladies' Olympic team.

At dawn I named a Delphic warbler and, better yet, a smallish brown bird henceforth to be called the beige *dolorosa*. I dozed off under a tree, and the nature of breakfast began to take shape. A nightwalker is entitled to a little wine, and there was a bottle of Borgogno Barbaresco waiting. The meal itself would be a modest pasta made with three pounds of frozen squid

I had brought from home. There were three tomatoes and a bouquet of fresh herbs I kept in a flower vase. A head of garlic and the somber character of Spanish olive oil would fill the bill.

As I headed home, I experienced a specific chafing problem known to many amateur naturalists, so I had to walk splay-legged. The new project unrolled its path in glory. I had no intention of becoming a neo-Dondi/Gandhi, but by the end of this new calling I would be a small brown man in a green coat looking for brown birds. "Deep in his throat, but perhaps it is a bird, he hears a child cry . . ." I quoted to myself, from a poem I wrote at nineteen.

1990

What Have We Done with the Thighs?

W here have all the thighs gone? Where are the thighs of yesteryear? This is not exactly a litany raised by many, but the heartfelt concern of a few. In recent memory I do not believe that I have entered a restaurant where thighs are allowed to stand alone proudly by themselves. I mean chicken thighs, though duck and turkey thighs are also lonely and neglected.

On a recent trip to New York via L.A. I tried to raise the thigh alarm in both places to show biz folks in *au courant* restaurants.

"God, what I'd do for a plate of thighs, you know, grilled in *paillard* form with a sauce made of garlic that has been roasted with olive oil and thyme, then puréed and spread on the crisp thigh skin. Alice Waters makes them that way."

"I think that's Mike Nichols's agent," a lady answered.

"Once on safari in Brazil I ate a big platter of roasted thighs with a blazing hot *chimichurri* pepper sauce in Bahia, then it was off to the jungle up the Rio del Muerto where we were trying to catch a big anaconda for the new Disney theme park in North Dakota. I was lost for thirty days and ended up using duct tape for toilet paper."

"I think I saw part of it on PBS," a producer in an Armani power blazer said. "In Taos where I met Dennis Hopper's cousin Duane. Duane Hopper. They're both from Dodge City, Kansas."

"Yeah, I've been there. The lady at the Best Western fried me three thighs for breakfast. With biscuits and pan gravy."

"Let me correct myself. That isn't Mike Nichols's agent. It's only Roger Ebert's agent. I heard R. E. just wrote a hot screenplay called *Naked Scouts on Their Birthdays*," the lady chimed in.

"I think chicken breasts are the moral equivalent of a TV commercial. I make Bocuse's *poulet au vinaigre* only with thighs," I insisted.

"The Budweiser Clydesdales are really getting dreary," she replied. "Dalmatians are cute in the snow."

"So are zebras." I watched as she ordered a poached chicken breast, insisting on flat-leafed Italian parsley on the side, as if it were intended to save this *filet de torpor*.

So I am a voice crying out in the wilderness. A casual inquiry to my brother, who runs the University of Arkansas library system in Fayetteville, and has contacts with Tyson, the world's largest producer of chicken for the table, revealed (hold onto your ass!) that the U.S. shipped 50,000 metric tons of thighs and legs to Russia in 1990! I fear I do not comprehend the mind that remains unstunned by this figure. It fatigues the brain, and deep in the forest on my daily hike I leaned against a lightning-blasted beech tree, a power spot, and imagined a thousand of these tons frozen into the shape of a prone King Kong in the hold of a giant freighter. I had gotten rid of one but had forty-nine to go. So many thighs, so many freighters.

Other notions began to spin off through the wintry air. Are we shipping our vigor, our strength, abroad? Would the ghost of D. H. Lawrence suggest that we fear thighs because of their proximity to the organs of reproduction and evacuation? Is it because we are still mummy's children and crave the anonymous, tasteless breast? Is it a subconscious fear of AIDS? Probably not, as sixty percent of those under thirty in America have never seen a live chicken and couldn't tell a thigh from Jon Bon Jovi's chin. Once I prepared quail for an actress of some note who doubled as a vegetarian. She was appalled after dinner to discover she had eaten a "living thing."

"Not after it was shot and plucked and roasted at 400 degrees for twenty-three minutes," I offered, suspecting Quaaludes.

Back in the forest I imagined the shark carnage that would occur if a freighter sank with such a cargo, the ship breaking up and the immense, frozen blocks of chicken thighs slowly melting in the saltwater. Strangely enough in the old days in Key West I once night-fished with a Cuban for sharks with a live chicken, the big hook bound to the hen's body with twine. For reasons of squeamishness I did not hold the rod with the live chicken bait but drove the getaway car. Soon enough we were eating broiled shark steaks and tending a shark stew laden with garlic and fresh tomatoes. Much of the hen was still intact though a bit of a mess to pluck. Not surprisingly, the shark had headed for the rear end where the flavor resides.

I left the woods and made my way over to Hattie's Grille in Suttons Bay, my favorite restaurant in the vast expanse of northern Michigan, though there are three others that could also survive in the competitive atmosphere of Chicago, or the coasts—The Rowe Inn, Tapawingo, and the Walloon Lake Inn. Naturally there are other good places but they have largely neglected a responsibility of first-rate restaurants, which is to educate our palates. Jim Milliman is the owner and chef of Hattie's Grille, assisted by Alice Clayton, a birdlike young woman who is breathtakingly deft in the kitchen.

When I arrived during the afternoon prep work Milliman was busy making three desserts, bread, and a pâté all at once. Then his wife, Beth, called and asked if he could whip up a white-chocolate mousse. He smiled and began chopping Belgian white chocolate. I poured a largish glass of Trefethen Cabernet, which is a steal, and was reminded again of the sheer speed that is demanded of the chef. I used to daydream of becoming one but the fantasy dissipates when reflecting on the exhaustion of preparing a dinner for ten. My own restaurant could only accept a daily party of four, at most. My hands are clumsy. I typed five novels with a single forefinger. Frankly, this limited my interest in revision.

Milliman doesn't go in for fancy names for his creations; his smoked whitefish pâté is called just that, and a lovely dish of his devising, medallions of Maine lobster in a tequila sauce, carries no frilly adjectives. He is particularly skillful with seafood though I enjoy his pheasant potpie, the garlicked veal chop on a wild-rice pancake, his chicken thighs braised in stock, cream and shiitakes.

I was strangely silent, sipping or gulping my wine, in hopes I would be asked what was bothering me.

"What's bothering you?" asked Milliman, who is accustomed to me in full babble about food matters.

I explained my thigh thoughts, ranging through culinary history down to the sociopolitical implications of exclusionary food faddism, the penchant for fey minimalism in the upwardly mobile groups. I finished with, "Do you think this all stands for something bigger?"

"Absolutely," Milliman said. Then we discussed approximately a hundred good ways to cook chicken thighs, branching out into turkey thighs (I favor the nutrition nag Jane Brody's way of poaching them in vermouth with fresh vegetables and a head of garlic). For duck thighs and legs you need go no further than Paula Wolfert's *The Cooking of South-West France*, or to Madeleine Kamman. Alice Waters bones rabbit thighs and grills them with *pancètta* and fresh sage. I prefer my thighs with two wines I got from Waters's husband, the wine merchant Stephen Singer: any Bandol, or a chianti called Isole.

On the way home I stopped at the grocer's for a slice of pork steak, a white-trash proclivity of mine. You pretend you're cutting off all the fat. It's the rare restaurant that offers pork steak. Doubtless it's being sent to China along with hard-to-find pig hocks. On the bulletin board in the grocery foyer someone was offering "Rabbits, Pets or Meat" on a three-by-five card.

This is a visceral world, I reflected, watching the carloads of deer hunters in bright orange milling up and down the country roads in the cold rain. There would be a big kill this year with extra permits given in lieu of extensive orchard damage. I have an orchard and couldn't shoot a deer for eating my young trees, but then I don't depend on the orchard for a living. On the rare occasion I deer hunt I hike the vacant Lake Michigan beaches where the deer notably aren't to avoid shooting one. This is horribly dishonest as venison is by far my favorite meat. I'm forced to hang around local taverns with a long face, saying such things as "If I hadn't lost my eye in the Tet Offensive (a fib) old mister swamp buck would've been deader than a doornail." Then I accelerate by asking for lesser cuts, the heart and liver, or the whole neck, including the bones, from which you can make a splendid *carbonnade* or *posole*. It usually works.

What we eat depends on where we live and how we have come to look at ourselves. An increasingly smaller part of our population has been raised within an age-old agricultural cycle where hunting and gathering are still a dominant, if waning, force in life. I find it disturbing to see recently all the life-style Nazis afoot prating about what one should drink, eat, read. Of course there is no dialogue. Given a choice between the NRA and animal rights I'll choose a rowboat anytime.

In his wonderful new book of essays, *The Practice of the Wild*, Gary Snyder says, "Our distance from the source of our food enables us to be superficially more comfortable, and distinctly more ignorant." Snyder is a Zen Buddhist and I doubt he would condone hunting except by native populations. The point is our "distance." I question the virtue of not knowing where your food comes from, whether it's the chicken on the conveyor belt clucking its way toward the knife, the steer waiting for the stun-gun, the fish gasping in foreign air among hundreds of others. On the goofy outer edge, researchers at Yale discovered that plants react when a shrimp is killed in their presence. Of course there is nothing so immediately rewarded in America, in the arts, entertainment, or public life, as a shrill and limited consciousness.

To be Christian, or something, maybe the Russians need the thighs more than we do. Once they're dead they may as well be eaten and for reasons involving the lack of soul we're not doing the job. I just worry that the Russians don't have the proper condiments—the fresh garlic and herbs, peppers, hot sauces, BBQ sauces, the wild mushrooms, leeks, and cream.

HOT TIPS—New product by Tabasco to make more-than-presentable chili quickly, called "TABASCO 7 Spice Chili Recipe (Spicy)." It will enrage the legion of chili bores we've all met. The best human thighs are visibly owned by Stephanie Seymour (*Sports Illustrated* calendars) and Madeleine Stowe (actress). As Pai Chang said a thousand years ago, "Just melt the inner and outer mind together completely."

1991

Travel & Sport

*With all its eyes the creature
world beholds the open.*

Rainer Maria Rilke

A Plaster Trout in Worm Heaven

I admit I woke up grousing; a lick from my Airedale pup Hud, named Hud to offend all people of good taste, did little to improve my mood. I reached up to the radio from the floor, where I must sleep forever since a 1,000-yard tumble while bird hunting savaged my spine. A newsman was reporting the accidental death of Herb Shriner, my favorite boyhood comedian. A girl in New York City once told me I talked like Herb Shriner. It takes many generations of rural indigence to make a Herb Shriner voice, long evenings of pinochle around a kerosene stove trying to pick up Chicago on a ten-dollar radio. There was a light rain against the windows, and I thought of a statement once made by a statistics nut to the effect that Michigan receives less sunlight than any other state.

I walked out to the barn and tried to look at Lake Michigan—on a clear day, few though there may be, you can see over thirty miles, way out beyond the Manitou Islands, and the hills are conceivably full of the sound of music. Because of the obtuse presence of the media, I often think of myself as living within a giant, beautiful, scale-model cigarette commercial. I sang a few bars of "It's Great to Live in the Great Lakes Country." The landlord looked at me quizzically from a tool shed. I waved. No time for embarrassment. I was going to a festival.

There appear to be a lot of small hat sizes around here, I say to myself, perhaps unfairly, entering the hotel bar in Kalkaska (pop. 1,475). One learns to mistrust locations where even a good hamburger is not available. But the drinks are extremely large and cost only fifty cents. Getting drunk here would be punching inflation right in the nose. The man sitting on the stool next to me in the crowded room announces himself as a former marine.

"Once a marine, always a marine!" I reply, attempting to placate his obvious hostility. The same may be said of Harvard graduates. They simply never let you forget.

Then the marine says, "If you don't love it, leave it," quoting the great Merle Haggard tune and eyeing my rather trim Pancho Villa mustache. His lips are flecked and stained with one of those nostrums used to combat stomach acid.

"Leave what?"

"The U.S. of A."

"I *looovve* it," I say, rolling my blind eye counter-clockwise, one of the few skills I picked up in college.

"Damn ajax," he replies, drinking deeply. Beer drizzles down onto his faded fatigue shirt.

"Do you favor the cattle prod as a fishing weapon?" I say, taking out my little steno pad and turning to him on the bar stool. He shrugs and leaves.

I reflect on the pioneer spirit and how it made our country what it is, and the odious Bumppoism that emerges for events like the National Trout Festival. The slogan of this year's festival, the thirty-fourth annual, is "This Land Is Your Land—This Is My Country," which is typical of the sort of hysterical chauvinism and contradictory rhetoric one finds in rural hardhats. At Jack's Sportshop, where the fish in the contest are to be weighed in, flag decals are for sale. It brings back all those articles I've read in the past twenty years celebrating the sportsman as a modern conquistador:

WE FIST-FOUGHT HITLER'S LUST-MAD LUNKER TROUT

"It seems that I was asked to go up in the High Lonesome with Bob, Bob Sr., and Bob Jr., partners in a Dairy Whip/insurance/real-estate/kapok-flailing operation in a little town next to the Big Woods in our state. We left at dawn after a hearty breakfast of fresh country eggs, country flapjacks, country bacon and country toast, all washed down with many cups of hot black java. I sat in the back of the nifty camper with the three white police dogs that would be used to guard us against those terrors of the local wood-lots, porcupines. The dogs were named Rin and Rin Tin and Rin Tin Tin to keep things simple. Next to a holstered .357, Bob Jr. wore a machete that he claimed made an excellent fish priest. We were towing a boat and an all-terrain vehicle and in addition had brought along four trail bikes, a dozen varmint rifles of various calibers, fishing gear and a case of good old snake-bite medicine . . . yuk yuk yuk . . ."

This might be called the brown-shoe–white-sock syndrome and is, I fear, the predominant attitude of fishing- and hunting-license buyers.

In what might be called the town square of Kalkaska, except that nearly all of the town is on one side and the railroad tracks are on the other, there is a statue. Not a Confederate general, a Union general, an Indian chief, a bronzed howitzer or a limp tank. It is a trout. I am told that it is a brook trout, and it is nearly twenty feet high. Curled and flexed, its enraged plaster strikes out of the smallish fountain at an imaginary giant fly, or more likely a worm dangling from worm heaven. Actually the fish looks like a cross between a smelt and a moray eel, or a sick alewife with a tinge of green creeping along the dorsal and the dread death spots beginning to appear.

But that is not the point. People passing on Route 131 may glance to the right and see the fish and muse aloud, "This is fishing country." The trout is continually bathed by water jets, but today there is a malfunction in the fountain. I cross the street with Cliff and Clint to see what's wrong. Clint Walter is to receive the Citizen of the Year award and is a benign and dedicated conservationist. Cliff Kimball is the president of both the festival and the Chamber of Commerce and is an unabashed booster. It seems the pump hole for the fountain is filling with water and if something is not done immediately the electric motor will short out. Cliff says it took a lot of pancake suppers to build this trout shrine. In small towns in Michigan, and probably elsewhere, pancake suppers, perch fries, ox roasts, chicken-gizzard barbecues, square dances and raffles are used to raise money for statues, PTA tea services, bank uniforms and school trips, like sending the senior class to Chicago or Milwaukee on the *Clipper*. Anyway, the fountain is fixed after some tinkering. Emergency ended. The fountain will spray throughout the festival.

The fire whistle blows and Cliff and Clint hasten off, both members of the Volunteer Fire Department. The bandstand, with its red, white and blue bunting, is deserted. I climb up the steps and walk to the microphone. My chance! There is a crowd slowly assembling for what the program calls Youth on Parade, with floats, pets, clowns, bands and attractions. I feel like the dictator of British Honduras and have a dark desire to bray some nonsense, such as, "The trout on my left is rabid!" or "The war is over!" But I recognize my urge as literary and blush.

I spot a man I watched a week ago in Leland snagging steelhead with gang hooks, a custom a bit more stealthy and subtle—and popular—than old-fashioned dynamite or gill-netting. I could yell at the oaf and expose him, but then the point would be missed on the gathering crowd, which now numbers at least 200. Cliff mentioned that approximately 70,000 people would be here or "in the area," as many as attend the Shenandoah Apple Festival but not nearly as many as are said to attend the Traverse City Cherry Festival. There are fibbers afoot in the heartland.

It is a glorious day, the mildest opening of the trout season to come to mind. A few years ago I sat huddled on the banks of the Manistee with a mixture of snow and sleet flying in my face, my hands red and numb from tying on streamers, and the guides on the rod icing up every few casts. The first day always seems to involve resolute masochism; if it isn't unbearably cold, then the combination of rain and warmth manages to provide maximal breeding conditions for mosquitoes, and they cloud and swarm around your head, crawl up your sleeves and down your neck, despite the most potent and modern chemicals. Early in the season the water is rarely clear, making wading adventuresome. The snags and deeper holes become invisible to a fisherman. You tend to forget that stretches of familiar water can change character within a year's time—last season's safe eddy below a pool measures a foot above the wader tops this spring, surely the coldest, wettest foot conceivable.

I walk over to the Chamber of Commerce office and have coffee with Cliff. He is pleased pink about the weather. Questioned about the crowd possibilities, he replies obliquely. *He* says that Kalkaska is the smallest town in Michigan with a full-time Chamber president. He allows as how his duties are so pressing, he does not have time for trout fishing—perhaps a little pike fishing later in the season in the Upper Peninsula when "things slow down." I reflect on this. It would be hard to create a slower village. Driving around Kalkaska County, you are reminded of those Jonathan Winters routines involving a hound with a bald tail sleeping near a gas pump and chickens scratching in a bare yard. But such places have an undeniable charm nowadays. Much of the popularity of country music is surely due to nostalgia for those drowsy days when "we didn't have much, but we had fun."

The village is beginning to fill. Some of the people are farmers in bib overalls on their traditional Saturday visit to town with their pickups full of sacks of feed and groceries. But there are many out-of-county and out-of-state license plates, and the bars and restaurants are full. I talk to dozens of people, and their reasons for coming are varied, ranging from "I never missed one" to "I like the parade" to "a chance to visit the hometown."

Everyone seems to know everyone else, but this is the sort of camaraderie caused by good weather and the prospect of a parade. It occurs to me that nothing really happens at a festival, no daring feats of excellence, but that no matter how artificial the point of celebration might be, these events provide entertainment, an excuse to go someplace, a break in what up here is the arduous process of making a living. Now that much of our countryside is less intensively agricultural, festivals compete with county fairs in popularity. A great number of misplaced farmers have gone south to the factories of Flint, Grand Rapids, Lansing and Detroit, and they look for any excuse to return to the country with their aluminum campers and pale city children dressed in what are considered locally as outrageous costumes.

I decided to take a short tour of the streams to see how the fishermen were doing. There are three reasonably good trout rivers within twenty miles of Kalkaska: the small Rapid, the medium-sized Boardman and the large Manistee. In addition, inside of a two-hour drive you can reach the Pigeon, Sturgeon, Black, Au Sable, Betsie, Platte, Pere Marquette and Pine, plus innumerable smaller creeks. A large stretch of the Au Sable has been brought back from relatively degenerate conditions by an organization called Trout Unlimited, which is the fly-fisherman's court of last resort. This provides adequate fishing for all but the most adamant whiners, among whom I number myself.

I was horrified in Livingston, Montana, last year to hear Joe Brooks, the famous angler, say that Michigan fishing was fine. After all, I had traveled nearly 2,000 miles to hit the honey buckets. There is no question that the streams are not what they were, say, before 1955. The reasons are the usual ones—newly developed resorts, cottagers, road builders, oil interests, industrial effluents, virulent pesticides.

None of these need cause irrevocable damage, but getting government aid is difficult. Other forms of fishing—trolling for lake trout and coho salmon, for example—have a larger constituency and command a larger share of the money and the attention of the state's Department of Natural Resources. And so the charter business is booming and the boat manufacturers are happy. Large coho and chinook are being caught in quantity, and it is difficult to begrudge their advocates the fun of catching them, though trolling seems to be a desperately boring form of fishing. The coho, however, have disturbed the steelhead fishing by jamming the mouths of rivers emptying into Lake Michigan with spawning fish in their death throes.

All the fishermen encountered on the Boardman complain about the warm and sunny weather except a young boy who has three nice browns, about fourteen inches apiece. Most of the anglers are using worms, and none flies. I drive over to Sharon (pop. two or three, seriously) on the Manistee. The story is the same—too much heat and light. It has often troubled me that, no matter, truly cunning fishermen invariably catch fish. Their methods must be plastic and unconstrained, perhaps unsporting. During July and August on the Boardman, when I mostly catch spiritless hatchery fish, a few crafty old men catch large browns by chumming the stream with quarts of grasshoppers, then placing a small hook to make one of the bugs a fatal meal. Though effective, this seems, to my way of thinking, a bit low.

Ernest Hemingway fished the Boardman as a young man and complained in a letter home that the swiftness of the water made wading difficult. I think this was part of the novelist's imagination, because there were, even in his time, four dams on the last twenty miles approaching Traverse City. The final two-mile stretch is now murky and exudes a shameful stench. And it is not simply a matter of saying that things "aren't what they used to be," which is neither helpful nor interesting. I am privately in favor of the death penalty for any form of pollution not speedily rectified. If you are keen on trout fishing, I advise that you log thousands of hours a summer, because the signs, short of radical ecological surgery, point to its demise.

When I return from my streamside tour around noon, Kalkaska is choked with people, though a wombat most assuredly can choke on a single kernel of corn, and I have no idea how many people there are. I park in a shady residential district and walk the five or six blocks to the center of town. The lawns are neat, the houses modest but in good repair. What do people do? Take in each other's laundry and throw festivals? Our land is full of incomprehensible wonder, and nay-sayers should be raspberried.

On Main Street, Cliff is up on the bandstand in a boater and a string tie. Hank Snow's country music blares from a public-address system that tweets and howls and screeches, drowning out the lyrics. Cliff makes some garbled announcements. He is a mixture of booster and carnival barker. I remember he once lured the International Sled Dog Races to Kalkaska for the slow winter months.

Perhaps in an age heavily flavored with the artificial and the often very distant spectator sport, a celebration of trout or dog is a good thing despite the heavy dosage of sheer hokum. A Silent Majority spring rite laced with streaks of yokel patriotism.

In front of the hardware store there is a kindly old man who tells me that many years ago a rainbow weighing over twenty pounds, caught at Bailey's Rapids, won the contest. Bailey's Rapids is a stretch of the upper Manistee near Fife Lake and not far from town. I have fished the area with some eagerness. It is unlikely that this fast, shallow stretch of water can offer good fishing much longer; too many cabins have been built on its banks in the past decade. The waters will inevitably degenerate from seeping septic tanks.

I feel melancholy reading the Official Program, which announces such events as a canoe race, a Grand Royal Parade and one last item, a Buick Opel Paint-In. I plan avoiding the latter but allow my mind to revolve wildly around its possibilities. I begin to think numbly of the many small communities in Michigan that throw one sort of festival or another to draw dollars before winter sets in. (Climate may soon be no hindrance; a few months ago there was a snowmobile festival.) We have a Bean Queen, a Strawberry Queen, a Cherry Queen, a Smoked Pickerel Queen, an Alpenfest Queen and a Red Flannel Queen from Cedar Springs, whom I am to meet later today. The new Trout Queen is Pat Christian, an appropriate name for a lovely girl from the north country. I wonder if in the swine provinces of Iowa they have a Pig Queen. Or if somewhere in our country there is simple Queen Queen. And do they have Queens in England other than the honest-to-God one?

At lunch there are many local politicians, and virtually everyone is applauded and gets an award except me. The fried trout is good. Fred Bear of Bear Archery is announced King of the Festival, and there is a hearty round of applause for King Fred and Queen Pat, who sit together in purple robes with bright-yellow paper crowns. Fred Bear has slain elephant, grizzly, polar bear and Cape buffalo with bow and arrow; he looks gaunt and fatigued, like a member of displaced nobility or an actual sultan at a Shriner convention.

There is an interminable speech by a state Fish and Game Department representative. He says that statistics show Americans spend more on outdoor recreation than they do on the Vietnam War. The comparison is boggling. We are told his department is doing a "yeoman's job" taking care of the resources that the "Omnipotent Being" and "Mother Nature" have given us.

During the Grand Royal Parade, I count fifty-six floats. Floats represent something truly inscrutable in our culture, and you may want to draw some conclusions of your own from this sampling: the sheriff of Lake County, King Fred and Queen Pat, a state senator, a team of sled dogs, three mobile homes (just plain mobile homes), a church bus with a banner proclaiming HEAVEN OR BUS-T, an old car, the National Ice and Snow Queen, a garden tractor with an STP sticker, an old plow, three marines, a large papier-mâché Holy Bible, the Kalkaska Sno-Packers (snowmobile club), the Missaukee County Dairy Princess, a posse mounted on horseback, the Liars Club.

I walk to Jack's to check on the fish entered in the contest. A Reverend Glick has entered a fine steelhead, and there are several good catches of browns, though one entry is suspiciously uniform and might have been caught at a planted trout pond. (When the dog days of August are around and the fishing is slow, it is great sport sneaking through the woods and poaching private ponds. I usually take along a bottle of whiskey for courage.) Looking at the pastor's steelhead, it occurs to me that an energetic and expert fisherman could catch in one day coho and chinook salmon and steelhead, rainbow, lake, brown and brook trout within fifty miles of Kalkaska.

While driving home after a fine, though terribly honky concert by Hank Snow, I begin to dream about what the caddis hatch will be like this year. I open the car window and restructure Carl Sandburg by yelling, "The People, No!" into the American night. Then I become humble, remembering a few weeks before blowing a cast to a world-record tarpon that was hanging still in a clear green pool not thirty feet from the boat. This is akin to missing the TV across the living room with a shotgun loaded with number eight birdshot. My partner and quasi-guide screamed and threw a fit until I became a small, very warm blob of molasses on the boat seat. I would return to Big Pine Key only in a full Groucho Marx mask.

The night is unseasonably warm for April, perfect for the spring absurdity that I had just witnessed. Tomorrow Kalkaska can count its change in peace. Everything has been talked about except the lowly trout. It may as well have been a Frisbee Gala, but that is held in July in Copper Harbor.

1971

The Violators

Picture this man on a cool, late summer morning, barely dawn: gaunt, bearded, walking through his barnyard carrying a Winchester 30-30, wearing a frayed denim coat and mauve velvet bellbottoms. He is broke and though able-bodied he thinks of himself as an artist and immune to the ordinary requirements of a livelihood. Perhaps he is. He is one of the now numberless dropouts from urban society, part of a new agrarian movement, the "back to the land" bit that seems to be sweeping young writers. But he hankers for meat rather than the usual brown rice. I myself in a fatuous moment have told him of my own 200-gram-a-day protein diet—meat, meat, meat, lots of it with cheese and eggs, plus all the fruit you can lift from neighboring orchards and all the bourbon you can afford during evening pool games. Who needs macrobiotics?

Anyway, back to the barnyard. The killer lets the horses out of the paddock and they run off through the ground mist. The morning is windless and the grass soaked with dew, ideal conditions for poaching a deer. He walks up the hill behind his house, very steep. He is temporarily winded and sits down for a cigarette. Thirty miles out in Lake Michigan the morning sun has turned the steep cliffs of South Fox Island golden. There is a three-foot moderate roll; the lake trout and coho trollers will be out today in all of their over-equipped glory. Later in the season he will snag lake trout from the Leland River, or perhaps even catch some fairly. He thinks of the coho as totally contemptible—anyone with a deft hand can pluck them from the feeder streams.

About 500 yards to the east, clearly visible from the hill, is a deserted orchard and a grove of brilliantly white birch trees. Beautiful. He will walk quietly through a long neck of woods until he is within 100 yards of the orchard. Except in the deepest forest, deer are largely nocturnal feeders in Michigan, but they can still be seen in some quantity at dawn or dusk if you know where to look. During the day they filter into the sweet coolness of cedar swamps or into the rows of the vast Christmas tree plantations. He sits and rests his rifle on a stump. He immediately spots a large doe between the second and third rows of the orchard, and farther back in the scrubby neglected trees a second-year buck, maybe 130 pounds, perfect eating size. He aims quickly just behind and a trifle below the shoulder and fires. The buck stumbles, then bursts into full speed. But this energy is deceptive and the animal soon drops. My friend hides his rifle, covering it with dead leaves. If you do happen to get caught—the odds are against it—your rifle is confiscated. He jogs down to the deer, stoops, hoists its dead weight to his shoulder and heads back to the house.

A few hours later his pickup pulls into my yard. I am in the barn wondering how I can fix one of the box stalls when my brother has bent the neck of my hammer pulling spikes. I hear the truck and when I come out into the yard he hands me a large bloody package. Everything is understood. We go into the kitchen and have a drink though it is only ten in the morning. We slice the buck's liver very thin, then drive to the grocery store where I have some inexpensive white bordeaux on order. When we get back my wife has sautéed the liver lightly in clarified butter. We eat this indescribably delicious liver, which far exceeds calves' liver in flavor and tenderness. A hint of apple, clover and fern. We drink a few bottles of wine and he goes home and I take a nap. That evening my wife slices a venison loin into medallions, which she again cooks simply. During the afternoon I had driven into Traverse City to splurge on a bottle of Châteauneuf-du-Pape. The meal—the loin and a simple salad of fresh garden lettuce, tomatoes and some green onions—was exquisite.

End of tale. I wouldn't have shot the deer myself. But I ate a lot of it, probably ten pounds in all. I think it was wrong to shoot the deer. Part of the reason I would not have killed it is that I am no longer able to shoot at mammals. Grouse and woodcock, yes. But gutting and skinning a deer reminds me too much of the human carcass and a deer heart too closely resembles my own. My feelings are a trifle ambivalent on this particular incident but I have decided my friend is a violator only barely more tolerable than the cruder sort. If it had been one of the local Indians—it often is—I would have found it easy to bow to the ancestral privilege. But my friend is not a local Indian.

Game hoggery is not the point. The issue is much larger than human greed. We have marked these creatures to be hunted and slaughtered, and destroyed all but a remnant of their natural environment. But fish and mammals must be considered part of a larger social contract, and just laws for their protection enforced with great vigor. The first closed deer season in our country due to depletion of the herds occurred in 1694 in Massachusetts. Someone once said, "The predator husbands his prey." The act of violation is ingrained, habitual; it represents a clearly pathological form of outdoor atavism. Not one violator out of a hundred acts out of real need or hunger. The belief that he does is another of many witless infatuations with local color.

I have an inordinate amount of time to think and wander around. Poets muse a lot. Or as Whitman, no mean fisherman, said, "I loaf and invite my soul." Mostly loaf. I have always found that I can think better and more lucidly with my Fox Sterlingworth, or any of a number of fly rods, in hand. I'm a poor shot, but I really do miss some grouse because I'm thinking. Recently I was walking along a stream that empties into Lake Michigan within half a dozen miles of my farm. It was late October, with a thin skein of snow that would melt off by afternoon. There were splotches of blood everywhere and many footprints and small piles of coho guts. The fish were nearly choking the stream, motionless except for an errant flip of tail to maintain position. And there were some dead ones piled up near a small logjam. They stank in the sharp fall air with the pervasive stench of a dead shorthorn I had once found near the Manistee River. Oh, well. Sport will be sport. No doubt someone had illegally clubbed a few for his smokehouse. Clubbed or pitched them out with a fork or shovel as one pitches manure. They are surprisingly good if properly smoked, though you must slice and scrape out the belly fat because of the concentrated DDT found there. But in the stream, in their fairly advanced stage of deliquescence, with backs and snouts scarred and sore and whitish, they looked considerably less interesting than floundering carp. How could a steelhead swim through this aquatic garbage to spawn? Tune in later, maybe another year or two, folks.

I walked back to my car and drove west two miles to the stream mouth. This confluence of waters has never produced any really big trout, but it is fine for close-to-home fishing. I rigged my steelhead rod, put on my waders and began casting into a mild headwind, which required a low-profile turn-over. Around here one learns to appreciate anything less than fifteen knots, though if the water is too still the fishing is bad. I am not a pretty caster and my ability to double haul, thus increasing line speed, is imperfect; when you flunk a double haul the line whips and cracks, then collapses around your head and you are frustrated and sad as only a fly caster can be, glad only that no one was watching. I hooked two small fish on an attractor pattern and lost them after a few jumps. Then I hooked a larger fish on a lightly weighted Muddler and within an asthmatic half hour of coaxing I beached it. I was breathless, insanely excited. A steelhead, maybe six pounds with a vague pink stripe and short for his weight, chunky, muscular, a very healthy fish. Yum. Then a retired contractor from Ann Arbor I know came along and began casting with a small spoon and light spinning tackle. He is a pleasant sort, mildly arthritic, so his sport exacts no small amount of pain—the water is cold and the wind is cold and moist. He fished for an hour or so before he hooked an ungodly animal, a steelhead that porpoised like a berserk marlin, easily the largest I had ever seen. It made a long lateral run and he followed it down the beach for a few hundred yards before the fish turned and headed out for South Manitou Island and, beyond that, Wisconsin. It cleaned him. We sat and talked about the beast and I could see that his hands were shaking.

Three more fishermen came along and began casting in my spot with huge treble-hooked spoons. One of them quickly changed to a heavy bell sinker to which he attached large hooks. They were using what is known in Michigan as the "Newaygo Twitch"; three easy turns of the reel and then a violent reef. It is a fine method for foul-hooking and snagging coho and chinook, even spawning steelhead and lake trout. The Michigan Department of Natural Resources has submitted to political pressure and ruled that foul-hooked salmon can be kept rather than released and this ruling has encouraged bozos by the thousand to use the twitch method to the exclusion of all other styles of fishing. I have seen sportsmen snag upwards of 200 pounds of lake trout—incredibly far over the legal limit—in the Leland River where the fish are in layers devouring their own aborted spawn below the dam. And these people have been led to think they are fishing. Anyway, I left the beach immediately. I stopped into Dick's Tavern to calm my abraded nerves. I often fantasize about bullwhipping these creeps as Mother Nature's Dark Enforcer. When my imagination for vengeance is depleted I think about moving to Montana where such yuks, I suppose, are as plentiful, but seem at least less visible. It is strange to see a government agency sponsoring acts that are a degradation of the soul of sport. It is as if the National Football League were to encourage and promote face-mask tackling. Take a firm grasp and rip his damn head off.

It is a silly mistake, I've found, to assume that rules of fair play are shared. I have met and talked at length with men who harry and club to death both fox and coyote from snowmobiles. It should not seem necessary to pass laws against so base and resolutely mindless a practice, but it is necessary. I suppose that in simplistic terms our acquisitive and competitive urges have been transferred directly to sport—one can "win" over fish or beast but, unlike what happens in other forms of sport, the violator disregards all the rules. A certain desolate insensitivity persists: I know some seemingly pleasant young men who in the past have gathered up stray dogs to use as target practice to hone their skills. This is not the sort of thing one can argue about. Neither can one question the logic of the hunting club members who bait deer with apples, corn and a salt lick, and then on the crisp dawn of the first day of the season fire away at the feeding animals. Or marksmen who hang around rural dumps to get their garbage bear. Or those who wander around swamps adjacent to lakes in the spring collecting gunny sacks of spawning pike; usually they are the same people who tell you that fishing "isn't what it used to be." To be sure, the majority of sportsmen follow the laws with some care, but the majority is scarcely overwhelming. More like a plurality with a grand clot of the indifferent buffering the middle. And silent, at best. Not to mention the chuckle-wink aspect, the we're-all-cowpokes-ain't-we attitude, of so many judges who mete out wrist-slap fines to game-law violators.

I think I was about fourteen when the problem first became apparent to me. It was late in November near the end of the deer season, very cold up in Michigan with a foot of fine powder snow, not bad to walk in as it burst around one's feet like weightless down or fluff. I was hunting along a ridge that completely encircled a large gully forming a bowl. At the bottom of the bowl there was a small marsh of tag alder, snake-grass, dried-up cattails and brake, and perhaps four or five slender tamarack. I sat down on a boulder to eat my lunch and watch the swale, thinking it might hold a large buck or even a young spikehorn. Across my lap I held an antique 38-40, the accuracy of which was less than profound but better anyhow than the shotgun and slug my friends used, which was an embarrassment to them. After an hour of sitting and staring, staring so hard that my eye tried to trace the shapes I wanted to see, four deer calmly walked out of the far side of the swale. I looked at them quickly through my peepsight. All female. They picked their way cautiously single file toward a sumac thicket on the side of the hill, trying to minimize the time spent in the open. But then an explosion, a barrage, a fusillade. The first doe made the thicket and bounded up and over the ridge. The second dropped in her tracks but the third, shot probably in the hindquarters, tried to drag herself back to the swale by her forefeet. Then she was hit again and was still. The fourth doe ran in narrowing, convulsive circles until she dropped.

I don't remember thinking anything. I only watched. Three men walked down the hill and looked at the deer. They were talking but were too far away for me to hear distinctly. I sat very still until their red forms disappeared. I didn't go down the hill and look at the dead deer. I thought the game warden might come along and think I had shot them and the fine for shooting a doe would be enormous for someone who earned at best $2 a day for hoeing potatoes. I hunted without thought for a few more hours, getting a hopeless shot at a distant buck, and then walked to the car where I was to meet my father when it began to get dark. All the staccato noise of the rifle shots had served to remind me of the Korean War and what it must sound like. Pork Chop Hill was much in the news in those days.

I think it was Edward Abbey who coined the phrase "cowboy consciousness" to describe that peculiar set of attitudes many Americans still hold: the land is endless, unspoiled, mysterious, still remaining to be overcome and finally won. So shoot, kill, bang-bang-bang. WOW! And city dwellers, it seems, who come to the country during the hunting and fishing seasons, are now more guilty of these attitudes than their rural counterparts, who sense the diminishing wilderness around them, the truncated freedom of movement. Every dentist and machinist and welder and insurance adjuster in Michigan either owns or wants to own twenty posted acres "up north."

But we are hopeless romanticists about this imaginary Big Woods—it simply no longer exists in any faintly viable form. Even one of the far corners of creation, the North Slope of the Brooks Range, is littered with oil drums. It seems funny, too, to discover that every American in the deepest little synapse in his brain considers himself a natural at hunting and fishing, a genetic Pete Maravich of the outback, wherever that is. We always tell each other that the deer are on the ridges today or in the swamps or clustered in the grape arbors or frittering away the morning behind the woodpile despite the fact that few of us could identify five trees at gunpoint. And every little rural enclave has its number of wise old owls who have spent a lifetime sipping draft beer and schnapps and are rife with such witticisms as "you greenhorns couldn't hit a bull in the butt with a banjo. Now back in 1938, why . . ." The point is that in the old days the rivers were stiff with giant bull trout and deer wandered the countryside in grand herds like Idaho sheep. You didn't even have to aim. This cowboy consciousness is so ingrained and overwhelming in some violators that they will suffer any risks. A poacher near here was arrested for the twentieth time, fined $1,000 and given 165 days in jail. An equal punishment was given to two men who dynamited a rainbow holding pond at a weir. I somehow doubt that this will discourage them.

I feel a very precise melancholy when I hear rifle shots in the middle of a September night; the jacklighters are at work after a tepid evening at the bowling alley. Picture this recent local case. A yellow cone of light is shining into a field. It is a powerful beam and nothing animate within a hundred yards escapes its illumination. Three teenagers are sitting in an old Mercury playing the light against the backdrop of woods and field as they drive slowly along a gravel road. One of them has a loaded rifle. If a deer is spotted the light paralyzes it hypnotically. The deer will stare without motion into the light and even the shabbiest marksman can pick his shot. But this will prove an unfortunate night for shining deer. A car approaches from the rear at high speed and swerves in front of the hunters to block any escape. It is Reino Narva, the game warden, to the rescue. In this particular instance all of the culprits are juveniles and first offenders and the sentences are light.

There is nothing inscrutable about the matter of violation. I fancy myself an amateur naturalist and have hot flashes when I think of the sins of my past, harmless and usual though they may be. I think of the large brown trout I caught at age twelve by illegal set line in the Muskegon River. Turtles had eaten all but its head by the time I pulled the line in. I nailed the head to the barn alongside my pike and bass skulls as if I had caught the fish by fair means. Or the roosting grouse stalked and shot with a .22. Or diving into a lake for weeks on end with a knife, handle in mouth, to carve the heads off turtles we flushed from logs. We thought they were killing our fish. Or shooting crows. Or shooting at deer in midsummer with bow and arrow, though I don't remember ever coming close. All the mindless sins of youth committed in the haze of reading Edgar Rice Burroughs, Zane Grey, James Oliver Curwood, Jack London and Ernest Seton; wanting to be a steely half-breed Robert Mitchum type with hatchet, revolver, cartridge belt and a long mane of hair trained with bear grease.

Gentle reader, rules will never stop the jacklighter and snagger, the violator. It is not so much that enforcement of the law is inept, but that respect for the spirit of the law is insufficient. And in Michigan there are fabulous ironies; a portion of any fine for a game violation is earmarked as "restitution to the state." But you might well be shining your deer in an opening in a forest that has been ravaged by the oil interests—public land doled away for peanuts by conservationists in a state with boggling population and recreation problems. Or you might get caught snagging a trout in Manistee Lake where a paper company belches out thousands of gallons of fluid waste daily into public waters so rank that a motorboat scarcely can manage a wake. Who is violating what? Or as René Char said, "Who stands on the gangplank directing operations? The captain or—the rats?" Not a very subtle distinction, hereabouts. The problems seem, and perhaps are, insuperable. The political-business-conservation relationship in Michigan often reminds one of old-style Boston politics; everyone gets a piece of the action but the pie itself suffers from terminal rot. Of course, this is ho-hum stuff now. Pollution is "in committee" everywhere and government is firming up its stand, à la kumquat jelly, with a lid of yellow paraffin. I have a dreamy plot afoot for a court test to be decided on Saturn wherein the Constitution and Bill of Rights would be made to apply to fish and mammals.

Finally, it is a very strange arrogance in man that enables him to chase the last of the whales around the ocean for profit, shoot polar bear cubs for trophies, allow Count Blah–Blah to blast 885 pheasants in one day. It is much too designed to be called crazy or impetuous.

Those lines of Robert Duncan's about Robin Hood come back to me now: "How we loved him / in childhood and hoped to abide by his code / that took life as its law!" The key word here is "code." Sport must be sporting. We have a strong tendency to act the weasel in the hen house. At dawn not a single cluck was heard. It might be preposterous to think we will change, but there are signs. Judges are becoming sterner and people are aware of environmental problems to a degree not known in this country before. Game wardens get more cooperation from the ordinary citizen than they used to. Violating is losing its aura of rube cuteness.

The true violator, though, will persist in all of his pathological glory. Even if there were no game left on earth, something would be devised. Maybe a new sport on this order: ganghooking Farmer Brown's pigs. A high-speed power winch mounted on a vehicle hood is required, and a harpoon with large hooks. You shoot the harpoon over the pig's back and press the winch button. Zap! You've got yourself a squealer. Precautions: make sure Farmer Brown is away for the day, and take your finger off the winch button in time or the pork will really fly.

1971

Ice Fishing, the Moronic Sport
A Michigan Journal

There are strange things done 'neath the midnight sun.
—Bob Service

We're not actually *that* far north. Yes, a small church in the Upper Peninsula had a Blessing of the Snowmobiles, and not a trace of irony was noticed. But the sense of the Arctic does pull on us; days shorten, men mumble, the euchre games at the tavern grow extended and violent. There is much talk in December and January of just when the bay will freeze over. It is the west arm of the Grand Traverse Bay they are talking about, a very grand bay indeed, containing some five by thirty miles of Lake Michigan's water. The east arm (they are separated by the forefinger of Old Mission Peninsula) usually freezes first, but the lake trout there, for unknown reasons, run smaller. Some years the bay doesn't freeze, but this is rare. And some years an oil tanker is brought in at an inopportune time, say if there is a steady offshore wind and a warming trend, and the ice breaks up and blows out of the bay. Until February 14, the date on which the ice is usually safe, sportsmen must be content to fish on smaller lakes for perch or crappies, or some of them take up the ancient art of pike spearing. But these activities locally are only considered as warm-ups. On inland lakes, many consider these forms of ice fishing adequate and cases are made for chugging bluegills with corn borers, a small obnoxious worm found in cornstalks. Houghton Lake, a resort area drawing much of its traffic from Hamtramck and other posh Detroit suburbs, throws a gala every winter known as Tip-Up Town, the "tip-up" referring, of course, to the crude rig positioned above the hole in the ice.

Years ago, when I was a temporary prisoner on Long Island and dreamed of a return to Trout Country, I thought of those hallowed winter nights that resemble Christmas cards, with large jeweled flakes of snow falling softly on humble farm animals and peasant faces upturned in wonderment and looking not a little bit like my relatives. But reality is a different pudding. BRAAAOOWILL is what we have, my transcription of what is called a snow-mobile "safari." Safari is when a dozen or so machines strike out in the night cross-country for another tavern. Let's have it once more: BRAAAOOWILL, as if a dozen burly chain saws were mating under a single tympanum cowl.

Walking out on any large expanse of ice has always been dramatic to me. After not many steps I tend to stumble involuntarily, as if I were an exhausted survivor of the Byrd Expedition. I frankly expect seals or polar bears, perhaps a wolf loping along the farther shore. But if I fall and roll over I can maybe see a 1969 Camaro passing on the road or a guy and gal in his 'n' her purple satin overall suits just cattin' around on their throaty Ski-doo. This brings me swiftly back to reality. Here are a few reality facts from the Great North: our unemployment rate this year is sixteen percent, giving many some much unwanted time off; snowmobiles, mobile homes and motels each outnumber the total population in 1977; most of my friends are unemployed and if I *did* have any money they would try to borrow it! I am led, though, by many people I meet to believe that they are mainly worried about the Communist Threat and how the "radicals are tearing apart the country." They tell me that they "worked for what they got" and "nobody gave them nothing." In periods of high unemployment the Great Depression again becomes a ruling fact of life. Yet many people up here strike me as more populist than conservative, and there is the kind of generalized suspicion of Big Government that one finds in non-urban Arizona. They are angry at Nixon for selling them that 1952 Buick, but then they hated Johnson, who is still blamed for everything but the tight-money policy, which is especially hard on a resort area, the only other large local industry being a state insane asylum.

Oh boy! I have been invited to go ice fishing by two of my friends, Richard Plamondon, who is a bartender, and Pat Paton, a carpenter and machinist and block layer. As I dress before dawn, I feel somehow patriotic wearing Air Force surplus arctic balloon boots and bib overalls over other trousers and thermal underwear and various sweaters and a goosedown vest and an outsized quilted coat from when I weighed 225 pounds. Eighteen articles of clothing in all, and when I got out of my car I found I could scarcely walk. I fell on the slippery ice with padded impunity, a big helpless doll of a trout slayer. The early morning air was bluish with cold, and as I waddled along I thought of the promised steak to come in the afternoon and the whiskey I would use to wash it down. But there I was being asked to spud some holes in the ice. One cannot refuse. Chores are shared. Pat and Richard were organizing the chuggers and tip-ups. Everyone spuds their own holes, a rule of the Big Ice. I felt the spud was too heavy after only a few chops. I wanted the ice to be very thick for my safety but thin for the spudding. It became apparent that we could have fished from the security of a railroad car. Over a foot thick, and I was wheezing and steaming and my shoulder ached. I knew then why construction workers liked the sport: they were able to spud the holes. Anyway, Richard tested the depth: 170 feet. A lot of dark down there. I peered in the hole and saw the reflection of a moon face, my own. Richard set a tip-up for me and told me to spud another hole to chug in. I couldn't believe it. I thought, whatever happened to the tradition of the gun bearer who in this case might be put to work, or some sallow, nasty teenager might be brought along for a pittance. But I spudded on. Finally I attached a Swedish pimple (surely the most elegant name for a bait) to a line, dropped it to the bottom, raised it five feet as instructed by Pat and Richard, who watched my motions critically, and began chugging. Sort of ghastly. No question about it. I had become a Chugger! A brutish act, and it was so cold except for my toasty feet in their big white warmonger boots.

Within an hour I had eaten both my sandwiches, roast beef with thick slices of onion. I had also begun drinking my apple wine. After the second bottle I felt quite happy. I was probably cold but I couldn't feel it. The ice had become a mattress against which I snuggled prone, still chugging. No nibbles. Then Richard's tip-up flag went up and we ran over to the hole. He let the spool run freely for a minute to make sure the fish swallowed the minnow, somewhat similar to the way you hook a sail or a marlin. But not too similar. Pat contended that the fish was large, as only a large fish made a long run. I watched the red plastic spool steadily unwind until Richard picked it up and lightly reefed the line. Then he began to slowly draw it in hand over hand as if he were retrieving an anchor or a used kite. I was jealous. Why didn't my flag go up? Perhaps I wasn't "living right," as they say.

Richard was gaining steadily on the fish. He announced laconically that it wasn't large. We stood peering down the twelve-inch hole until, shockingly, a trout popped out with the tail of a minnow sticking out of its mouth. Then, horrors! It flopped on the ice and gave off a prolonged BELCH!, a sort of berserk flatulence. I was deeply shocked.

"That pressure sure gets to them," said Pat sagely.

"You're not just a ———," replied Richard.

The point was that the fish had been pulled up precipitously from 170 feet and the variance in pressure was explosive in a minor sense, somewhat like the gas released by a semi-impacted bucking bronco at a rodeo. The trout weighed about three pounds, a good eating size. His eyes bulged and quivered in utter defeat, the ultimate tummyache and bends. I went back to my chugging hole after breaking up the thin ice that had gathered in the cold around my tip-up. I wanted to catch a fish and bring it home so that my daughter wouldn't peer over the top of her Wonder Woman comic and say, "You didn't catch any!" and my wife wouldn't ponder, "Did he go to a bar and play pool or did he really go fishing?" To no avail did I chug until I got tennis elbow. I grew bored and cold and began playfully throwing chunks of ice at Pat and Richard. They were not amused.

We finally quit by mid-afternoon and drove to a restaurant where the waitress giggled extravagantly over my balloon boots.

"Are your feet *that* big?" she asked.

"I'm an American Ice Fisherman, bring me a drink," I shouted wittily. The jukebox was playing a merry polka.

When she brought the drinks she rolled her eyes again at my feet. I told her then that I was a veteran of many polar expeditions and had tracked the wily seal to his air-conditioned lair. She asked if seal meat was good and I said yes if they take the ball off their noses har har har. Richard and Pat were sullen as the pretty waitress wasn't interested in them but in my feet. *Tuff*, I said. So it goes, this sport of the north, fit mostly for the hardy unemployed, those who dare thin ice with their snowmobiles and often plunge (eight last year) to a gurgly death amidst the very fishes they sought with pimples and corn borers, red worms and dead smelt (two for a quarter).

A few days later I got a call from Richard saying that a group of locals were going out the next morning and I could meet them on Route 22 about 300 yards south of Chervenko's Rung & Bung Works (coopers to the fruit-orchard trade). I was several hours late due to sloth and invented errands. I spotted them with my binoculars a mile or so out on the ice. But farther up the bay a Coast Guard icebreaker was leading in a tanker with a rather eerie succession of resounding crashes, like hearing a battle from a distance. The ships were well beyond the fishermen, but I decided that the ice looked a trifle soft. Definitely unsafe. Perhaps I would go home and treat myself to an extended nap.

I began to think of ice fishing in the old days. It is, after all, no modern invention. I have a Currier and Ives print of some pilgrim types hauling shad from the ice. In the 1930s great cities of ice shanties were erected on large northern lakes. Even electricity was available. Recently I was in Minnesota, a state that along with Wisconsin can readily be confused with Michigan, chauvinists notwithstanding. In St. Paul an old-timer told me many yarns. He said that entire cottages especially built for the purpose on skids are pulled onto the ice by diesel tractors. From the comfort of kitchen, bedroom and the living room the fabled walleye is fished for. Imagine your own living room with a big hole in the floor. You're lolling in an easy chair fishing through the hole, with a couple of lunker walleyes on the floor beside you. Maybe you have the TV on, and Jack Nicklaus is grinning his Ohio grin on an eighteenth green somewhere. You will cook the walleyes for dinner. They taste better than any fish I've eaten, better than mountain cutthroat, Dover sole, swordfish, lake trout or pompano or lungfish. Perhaps Myrna in her tattersall negligee is bringing you a cold one or just plain Mom is across the room knitting. It is imperative for obvious reasons to have your cottage dragged off the ice before it thaws. I might add that the "walleye" got its name from its particularly weird stare, but then you don't have to eat the eyes.

In my own "old days" we knew none of these sybaritic pleasures. I suspect my father thought if comfort were involved it wasn't sporting. So we would get up before dawn, drive out through the snowdrifts along a logging road and fish all day long in the bitterest cold for a mess of bluegills and perch. Nothing sentimental here. It appeared fun because it was supposed to be fun. Kids are doggish, and if you say, "Come kids, let's pick the dump," they will jump at the chance.

Earlier in January I sat with Richard for three days in his shanty on Lake Leelanau looking down through a hole at a foot-long live sucker minnow dangling from a line. The shanty is kept totally dark. The hole in the ice for spearing is usually about three feet square. The visibility is amazing—a window on the freshwater netherworld, which, though the life doesn't compete with the multitudinous saltwater variety, is nonetheless a lot better than staying home and waiting for winter to go away. Anyway, the sucker minnow was supposed to attract the great northern pike, or Mister Big Teeth as he is known in some quarters. When the imaginary pike drifted into our rectangle of vision for a sucker supper, the spear would be thrown at him. The spear was somewhat larger and certainly more cumbersome than the tuna harpoons used off Gloucester and Block Island. Poor pike. But only one appeared in the three days and we were caught unawares, and when Richard lunged with the spear the pike was driven against the bottom and squiggled out between the spear tines. So much for pike spearing, which is in danger of being outlawed. But it was pleasant sitting there in the dark shanty, warm with a propane stove and copious supplies of food and drink.

We would occasionally chug for perch with small minnows while we watched our decoy. In addition to the meat of the fish, perch roe lightly fried in butter is delicious. I suspect that it is healthy, too, though I have no evidence. But some I know who eat it are huge, a trifle fat, in fact, and can drink fifty glasses of draft beer in an evening. It's never boring in an ice shanty. You talk idly while your head sweats and your feet freeze. There is all the husky camaraderie of the locker room. A sample:

"Do you know *that* girl in Sutton's Bay? You know the one I mean."

"Yup."

"Well I would ——— ——— ———."

"She's built like a rain barrel."

"Pass the wine."

I would like to make an elementary contention here about expediency and sport. In this locale, winter begins in October and runs unremittingly until the end of March. My friends in warmer climes won't believe we had sixteen and a half feet of snow this year. After a while you no longer believe there's any earth left under the snow. The ground is a fib. It was still possible to fish on the part of the bay nearest Traverse City in early April. In fact, a large school of young coho salmon running between two and three pounds were discovered in the shoal water near the power plant. A healthy adult with an interest in the outdoors has to do something during these five months. The snow is almost immediately too deep for rabbit hunting—the beagles flounder on their short legs. Even an instinctively arch and lazy whiner like myself doesn't want to spend the entire winter looking out the window dreaming of Cozumel, Cabeza de Vaca, Belize. And you worry too much: a night when it is below zero and the wind off Lake Michigan is at forty knots and the car is buried in snow, and you count and time the weird thunks and squealings from the furnace, which inevitably breaks down. The weather seems to lose its threat when you spend time out in it, and if you're not geared temperamentally to skiing or snowmobiling, you're left with nothing to do but fish.

The true force behind ice fishing is that it is better than no fishing at all. In extremis, an addictive fisherman will shoot carp with bow and arrow, set up trotlines for carp and suckers, spear dogfish on Pig Trotter Creek, chum nurse sharks within rifle range. He will surround the crudest equipment with a mystique and will maintain to the uninitiated that there's no sport quite like fishing rainbows with bobber and marshmallows.

And ice fishing has its strenuous converts. Pat told me that a year ago in April, just before the ice broke up, he was chugging out on the bay when a Coast Guard helicopter came over low and motioned him off the ice. He stayed until he got three fish and the helicopter returned. Then he noticed that the ice beneath his feet was sinking a bit. He grabbed his fish and ran and the ice for a mile around began wavering and rippling and heaving. The groans made in this situation convince one that there are prehistoric monsters under the ice trying to get out. It is chilling.

One day I drove up along the water through Pshawbetown, a small enclave of Chippewa and Ottawa Indians who are much the worse for wear. Naturally at one time they owned all the land around here. Now there is little or no running water, few indoor toilets, a ghetto shabbiness if it weren't for the fact that there is space to roam. Most of them are kept busy in the winter cutting wood for their stoves. An uninsulated shack can use an astounding amount of wood. I glassed a small cluster of fishermen about a mile out. In the tavern the night before someone anonymous (I must protect my sources) had claimed he had taken seventeen lake trout with a combined weight of over 100 pounds in just a few hours. This is well over the legal limit, but there is simply too much ice for the game warden, Reino Narva, to cover adequately. Concern is minimal, however, as the lake trout population is approaching the vastness of earlier in the century through concerted plantings, lamprey control and stringent but perhaps unfair regulation of commercial fishing.

I cut across the peninsula to Leland, a beautiful little harbor town. People here are upset over the government's acquiring 70,000 acres of local land for a National Seashore. Of only slightly less concern is Bill Carlson's attempt to regain some of the commercial fishing waters taken away by the Department of Natural Resources. An additional severe irritant is the state and federal DDT regulation: most varieties of Great Lakes fish have close to ten parts to the million, which is above the legal allowable limit for shipping. I eat all the fish anyway because I am young and fat and reckless and love the forms of danger connected with eating. I feel sad, though, when I watch the magnificent steelhead leaping against the dam in Leland: all subtly poisoned, though expensive equipment is needed to determine the fact. They still *look* like steelhead. The breakwater is mountainously covered with ice, but still some waves break over the ice, pushed by our third gale of the season.

Bill Carlson is a fourth-generation fisherman. The nets around his shack remind me of Cape Ann. But far out beyond Cape Ann the swordfish are gobbling mercury below waves dotted, according to Heyerdahl, with eraser-sized gobbets of oil. And then above them a storm petrel or sooty shearwater or plain old herring gull wheels in ordinary gyres carrying a special freight of poison. There is a certain boredom in anger.

I was down on Good Harbor Bay when the ice was breaking up. The bay is about five miles wide and the equal of any tourist-photo bay I know of, though ungraced by Noel Coward and suchlike who go to Montego. A few days before I had walked out two miles on the ice to see Richard and his father Dick and Bruce Price. I followed Bruce's footprints as he weighs nearly 300 and I wanted to feel safe. I stepped over a two-foot-wide crack and peeked for a moment down into the dark clear water. They hadn't had any luck. And Richard was angry. He had dropped a twelve-dollar augur while spudding a hole, and there it would rest permanently 100 feet below us. I said that I had stepped over a crack and they said the crack hadn't been there in the morning. But there was no offshore wind that would drive the ice out toward South Manitou Island. I felt edgy and got the creeps as if Lon Chaney were under the bed, turning into a man-wolf hybrid. I neatly tip-toed back to the car, listening for any rumbles or giant sighs that would announce my death by cold water. POET DROWNS, the local paper would read. Or probably MAN DROWNS, as there is a prevalent notion in the upper Midwest that poets are invariably "dead people."

Back on shore a man was whistling hopelessly at his Labrador, who was busy sniffling around the juniper bushes that abut the shore. Dogs. I had recently apologized to a neighbor about my male Airedale Hud "covering" his own dog, but he said it was okay because his dog was male, too. Nature! Then the Labrador came over and sniffed my leg, smelling my penned bitch Justine. He looked at me soulfully and I quickly removed my leg to the safety of the car.

I drove to the tavern in the evening, and Richard said he had called the Traverse City Chamber of Commerce and asked about a petition that would attempt to keep the oil freighters out of the harbor during the prime fishing months of February and March. An unnamed party suggested that the malcontents should be out looking for work. Bumpkin vigilante action has been talked about—say a string of snowmobiles in a freighter's path. Count me out. The ice fisherman is low on the economic totem ratings for logical reasons. One can equip oneself for five bucks. And ice fishermen aren't big spenders in the tourist operations. A five-dollar frozen steak is for Detroiters.

I got up at 5:00 A.M. to go steelhead fishing, but when I got there my rod guides kept icing up and the line wouldn't move freely. But a week before I had stood on the discouragingly thick ice and cast my fly, a mylar dace, and lost it to a floating iceberg. Oh well. Last year I had broken a rod trying to cast strongly in the bitter cold. Will real spring never come? I said to myself, echoing the poets of yore. I meditated on the difference between a fly rod and a chugging paddle, which resembles a fraternity (or sorority) paddle with no initials carved on it. Pulling a fish in hand over hand has an atavistic glee to it; the fish imparts directly to the senses his electric struggle far below. Meat on the table! The provider! The "little woman" will be right proud of her jolly though indigent hubby. Pull that lunker out on the ice and cover him with snow to prevent the effects of dehydration and fish sunburn. I wandered around the creek estuary until I tore a foot-long hole in my waders. The water pouring in was horribly cold. I walked up the shore to an empty cabin, and a thermometer on the porch read twenty-four degrees. How stupid. I built a small fire out of driftwood and warmed my foot, watching some buffleheads circle above. From out in the bay, the birds were barely visible. I could hear the tremulous cry of two mating loons. I was frankly tired of cold weather and I imagined that the loons were also tired of running into icebergs, and the steelhead were tired of dozing in the cold water with their brains asleep to the spawning run.

Now the ice is gone and the snowdrift on the hill across the road shrinks daily. I have had two fair weeks of steelhead fishing and am gathering my equipment for a trip to Key West. Fantasies of a record tarpon are rife, though as unlikely as a record starlet. I feel somewhat benign about the preposterous winter I have endured. A crocus has appeared in vulgar purple glory. I will avoid hammerheads and moray eels and rattlesnakes and other imagined dangers, and go through more winters not unlike this one, where the depleted imagination narrows to a singular point. Fish. Anywhere and almost anytime. Even when trees split open from cold and the target is a bowling-ball-sized hole in a lid of ice.

1972

La Vénerie Française

Apprehension. And not the simple white-knuckled variety but another sort of another degree: super-taut purple knuckles. The Leningrad airport was in the middle of a blizzard and the Aeroflot jet—I was sitting far in the rear, ideally the safest place—seemed to swerve and veer on a runway which looked much like a mile-long skating rink. *Vodka* my soul cried out, while my hand reached for a vest flask.

Then six hours later, after floating through the blue snowless air, I landed in Paris and found that the temperature was in the low seventies and my adrenalin glands had shrunk from their all-too-frequent volleyball size back to the manageable configuration of Ping-Pong balls. I wandered around Paris for five days in the rare late October warmth, the sun creating a beautiful golden haze out of the auto exhaust, which seemed to exceed that of New York. I walked at least a dozen miles a day but only for the exercise necessary to create appetite. After a month of travel I was fatigued with all monuments excepting restaurants and those chichi girls who were strutting like cheetahs between and around the Place Vendôme and the Place de la Concorde. I spent two minutes watching the Soviet leader Brezhnev's motorcade pass and my thoughts were drawn to Frederick Forsyth's *The Day of the Jackal*. I felt very mysterious for a few moments, secretive and gloomy, but returned to the Lotti for a five-hour nap. Dinner would be extensive and required rest.

On my fifth afternoon in Paris Count Guy de la Valdène, a friend I fish with in the Florida Keys, picked me up for the ride seventy miles out into Normandy to his mother's place near which a stag hunt would take place. Guy usually eschews the title "Count," claiming that it is mostly handy for making difficult restaurant reservations. The trip out of Paris seemed maniacally fast; even through the gentle Bois de Boulogne most Frenchmen think of themselves as Grand Prix drivers, even if in a humble model of

Renault or Citroën. We talked of the coming tarpon season, still six months away, but the stag hunt, the knowledge of which was limited in my poor brain to old tapestries in art books, was also discussed. Guy kept using the French pronunciation for the word "equipage" (ek-kee-pajjh) and rather than admit my ignorance I chose to think of the word as a description of a malaise, say a virulent form of hiccups, though of course my associations fit into none of Guy's sentences. I had decided days before that my two years of college French, taken a decade before, were sloppily insufficient. All other attempts had been met by querulous stares from waiters, bartenders, the concierge, even the gendarmes, who after slight bows and responses would glare snottily at my long hair and Pancho Villa moustache. Perhaps they took me for a student bent on loosening a cobblestone to throw through the Van Cleef & Arpels window. Or perhaps in preparation for Brezhnev—there were a million Soviet flags flying—they too had read *The Day of the Jackal* and were sizing me up as a potential international bad guy. Most likely though, subtracting the drama, I was thought of as just another dumb-dumb tourist asking dumb-dumb tourist questions. I asked Guy what would happen if you walked up to one of those De Gaulle–sized cops in front of the American Embassy and called him a *pig*. He said that you would have to start running immediately, hopefully like Bob Hayes out for a sideline bomb from Starbuck. Guy was very irritated at missing the pro-football season.

We finally drew up to the small village of St. Georges-Motel, if drawing up is an accurate phrase for one hundred kilometers per hour. We stopped before an enormous iron gate and an old lady ran out from a rather attractive cottage and opened the gate. We drove down a long double aisle of trees and turned left, crossed a moat and entered a large courtyard. In the twilight I could see a huge dwelling which I recognized from years of moviegoing to be a château. My efforts toward nonchalance were rather weak, and when we walked in I uttered a not very appropriate "nice place you got here." After changing my clothes and a quick drink—I was wishing I owned a cape or something similar—we went out to eat at a pleasant little auberge down the road, the inside of which resembled a florist's shop. Guy and his lovely wife Terry ate rather simply but at their insistence I had a woodcock pâté, a heavily-truffled omelet, and a huge serving of wild boar, plus fruit, cheeses, a few bottles of wine and a tasting of several brandies.

The next morning I awoke early with severe indigestion. Why must good food in quantity exact pain? I meditated on Igor Stravinsky's fabled digestive powers and the gourmandizing of Balzac and Diamond Jim Brady, who had willed his enormous stomach to a medical school for study. Perhaps I am not cut from such cloth, I mused while shaving. I opened the drapes and looked out on some rather mammoth formal gardens and a colonnade a quarter of a mile in the distance. I tried to slip out but was slightly delayed by a kitchen girl with coffee and croissants. I was eager to walk around the grounds. Guy had mentioned in passing that his mother raised horses and I wanted to give them a look. With my years of familiarity with the animals (we keep three on our own little farm) I can instantly tell between a Shetland pony and a draft horse, and after many nasty falls and doggish bites I have settled on looking at these creatures from a distance as if they were ambulatory paintings.

I walked around for several hours. There were swans in the moat and several ponds and also a large flock of wild mallard ducks. A fair-sized river and several brooks meandered through the grounds which were covered with huge beech and oak trees. The stables, paddocks, and neatly fenced pastures appeared to take up several hundred acres and I counted some forty horses including foals, fillys, colts, and mares. In the stable courtyard I tried some of my French on a man who quickly explained in good English that he had received some of his training at racing stables in the United States. Guy's mother, Diana Manning, shares an interest in thoroughbreds with her brothers Raymond and Winston Guest. I decided I liked the horses. They trotted up to the fence to be lovingly petted and lacked the gestures of hostility I associated with some quarter horses (offer a carrot and lose a finger). Despite their gentility and beauty I still didn't want to ride one. A particular mare that had just returned from training and had proved a bit recalcitrant was running around her pasture at a speed that closed on fifty knots. Only a tenacious badger could have stayed on her back.

I returned to the château thinking of Hemingway's fascination in his Paris days with horseracing and how he often considered his winnings as "funny" money, like winning unexpectedly big at a poker game. He would treat a group of friends to a long meal and drinks. My single experience at Saratoga years before had lost me a considerable amount and purged me of this sort of gambling though I enjoyed the beauty of the track. I walked up to the third floor where there was a charming room decorated in the manner of a small American cocktail lounge, a place to escape from the elegance of the rest of the place. I had a not very moderate Armagnac and played Pink Floyd's "Atom Heartmother" on the phonograph which made me a trifle homesick. I momentarily longed for my Merle Haggard albums and my home where the grouse season was in full swing now, as well as the steelhead fishing I alternated with the grouse. I walked back downstairs and took one of Guy's fly rods and cast from a bridge into the moat for several hours. There were no fish other than minnows in the moat but I figured that I wouldn't fly cast in a moat very often during this short life.

That afternoon we took a long drive through the forest where the hunt would take place. There was a startling resemblance to some of the good grouse and deer areas in Michigan with swales and brambles and stunted oaks, the acorns covering the ground. Our drive ended at a pentagonal tower with a lawn in the center of the forest, the pavilion from which the hunt would begin. Just down the road from the pavilion we stopped at a white-stucco farmhouse with a huge kennel behind it and met Serge Hervé, the head working man of the hunt, and his wife and daughter. Serge Hervé exudes an impression of strength and incredible vitality—he doesn't walk, he struts and trots and bounces. We looked at the stag hounds which are called *chiens de meute*. I asked if they all were named and was quickly introduced to Massena, Sombrero, Rubens, Tintoret, Quasimodo, Plantagenet, Tarzan, Potemkine, Offenbach and Opium, among others. I asked to see the best of the hounds and Serge entered the kennel and brought out Kroutchev, a fourteen-year-old with grey whiskers. Serge hugged and kissed the dog before returning it to the pen. The latter is a gesture I find common among the best dog trainers the world over. The markings and tickings were varied—some of the hounds resembled outsized foxhounds and others looked like blue ticks and walkers—and sizes were impressive, running from sixty pounds up to one brute that struck me as weighing over a hundred. Their dispositions were sweet and Serge had complete mastery over the whole lot, something I hadn't managed with a single pointer or my two current Airedales.

We entered the clubhouse to see some of the trophies, the largest of which was hanging over the fireplace. The head approached the size of an elk's though the spread and size of the rack wasn't nearly as large. Serge whispered, "*C'est un Monsieur,*" which is the ultimate compliment, meaning a noble and huge stag that provided a difficult hunt. Then Serge showed us another head collected only two weeks before. He cursed the rack with some humor and explained to us that the stag had tossed him high over its head with its antlers when he had "served" it. When a stag is brought to bay by the hounds part of Serge's job, certainly the most dangerous aspect, is to approach the stag and plunge a silver dagger into its heart. Often the stag isn't as fatigued as he might appear and Serge has been gored and tossed a number of times. The act of "serving" requires bravery of a rare sort. Anyone who has watched two male deer or elk arguing over a harem before the rutting season will understand the butting and goring power of these animals. Or if you're not familiar with these beasts try to visualize being charged full tilt by a four-hundred-pound mastiff with a set of well-honed horns on its head.

I loitered around for two more days, picking up information on thoroughbred breeding and any incidental lore I could comprehend on the hunt from the ancient books in the château library. But the weather was too splendid to read after a month-long dose of Soviet snowstorms. We made a desultory attempt at a duck hunt on some of the many ponds but the ducks were near the pastures and one doesn't fire shotguns near a dozen foals, the net potential worth far exceeding what I'll earn in my own lifetime. I was also apprehensive about scratching up a mint condition Holland & Holland, a shotgun that bore no resemblance to my own battered and overused bush double. There were a minimal number of brown trout in the river to cast to, most of them having been destroyed several years before by an effluent release from an upstream factory. How like home!

The evening before the hunt we dined with Pierre Firmin-Didot, who is the *maître d'équipage d'honneur* of the local hunt syndicate, the Normand-Piqu'Hardi, the costs being shared by the twelve full members. For many years Pierre Firmin-Didot had owned a private hunt which was called Rallie Normandie. He proved a splendid source of information and had hundreds of years of the history of *la vénerie française* at memory's tip. Unfortunately for me he lapsed immediately into intricate French after explaining that such a splendid tradition couldn't be described in my own humble language, a point over which I expressed some quarrelsome doubt. But Lorraine de la Valdène, Guy's very beautiful sister, and her friend Christian, a Paris film-maker, translated all the germane information, while I mostly daydreamed about the after-dinner champagne we were drinking. Earlier in the day we had retrieved it along with the dinner wines from the cellar where there were dozens of cases of musty, soiled bottles. All of the wine back home comes in squeaky clean bottles and doesn't taste nearly as good. Guy was off talking horse business to his mother and stepfather who were on the verge of a trip to Argentina. I kept thinking of how we were to get up at five A.M. for the hunt, an hour of horror I reserve for only the most promising trout fishing, and even then I usually only manage it by staying up all night after fishing an evening hatch.

Very early on Saturday morning, when the sky lacked even a trace of light, we drove the half-dozen miles through the forest to the circle around the pavilion which looked splendid in the headlights. I thought of Diane de Poitiers waking on the morning of a hunt hundreds of years before in her nearby château, then riding with the others on their mounts to this same pavilion. I momentarily wanted some share of a glorious history, a history with what is called "class" rather than the casual 30-30 bushwhacking of deer moving along their feeding runways back home. We always called it "meat hunting" and there was not even a vague pretention toward a search for a trophy. We pulled up in Serge's yard and the lights were on. The hounds, all forty-seven of them including the aged Kroutchev and a timid dog named Oxford, set up a bellowing that deafened. Serge stepped out of the kitchen door and yelled and they became silent and stood at attention. Even the small pet terrier that trotted along the outside of the kennel fence as if these huge hounds were part of his fiefdom paused for a moment— fortunately terriers aren't the size of Great Danes or they would rule us all.

The kitchen was warm and yellow with light and we accepted a half cup of coffee which Serge with promptness topped off with a big lashing of calvados. Calvados at dawn? Oh well. I finished mine in two gulps which proved a mistake as the cup was immediately refilled with another half-and-half. Even my lungs felt the heat and I thought of my dad's term for the homemade whiskey he used to drink, "pop-skull." There were five of us around the table including Guy and myself. Serge and the other two trackers spoke in a rapid patois of where best to locate a stag. We all stared at the calvados bottle which had just been refilled in the back room by Serge's wife. It was a party bottle, evidently a prized possession. Serge's shy little daughter Jeanette picked up the bottle and wound a key in the inverted bottom. A small porcelain ballerina twirled in a circle in the center of the amber liquid and the miniature music box that surrounded played "Lara's Theme" from *Dr. Zhivago*. I was overwhelmed, though my emotions might have been a victim of the instant fire of the calvados. I began to daydream, unable to pick up a word of the rapid colloquial French. Two weeks before in the Sadko nightclub in Leningrad the band had closed the evening with the very same song and several hundred people stood and cheered. Bad champagne flowed. And the movie and the book and the music were banned there and the song was anyway written by a Frenchman, Maurice Jarré. But the Russians somehow knew and loved it and lacked my stiff and priggish cynicism.

We stood and went outside. Serge sorted out the tracking dogs, three hounds that were especially trained to bay at a stag scent. We wanted to locate a likely animal for the hunt which would begin in three or four hours. The information we gathered would be presented to Jean Ferjoux, the *maître d'équipage*, who would select from the three searchers the most likely stag for the chase.

Guy and I accompanied Serge and his daughter down a small lane on the other side of the pavilion. Our hound, Ouragan, was anxious and we walked at an alarmingly fast pace. This speed was to continue for the next three hours, during which we would crisscross dozens of lanes for well over ten miles. It all seemed excessively swift to me, having overeaten again the night before on some fresh pâté de foie gras with a big chunk of truffle in the middle (with a '28 Anjou), a poached trout, a serving of the small forest deer known as the *chevreuil* and a quantity of cheeses, the last being a rank goat cheese I would retaste for the next several days. But then one doesn't travel to France to be temperate when one can be temperate in Michigan without even trying.

It was still the first pale morning light and Serge was pleased with the slight ground fog—the moisture in the air and the heavy dew would make it easier for the hounds to follow a stag. An unsuccessful hunt often hinges on extremely dry weather which provides poor scenting conditions. We found frequent tracks among the stunted oaks but the hounds are trained to the peculiar scent of the male and Ouragan dismissed the tracks as female. Then at the edge of the forest in a tilled field we found our first stag tracks. Serge and Jeanette and the hound became very excited but Serge knelt and judged that by the splay and size of the tracks that the stag was too small to bother with. The incident reminded me of a hunting friend in Michigan who could likewise accurately judge the size and sex of a deer by the tracks.

We continued on at what I thought of as an even brisker rate and out of pride I tried to conceal my wheezing. I had imagined myself to be in good shape from summer backpacking in Montana and the early grouse season back home but I was clearly outclassed by Serge and the ten-year-old Jeanette. I was very pleased when Guy dawdled with his cameras, and I desperately wanted a forbidden cigarette but the smoke would be scented easily by the stag and make him a bit edgy, perhaps moving him out of our section of the forest. After another two miles or so the hound picked up a good-sized stag and we spent an hour on a stratagem that would locate the hundred-acre plot of forest where the stag was hiding. We walked a square of four lanes and saw where the stag had crossed one path but had failed to emerge onto the other three that made up the rectangle. Serge and Jeanette were happy, and so was I as it meant we could return to the pavilion where I would smoke several cigarettes consecutively and rest my tired body. But on the way back we met the other two trackers and were mildly disappointed to discover that the one with Oxford had located a very large stag indeed, his proof being a chunk of fecal matter which indicated a stag with ample bowels. After seven hundred years of hunting in essentially the same manner no tricks are missed.

Back at Serge's we had another drink and spoke with Michel Pradel who was to drive us during the hunt in his small, sturdy Pibolle Citroën. Then we went back to the château and ate an enormous breakfast. Someone in the kitchen had packed our picnic basket for the afternoon and I snooped through its contents: some fruit, mineral water, two bottles of Margaux, Dutch beer, a variety of ham, cheese, and pâté sandwiches on miniature loaves of bread. Oh boy, I thought in my capacity of Mr. Piggy. How unlike the tawdry junk I carried along while grouse hunting, or what had been my father's favorite, incomprehensible deer-hunting snack—a baked-bean sandwich with a half-inch slice of onion. I reflected on how horribly my feet ached in my cowboy boots which have, of course, no sensible relationship to the act of walking but were the only boots I'd brought along to Europe.

A thuggish type in Moscow had offered me seventy-five roubles ($80) for them and I wished that I had taken his kind offer.

When we returned to Serge's at eleven the hunt was nearly assembled and Michel was waiting for us with his friend Lorette. Michel had a small silver hunting horn called a *corne* over his shoulder. Though a university student Michel is an addict of the hunt and knows the forest intimately. Guy might have driven but he confessed that we would probably have become lost and he needed a free hand for his cameras which some of the mounted hunters were busy staring at. They shun publicity as it is mostly bad, the hunt being generally scorned by the fourth estate and the intelligentsia, the situation bearing some similarity to the United States. As an instance, whenever most fellow writers of assistant professor mentalities learn that I hunt and fish they usually say something on the order of "Oh gawd, the Hemingway bit!" The grand one from Oak Park has made it difficult for others in his craft. In any event my usual response to the quip is non-quotable.

Half of the hounds were loaded into a truck to act as replacements later on and in the cramped quarters some fighting broke out which was quickly stopped by a shout from Serge. Ferjoux, the master of the hunt, was standing in the courtyard with everyone assembled in a closely packed circle. The three trackers with hats in hand made lengthy and elegantly descriptive speeches on the possible virtues of the stags they had located. Ferjoux was preoccupied with the minutest details and asked many questions. We were still disappointed when our stag, as expected, wasn't chosen. The timid little Oxford had won out.

Michel knew precisely where the hunt was to begin and we drove around the forest through the small villages of Saussay and Montagnette and then on a lane deep into the woods. I was frightened at the speed at which Michel drove the lanes but Guy assured me that it was nothing compared to what would come later. But the rather solid-looking trees were whizzing by only inches from my window in the front seat and with each bump my head narrowly missed crashing into the roof of the little car. We parked and stood around for a few minutes, then saw with excitement the approach of the mounts, usually a mixture of Arab and thoroughbred, followed by the hounds. Serge located the tracks with no difficulty and gave a blast of his horn which was answered by the horn of Ferjoux. In Serge's capacity as master of the hounds he follows the hunt on foot, something I couldn't comprehend after the morning's jaunt. We were idly talking and smoking when not fifty yards away the stag and three females suddenly broke from cover. The females raced across the lane but the stag paused, then circled back within his own block of woods. Michel signaled with his horn that he thought that he had seen a stag but wasn't absolutely positive. One must be sure. A day chasing the wrong stag is the worst of form. The fifteen or so hunters with Ferjoux well in the lead descended on us and I dove for the brush to avoid a trampling. A quarter mile off we could hear Serge bellowing at his hounds, then a signal from his horn that it was indeed the correct stag. The hunters were deployed by Ferjoux to visually cover any escape as the hounds drew nearer; the first few hounds to reach the stag would drive him from the cover, unless he chose a quick standoff in which case a few hounds might die.

While we waited I thought again of how a whitetail buck will send a doe or a number of them through a clearing first to test for any conceivable danger. Not very noble to use your mates as decoys but then you don't get to be a great big buck or noble-sized stag by acting stupidly. I was told that an experienced stag will often follow a smaller one, butting him on by force for several miles, then veer off in an attempt to fool the hounds by this intelligent ruse. But then the beast broke full tilt across the lane not far from us and Michel gave a definite horn signal to Ferjoux, who answered and gathered his group with some beautiful blasts from his hunting horn, the golden *trompe de chasse*, and they were off within seconds. As we walked back to the car I reflected on the natural authority Ferjoux seemed to possess, a sort of unassuming "macho" and uprightness that demands immediate respect and obedience: the master of the hunt has the dictatorial powers of an eighteenth-century sea captain and there is simply no breaking of the etiquette of *la chasse*. The horns over each hunter's shoulder reminded me of the walkie-talkies often used by those who hunt bear in Michigan's Upper Peninsula with hounds, the only local place back home where it is permissible. They always reminded me of huge teeny boppers with transistor radios pressed to their ears: picture the wiley Chub "Dink" Farley with his *10-4 10-4 10-4*, then shrieking into the machine that "Big Bruin" just crossed the road. This unsavory bit can be contrasted to the one-armed Roy Close from Emigrant, Montana, who will alone enter the mountains for weeks at a time to destroy a rogue grizzly with an excessive appetite for domestic beef. But then the stag hunt is as ritualized as the bullfight, the only apt comparison, though the hunt is incredibly less cruel.

We stuffed ourselves back into the car and Michel and Guy began guessing the stag's next move. We drove even faster this time toward an area where Michel expected the stag and hounds to emerge. I thought of how any respectable wine steward would express disgust at the way we were drinking the Margaux straight from the bottle as the car jounced along. We loitered around a recently timbered area of the forest for a half hour until the baying of the hounds far in the distance told us our guess had been wrong by several miles. We perfected a manner of jumping into the small car within seconds, a performance we were to enact a dozen times in the next few hours. We began to enter hilly country, plunging down narrow aisles into what could be fairly called gorges. Occasionally we spotted a stray hound that had apparently lost its way; the hound would look at us, then immediately act very intense and interested, much like a bird dog that is either too lazy or tired to enter a briar patch but still wants to present a good appearance. Along a ridge we saw a dozen or so hounds pass in front of us. We jumped out of the car and ran over the top of the ridge to find that it overlooked an entire valley and the village of Montreuil with the river Havre running through the village. It was evident that the hounds had chased the stag straight through town and across a wide field of hay stubble, at which point the stag plunged in and crossed the river. In the distance from our hilltop we could see the riders regrouping to Ferjoux's horn, the sound echoing melodiously throughout the valley. We plunged down the roadless hill, fairly flying in the car through thickets and over rocks, and passed through Montreuil to the point of reconnoitering. Guy was worried as we were drawing near his mother's estate as it would be impossible to allow the hunt to enter the château grounds. Stag hounds and hunting horns don't make a wise mix with a breeding farm—one could imagine an errant hound nipping the heels of a colt destined eventually for Longchamps. Fortunately the stag had headed off through a cornfield toward Dreux, the largest village in the area, actually a small city of some 25,000 people. But this was a bad break for the hunt as the area surrounding Dreux is a semi-urban sprawl and a major four-lane highway, "National 12," is in the area.

While the hunters paused to discuss tactics with Ferjoux, Guy and Michel told me how lucky I was to see a *débucher* (the stag leaving the forest for open country) as it makes for a more varied though certainly less classic hunt. Some consternation could be sensed on Ferjoux's face as the hunters headed at a gallop toward Dreux. At another small village we paused for a moment, and a gas station attendant told us that the stag had passed through town and had headed across a large field and through a woodlot toward a sanitarium we could see in the distance. I had a rather dark, surrealistic image of the stag jumping the sanitarium fence and bursting through a group of strolling loonies with the hounds in pursuit, scarcely an aid to therapy. But it turned out to be a tuberculosis sanitarium surrounded by a fair stretch of forest. We continued down through another valley where we spotted several hounds swimming across the river. Down the road a group of cars had gathered, full of people semi-attached to the hunt, and all were discussing stratagems. Serge and the riders looked fatigued and everyone had a worried appearance. One of the women present had spotted the stag recrossing the river and heading back toward the sanitarium. She said she had seen the stag pause in a field for a rest, having temporarily outwitted the hounds.

An hour of utter tenseness had begun. The stag had hidden himself in a small patch of forest, perhaps a hundred acres, and Ferjoux entered with the best of the hounds in attempt to flush the beast. But if the stag ran the wrong way he would be headed toward the freeway not to speak of a smarmy Americanized housing development and after that, the possibility of a flight through downtown Dreux, which would make for very bad publicity indeed. Luckily while we were waiting near the housing development drinking wine the stag reversed himself again toward clear country. Michel ordered us back into the car. I sort of wanted to stay, having spotted a very pretty spectator to whom I asked nasally, "Où est le stag?" She giggled and shrugged but then Guy told me discouragingly that she didn't have the foggiest idea what I was talking about.

Michel and Lorette and Guy seemed to think the hunt was nearing the end. We retraced our lane to the river and while crossing the bridge saw on a not-too-distant hill the stag and the hounds close behind, with the riders straggling a hundred yards back. By the time we got to the hill, a matter of minutes, the stag was standing at bay while Ferjoux and his riders watched from a few yards back. With great ceremony Serge drew the dagger from the scabbard and walked past the wary hounds, many of whom had been gored in the past. The stag appeared in shock and Serge quickly plunged the dagger into its heart. The stag dropped at his feet.

There was perhaps a minute of full silence except for the shuffling of the lathered horses in the dry grass and the guttural mutterings of the hounds, which Serge kept away from the fallen stag. However stunned and confused

I otherwise felt it was good to see that old Kroutchev was one of the few hounds to complete the hunt. This would be his last year. Then a strange pandemonium broke loose: all the hunters unshouldered their horns and began playing a particular melody in a modal chord that resounded and returned from the far hills on the other side of the valley. The hunters played with a glazed intensity, truly the moment they had been waiting for. A young man in a long army surplus overcoat and very long blonde hair began playing with more capability than the others. He owned no mount so I assumed he was playing for the joy of it. One of the trackers stooped over the stag and cut out its testicles and threw them in the grass. I wasn't sure if this was a ritual gesture or an act to protect the venison from the strong scent. Many cars began to arrive and a large group of farmers, local workers and those who had followed the hunt stood looking rather blankly at the fallen beast. With the mid-afternoon sun glittering off their horns the hunters profusely congratulated Ferjoux, whose face had lost its apprehension and was now glowing. The stag was loaded with effort into the back of a station wagon but not before the largest of the hounds had grabbed a leg and pulled the three hundred pounds of dead weight several feet, a show of strength for which he was punished only lightly. We got back into the car for the ride to the pavilion, some fifteen miles distant, where we would meet the hunters for the ceremonies that would end the day.

At the pavilion a crowd of a hundred or so had gathered. Guy was rather irked, claiming that the crowd was there, much like those who surround auto accidents, only to watch the gutting and caping of the stag. There would be an hour's wait while the hunters returned on their horses, washed up and had a brandy or two. We sat in the car drinking from a good bottle Michel had produced and finishing the picnic basket. Guy fiddled with his cameras and talked of hunts he had witnessed in his youth. He said that a decade ago he had allowed a few men from the hunt to enter the château grounds to dispatch a stag at bay. Guy had been very nervous about the race horses and then the man, not Serge, who was to serve the stag lost his nerve and the brother of Pierre Firmin-Didot had dismounted and in his elegant hunting clothes had directly done the serving, narrowly missing a thrust of the horns. I've always been interested in this primitive form of courage, never having felt much of it in my own bones. An angry dachshund can be an overwhelming threat to a former paperboy.

The trackers arrived with the stag and quickly gutted it out and performed the deftest skinning job I had ever seen. Some in the crowd were offended by the smell, which was actually sweet compared to butchering a Michigan deer that had received a gut shot from a 30-06. The trackers carved the meat, skillfully stripping the loins and placing it in a large burlap bag, leaving only the sparsely meated trunk and the intestines which they covered with the hide, propping the stag's head in an upright position.

The hunters emerged from the clubhouse and took their places a dozen feet behind the stag. A short, gracious speech was made by Jean Ferjoux and then Serge arrived with about half the hounds, perhaps twenty or so. The hounds became berserk at the smell of the carcass and surged and growled within the circle of spectators but were easily controlled by the tracker who cracked a whip above their heads. Then the hide was pulled back and placed near the hunters and Ferjoux gave the order for the hounds to be released. Within an instant an indescribable squabble took place: the innards and trunk were pounced upon in unison by all twenty hounds. Fights over morsels were broken up instantly by the whip cracking well above the hounds' heads. Ouragan trotted away proudly with a lung, a reward for his early-morning labors. He evidently held a high place in the kennel pecking order as no other dog challenged his prize. In a few minutes the remains of the stag had disappeared except for a well-chewed thick white spine. Even the sturdy ribs had been ground up and swallowed. Then Serge returned the obedient hounds to the kennel in an orderly group.

The hunters with horns in hand organized themselves in an order evidently based on seniority, with Jean Ferjoux standing in the middle of the group with his hands behind his back. They took turns playing solos, then choruses: this music, which was to last an hour, was a complete retelling of the four-hour hunt in song. There are over three hundred possible melodies to describe particular incidents including the *débucher* and the crossing of the river. Ferjoux requested several tunes that apparently characterized the parts of the hunt most pleasurable to him. The young man in the long army coat again played with great beauty and intensity. When the music finished the forest began to darken and the crowd and hunters shivered in the evening coolness. The hunt disbanded.

That evening we sat and rather drowsily talked about the hunt: our natural sorrow and empathy for the stag that all but the most moronic hunter feels for his quarry, but also our sympathy for the hounds, also noble beasts in whose blood runs this ancient urge for the quarry—dogs that had begun anyway as predators and had their instincts refined by man to hunt a particular beast, just as a good bird dog singles out his grouse. The sport is nearly a millennium old in France and in some parts of the world dates back five millennia, as in the stele I had seen in a museum of the great Abyssinian lion dogs upon their own quarry. There is no apologia now for hunting except that the desire is in us. Some are born hunting and rarely in our time out of need. I thought of the painting I had seen last summer in Browning, Montana, of a Blackfoot Indian delivering an arrow while riding full speed along a buffalo's side. Of course then it was what is called "necessary" but at the very least *la chasse* had preserved the ritual dignity of the hunt. It wasn't a million licensed hunters in my home state wandering around the shrinking woods, probably killing more trees with their stray shots and target practice than the sixty to ninety thousand deer taken yearly. Without becoming stupidly atavistic one might say at base that we are meat eaters still and some like to kill the meat they eat, which is not far removed in dignity from letting someone else do the killing.

Early the next morning on the way to Orly at two hundred kilometers per hour (I'm not kidding), my emotions left the remnant of the sixteenth century and reentered the twentieth. The hunt would be finally doomed not by its outraged opponents but by the fact that there is simply little room left in which to "chase" an animal. Dreux, the sanitarium, National 12, housing developments and villages left its edges a bit frayed. So the already minuscule remnant of the past suffers further attrition from the usual bane of population. And the motorized cavalcade that follows each hunt confuses the hounds with auto exhaust, diminishing the privacy of the sport. Cars. Population. My eight-hour jet took me from Orly to Detroit, another French name, and in part the ironic source of the problems, the coming end of it all. Even noblemen seem less interested in being regarded as "noble," what with the force of all of us in the middle who inadvertently will deny them by our press of numbers their ancient pleasures.

1972

A Memoir of Horse Pulling

*W*e thought we would have a swim and Jack quickly shed his clothes and I followed him into the small shallow pond covered with pale green algae, the water nearly strangled with weeds. We were perhaps seven and within the logic peculiar to young boys and pigs, muddy water is better than a hot August afternoon sun. When we got out we tried to scrape the scum and slime from our bodies which had begun to itch. Jack caught a watersnake and slapped its head against a fencepost; the snake's writhing ceased in his grasp and he dropped it. We looked over to the small pasture's woodlot fifty yards or so away; half emerged from a grove of tag-alder trees was an enormous bronze horse, the back of him invisible in the shade and the full sun falling on his great head and neck and flaxen mane. Jack said that is my dad's new horse and it will pull at the fair. It was so much grander than either part of my grandfather's team, which were lightweights and used only for farm work. I stood there and Jack walked along the fence toward the woodlot saying I'll show him to you. He struck the horse on the flank with a stick and yelled and the horse exploded from the trees running along the fence in my direction so I ducked under the fence. I could feel the hooves pounding in the ground and he galloped past me splashing through the edge of the pond so huge and close and tossing his head and mane and neighing. Then twenty yards or so farther on the horse stopped and fed calmly in the grass.

I would like to avoid any sense of "nostalgia"—the word has the attractiveness of a viral infection to my generation; those who wander about the age of thirty and having reached maturity during the Eisenhower lassitude feel lost within the energetic radicalism of the young, with their apparent willingness to change life-styles on a monthly basis or even more frequently. "Nostalgia" seems to involve the savoring of something permanently lost: the way Doc Blanchard ran, Big Daddy Lipscomb necktied, James Dean talked and drove a Porsche, Ben Hogan endured, or Ali jabbed.

I value my memory and find it as fascinating as life in the present; they mix together, coexist, live a comfortable life, confuse each other, and finally, have a sweet and permanent marriage.

Until the age of fourteen I lived in what now seems the nineteenth century in a small county seat of 1500 people in northern Michigan. My father, Winfield Sprague Harrison, was the government agricultural agent dispensing advice to farmers in a hopelessly unfertile countryside of jackpine, scrub oak, cedar swamps, and fields where gravel, sand and marl lurked altogether too close to the surface. The area was short on topsoil and money, but long on its efforts at the time to aid our boys who were fighting World War II by saving squashed tin cans, tinfoil, bread wrappers, picking milkweed pods for life preservers, and holding frequent blackouts and air-raid warnings in case the enemy should choose to attack us, though I suspect that it was agreed upon that we were a less than primary target. There was the usual plugged cannon on the courthouse lawn.

My father ran the annual county fair with Francis Godbold, the 4-H (Head, Heart, Health, Hands) director. My father loved his work, having come from many generations of unprosperous farmers; he had worked his way through what was then Michigan Agricultural College and considered farming an applied science and his job that of a missionary who spread the good news of effective farming methods. The fair was always held in late August on three invariably hot and dusty days. There were produce and crafts tents with vegetables stacked neatly, and canning, needlework and sewing with ribbons attached to the winning exhibits. And long sessions of milk cow, beef cattle, calf, pig, sheep, and even chicken judging took place. I took little interest in these; there was a small midway with games of chance and a few rides, a ferris wheel and merry-go-round, plus at least one implausibly frightening whirl and puke sort of machine. And a freak show where one paid an extra dime to see a hermaphrodite, an experience I might add that didn't mar my young psyche. We only argued whether or not "it" could do "it" to himself or herself. Farm children then, before artificial insemination, had a built-in sex education in the barnyard. But before noon each day I would have spent my miserably small allowance and would walk around looking for lost tickets on the ground, envying those who were drinking cold pop, and then I would find and pester my father for more change though he was busy judging everything imaginable, making sure the fair went smoothly. I looked forward only to the 4-H talent show in the evening though I was without any talent and anyway would have been too cowardly to enter. But a little girl I was fond of would sing "Candy Kisses," someone would play the musical saw, four older girls would imitate the Andrews Sisters, a young man with greasy hair would strum his guitar to the latest Grand Old Opry hit, and then a small boy would attempt "Flight of the Bumblebee" on the accordion.

But the main event, the most exciting spectacle to the adults, was the heavyweight horse pulling contest. The small grandstand would fill early in the afternoon with farmers and their wives talking and shading their eyes with the mimeographed programs. Out in the infield and across the track from the grandstand, a dozen teams or so would be standing, their owners since mid-morning having gone through the involved process of unloading them from trucks and putting on the harness and "working them out" a bit. I was always in the infield and watched the action with no great interest. Horses were simply as common as dogs or hogs to me. I was perpetually wary of the fabled cocked hoof which all my friends knew could kill in an instant, just as they knew men and sheep could breed sheep-humans. Someone had always heard of a recent rumor of a case where a child or man had been kicked through the side of a barn by a giant, angry hoof, "killed dead," as we used to say. The teamsters would be talking to their horses, straightening and adjusting the harness, chewing tobacco which would bulge one cheek and distort their faces. Later I learned they took snuff or chewed tobacco because it was cheap and nobody ever smoked in a barn, the largest of tinder boxes; smoking in a barn was a taboo on the level of incest. The teams would finally be marched out and people would clap for their favorites. The teams in turn would attempt to pull a loaded stoneboat a certain number of feet. A man with a clipboard would mark their progress, weight would be added and contestants eliminated until what I thought was hours and hours later a champion would be proclaimed. All the people in the hot grandstand would rise and applaud madly and the winning farmer would beam and blush and accept his trophy and the horses would stand there sweating and bored, waiting for the reward of feed and water.

These are first memories, hazy, probably inaccurate. It is lucky though for the world of books that those preadolescents perhaps genetically disposed to be writers don't keep journals. Think of the sheer, mimsy glut of sensitivity that would flood the market. But after the inevitable rejection of everything my parents seemed to value, an alienation lasting a decade, I came back to horse pulling contests; I go to them, few as there are, whenever I get a chance. I stand in the infield and take my clumsy pictures, talk to the farmers, the teamsters, and the beasts still look huge and magnificent; in reverse of the usual childhood memory they have become grander with time rather than diminished.

I was talking about the sport the other day to Leonard Erickson who lives down the road from me in Leelanau County, a fruit-growing area in northern Michigan. The county is a peninsula jutting out into Lake Michigan and the immediate presence of a large body of water tempers the climate and makes cherry growing possible. Aside from being a gentleman, a cattle dealer and fruit farmer, Erickson was for years a competitor and has a knowledge of horse pulling lore not a little less than fabulous. The sport for the "insider" has intricacies that remind one of fly-fishing or grouse hunting, subtle and arcane strategies, and superstitions that would fail any vaguely scientific test. There are cruelties, too, that reflect badly on a very small minority of practitioners.

The Belgian, with origins back before William the Conqueror's warhorses, that day's equivalent of the Sherman tank, is the strongest and most popular breed in heavyweight pulling contests. (I dwell on the heavyweights for the same reason I preferred watching Marciano to Basilio. The Percheron is the most frequent breed in the "lightweights," the cutoff point being a combined weight per team of 3200 pounds.) But the largest team does not necessarily win; conditioning is the main factor and natural strength, daily workouts, how well the horses pull together as a team are tremendously important. A well-trained team often beats a stronger and heavier one—in fact I have seen a disciplined pair of 4275 pounds beat an ill-prepared, fat team of 5200 pounds. As with dogs there is a great variation of size with the breed. At present there is an attempt being made to breed "more light" Belgian pullers, to sacrifice a bit of their compactness for a rangier horse. Pulling horses are nearly always geldings or mares for obvious reasons. One scarcely can tell a sexed-up bull elephant to "calm down" if there's a female in heat in the area. It is difficult for the neophyte to comprehend the strength of these animals. It has been accurately estimated that a team of championship quality can pull the equal of a rolling load of 110 tons, a deadweight stone boat of around 10,000 pounds, or a seven-bottom plow for a limited distance.

A device called a "hydrometer" mounted on a truck is used in major contests for absolute accuracy. The hydrometer though is unpopular at many county fairs. The audience enjoys the visual drama of the pig iron being gradually added as the contest continues. Usually there are many arguments and much stalling, false passes are made at the hitch, but all of this constitutes a tactic to allow the bottom of the boat to cool, thus reducing the friction of heat caused by the previous contestant. Most teams are keyed to start pulling by the sound of the clank of the hitch when the hook drops in rather than by the shout of the teamster. Two assistants carry the ends of the eveners as the team swings up to the boat, the teamster seats himself holding the reins tightly; then with the clank or shout their flanks lower and the horses strain forward against the weight, tearing out clots of earth with their hooves. When the twenty-seven-and-a-half-foot distance is reached a whistle is blown. Until then the audience refrains from clapping as the horses associate applause with success and will stop short of the distance. Anything short of a full run is measured to determine positioning among the teams.

Horse pulling can be an extremely expensive sport. The prize money is so pitifully small as to make the sport virtually amateur—top prizes rarely go over $250. A pulling team which will be in its prime for only about five years can cost anywhere from $400 to $20,000, the latter amount being the most I've ever heard paid for a team and this particular pair died a few months after the purchase from bloat. To this initial expense must be added the cost of hauling the team from contest to contest, the feeding of animals which eat four times as much as race horses, the not inconsiderable price of the custom harness required to pull the vast weights. It is simply a sport practiced out of love rather than for profit.

I have thoughts, usually dim and morose, about the mechanization of sport. One of the delights of a long trip into the Absarokas in Montana was the meeting of a Natty Bumppo sort of wilderness crank who openly admitted to the vandalizing of trail bikes because he hated the noise. He would stalk the riders until they left their bikes to climb or fish then smash the sparkplugs and carburetors with a rock. No matter how far into any mountain range we go we see jet contrails or are suspicious that we might step into a missile silo by mistake. In Michigan some sportsmen harry coyotes and fox from snowmobiles. Add to this the Alaskan amusement of shooting wolves from helicopters.

But even the sport of horse pulling owns some cruelty. A few teamsters use electric cattle prods to encourage greater effort in training. While it is true that shock collars are an approved though unpleasant method of working with bird dogs, I have heard of an incident where a difficult horse was shocked into prone limpid exhaustion by a 110 volt application of discipline. Though these animals are instinctively docile—they were used as workers so long the ugly streaks were bred out—there is an occasional exception. These "outlaws" are often prized as their willfulness makes them good pullers. Usually the sound of the whip cracking is enough just as a rolled up newspaper works with a dog. The sound helps "wind them up," convinces them that if they don't want to pull they have to pull. Unfortunately the inspiration of an amphetamine dose is also detected once in a great while.

I suspect that the sport of horse pulling will disappear with inevitable slowness, probably in my own lifetime. I don't mean that the breeding of draft horses will be discontinued. There is a large auction held several times a year in Waverly, Iowa for regular draft horses. There are still limited functions for the animals: the Amish refusal of tractors, the pulling in of seine nets on the Pacific Northwest coast, parade and general entertainment uses. Two local competitors, Larry Reed and Charles Van Borst, use their pulling horses in the winter to skid logs out of the woods in their lumber businesses. But few people of my own generation are even aware that draft horses exist other than the grand Budweiser Clydesdales they see on the television commercials. The Busch family will continue to breed them because they are beautiful, and, the best reason of all, they exist. But the sport, I'm sure, will suffer a natural degeneration as organic to our time as the death of jousting was to the Middle Ages. One might even assume in a framework of radical or visionary ecology that there won't be enough food in the year 2000 to feed such appetites. I don't know. Things change so strangely, catch us in errant surprise. My first innocent deer hunt fifteen years ago has been replaced with sampling at checkpoints by the Department of Natural Resources for DDT in the fatty tissues of the destroyed animal. There is no sentimentality here. Our own sport must finally assume the selectiveness and regimentation of Europe's. England had 1,000,000 draft horses in 1930 and in 1960 there were 70,000. Of course the war. . . . But the contests—how do we keep what we love when so few of us seem to love them?

Meanwhile back at the fair, the audience grows older and sparser. A casual survey of the grandstand, admission to which is free, makes it appear as though a retirement colony is having a holiday or a geriatrics ward was emptied for the afternoon. Horse pulling cannot compete with "Dan's Hell Roaring Devil Driving Car Smashers," the feature attraction of this year's fair.

I am forced now to think of my grandfather, John Severin Wahlgren, who traveled from Sweden to Illinois in the 1890s. After a number of years of saving he bought a farm "up in Michigan." When they moved northwards on a milk train that took two days to travel 300 miles my grandmother rode in a coach with the children, and John rode in a cattle car with a team of draft horses he had bought near Galesburg. They got off in the middle of the night at a railroad siding and a friend took Hulda and the children home for the night. But John walked the horses the seven miles to the farm. I think of it as a late April night with time left for plowing; the moon was in its third quarter, the pace was slow and the reins held tightly, the road narrow and perhaps a bit muddy with rain and there was a heavy scent of grass and weeds and the sound of frogs and crickets, the sound of horses' hooves muffled but heavy with fetlocks rising above the ground mist.

I have an old photo of my father, dead now as is my grandfather, leaning on the plow handles looking very jaunty with the reins over his bare shoulder and an old gangster-type fedora cocked on his head. He always helped with the plowing during the Depression when he was unemployed. The harness is stored in the chicken coop, moulding beyond repair. But I've often thought that if I ever get past the "renter" stage and own a small farm I'll buy a Belgian yearling just to look at and let grow quietly lazy and old.

1973

Bar Pool

Manhattan cocktail lounges and bars are notable for their lack of anything for the customers to do. Except drink, of course. And a drink can cost you a buck and a half or three dollars if you drink doubles, long a habit of mine as I crave the substantial in life. So you sit there if you are unlucky enough to be alone and perhaps pretend to be someone interesting like a spy, a lesser celebrity, a solitary businessman concocting a deal that will make a lot of people truly sorry. To your untrained Midwestern eyes the bartender always looks like a criminal or at least a pimp. But there is finally no real reason to be in a bar in daytime except to booze and look out the window at the burnt and umbrous haze that is New York air.

Way up in Michigan, officially known as the "Winter-Water-Wonderland," there are admittedly no French restaurants, very little theater, and the first-run movies are a few months late, but the bars serve as local clubhouses and there are games to be played. To be sure, it's not like Elaine's, where you can drop twenty bucks and pine away hours trying to exchange a single glance with a fritzee brunette in a transparent blouse. Hereabouts such costumes would cause a riot of bumpkinry. In most northern Michigan bars there is a shuffleboard, often a bowling machine, frequently a pinball machine, and always a pool table, bar-sized, usually about four by seven feet. And in many bars that table will be continually busy from late afternoon until closing time at two A.M. and kick-out time at two-thirty.

It is a game of infinite variables: after you break the rack the configuration of balls and the stratagems necessary to clear them never precisely repeat themselves. It is a game of inches and the calibration of stroke and English on a small table require even more patience than the larger table of the pool hall. True excellence is rare and vanities are punished. Gambling for a game of pool is illegal in Michigan but some sort of harmless "I'll play you for a drink" action goes on and in the downstate urban areas it gets a great deal more serious. With all those lovely auto factories they have more money to play with. It is a benign though demanding sport. You won't see the Johnson City big-time act with tuxedoed players owning the temperaments of concert pianists. A very few players like to surround pool with the aura of the badass; it's not unfair to portray their hokum in all of the shabby colors of nickel-dime evil right down to the cue case with a decal of a cobra stretched along its length.

I first came to bar pool as an unhappy graduate student who picked up his grocery money teaching English to foreign students in mixed lots, with as many as fifteen language backgrounds in a single class. My car trunk was stuffed with uncorrected papers. My heart was heavy. Each day was a fresh hemorrhoidectomy. The proctoscopic years. But in a half-dozen bars around East Lansing I began to learn to play pool, which quickly replaced bridge though the mania for both shares similarities. And with both learning is miserable. "You didn't finesse, you fool," your partner says as you slump down in your chair like a sick turtle. Or in front of thirty people in a bar, some of them pretty girls, you scratch an easy eight ball shot and the subsequent giggles fill your ears with blood. You always lose when you're learning and as Woody Hayes would have it, only losers are good losers.

It is obvious to me now that the earlier one starts the better, especially if good coaching is available. You see people who have played a dozen years using an open rather than a closed bridge on the cue, affording much less control of the stick. Most bar pool is incredibly clumsy. There might be one or two local dudes who beat everyone else quite consistently but they would usually be utterly lost against an average player in a pool parlor. A good large-table player can easily adapt himself and a snooker expert is deadly on a bar table. A three-cushion billiard player can rarely get used to the soft stroke required.

It is easy to stay on the same plateau of skill for years, even drop one or two steps for periods of time. The better players are able to shut out the world other than their immediate *querencia*, their place of strength which is described by the circle of light cast by the lamp above the table. Those who lack this self-absorption and ability to concentrate never improve appreciably. You can usually connect very bad evenings to a cause, the most obvious of which is that you had too much to drink. You were playing with a good friend and neither money nor pride was at stake. One of those rare miniskirts was sitting at a stool humming. And a raft of other possibilities: general depression, excessive happiness, an argument, a tranquilizer that removed your aggressiveness. A dispute with a wife or friend can throw your grouse shooting totally out of whack and the damage on a pool table is even more direct. But sometimes as with so many other sports the faults are inexplicable: a few years ago I led the local tournament for eight weeks, only to blow up in the final two matches, dropping the contest and purple bowling trophy to a bluegrass banjoist from New Haven, Connecticut. A foreigner got the apples. I brooded darkly.

Though I had played for a long time I didn't begin to understand the subtleties of the game until I met Benny Boyd a few years ago. At the time he was a college instructor and one day I caught him unloading several cases of liquor out of the backseat of his car. An unlikely act for a college instructor. He said he had won five hundred bucks in a pool game at a local bar and was stocking up. That seemed like a lot of money then and still does now, especially for an afternoon in a bar where one might be spending the afternoon anyway. I found out that he had won the Michigan Pocket Billiards Championship in 1966 and when in college had taken second in a national tournament run by the NCAA. After that he played professionally for a while. When Benny lost his teaching job in the economic bite put on universities he moved north and got a job bartending. Watching him play I learned that the trip between good or average and excellent was an impossible one. You simply can't beat a good player like Benny when he's on "dead stroke" as they call it. You might pick up a game or two by accident but you simply haven't paid your dues and in this case the dues are literally thousands of hours of intelligent practice.

I've only really gambled at pool once and didn't like the sensation. I mean gambled so that my pocket hurt as the fivers vaporized. It is similar, say, to a time-limit poker game where you are perhaps playing for a dollar, three raises to a man. There's only a half hour left and you agree to temporarily raise the stakes. The winners agree because they feel arrogant and in control and the losers quite simply want some of their money back. There's an almost palpable ozone in the air, acrid and suspenseful. Now people can be hurt. The pots are mountainous and the feeling of safety is gone. A pleasant evening of cards has exploded into something else and when your flush loses to a full house you are sitting in a bathtub into which some masked man has just dropped a radio which he neglected to unplug. I'm not geared for that sort of excitement in either poker or pool and doubt I ever will be.

I was playing eight ball in a bar in Livingston, Montana last summer with country-rock singer Jimmy Buffett, whose appearance is a bit bizarre for even the new west. He was leaning far over the table for a stretch shot when the witty bartender threw a firecracker at his feet. The blast was accompanied by a truly wonderful freak-out but it was hard for Buffett to get his stroke back so we watched the bartender toss some more firecrackers at two sleeping drunks at the end of the bar. Only one of them woke up, though the blast within the confined walls equaled a twelve-gauge magnum. We decided the other was dead but were afraid to check. Actually the bartender is a nice guy with an elfin sense of humor. He told us a story of how his Arabian stallion mated a mare over a picket fence and when she moved away the poor stallion was hung up over the fence and the fence had to be destroyed. "That's what can happen in love," said Buffett, I thought not too appropriately.

I don't find it strange that bar pool is openly and stupidly male. Games of skill often are and bar pool is transparently so with its definite pecking order in any single location. You don't mind getting burned by Benny but if some cretinoid hod carrier beats you badly you want to hide out in your bedroom in a penance of Dagwood boredom. In a hotel outside of Salinas, Ecuador, down near the Peruvian border, there was a bar table. And for a week a photographer and I would spend the evenings playing eight ball. I had an edge on him and could salve my poor hands and spirit, blistered by fighting marlin. The photographer would fight his marlin standing up while I required the strapped-in security of the chair. It was a very small thing to get back at his superb angling on the pool table with all of that warm, liquid equatorial air pouring in over the table through the open doors, the crash of surf in the background, and the moisture so heavy from the spray in the air that you would wipe your cue stick with your shirt after every shot. We played for drinks and unobtainable women and riches. It's fun to announce "This one's for Ava Gardner" and then swiftly win. "This one's for Annette Funicello" doesn't have the same Bogartian resonance.

Boston bars tend to resemble those in Manhattan. Once after moving my family into a new apartment I checked out the local tavern. No pool table. But there were several pay phones. Why all the pay phones? I even asked the bartender who looked at me as if I were Mortimer Snerd made flesh. Better to drop your change on pool than dialing a number for the horses across town, I thought. Telling the booky I wanted twenty on Marmalade in the seventh was a trifling pleasure compared to running seven stripes against that sea green felt.

And you see some funny things happen. Down in Key West one evening I watched a game in a freak bar only recently torn down. There was a large shaggy crowd of players evidently wired on downers, probably Seconal, and each game was a somnambulistic nightmare with all the shots requiring minutes of meditation and endless practice strokes with the cue. Then pensive reconsiderations. It was a hopeless, slow-motion game until a Cuban shrimper came up and ran successive racks with hyperthyroid speed. There was much mumbling and a general desertion of the table.

Huston Cradduck, who operates the grain elevator in Lake Leelanau, told me a story about a game that took place in Peach Orchard, Missouri. A hustler friend of Huston's daddy had spent a whole afternoon dropping games to the local sharpies, pretending to be very drunk and a total sucker. He dropped a number of hundred-dollar games, even fell against the table, cracking open his lip, until he drew in a high roller for five grand at which point he ran the table. He left with his money in a hurry to save his life. I thought that must be a record for a bar game but Benny said that a few years back he had watched a two-day match downstate where thirty-five grand changed hands in a bar mostly in one direction: toward a nationally famous player and his backer.

Violence in bar pool is a rare thing. The issues are settled on the table. I have had the 600-pound table moved during a game by some people having a friendly argument over a euchre game. After a lot of bluish epithets the older man, a plumber, called the younger a "college student." And the younger man called the plumber a "charlatan" which puzzled the spectators. While the plumber began to thrash the young man I looked in despair at how they had jostled my perfect setup on the pool table.

1973

Guiding Light in the Keys

Say that you have been driving south for two days and despite road exhaustion you are delighted to escape the flinty April cold of Michigan. Just outside of Miami you make a jog on the Palmetto Expressway, then another jog through the truck farms and you are past Homestead. Closer now. In the immenseness of its greenery the flat swampy terrain resembles nothing so much as a giant snake farm, but you know that not far on the left is the Atlantic and on the right, out beyond the miles of mangrove and saw grass, is the Gulf of Mexico.

Route 1 is slacked with trailers; from the air it would appear that you are trapped in a slow crawling trailer caravan, an imitation freight train hauling the weary to the sun for an Easter weekend rest. But you don't want to rest. You want to fish for a month, every day all day, way past the point of boredom or exhaustion or possible sunstroke or disgust. At Key Largo and on down to Big Pine you keep noticing there's a steady breeze out of the southeast, maybe twenty knots, and it has roiled the water and you hate it, but even this doesn't matter. You itch to be out there, to be staked on the edge of a flat in a skiff looking for tarpon or permit or bonefish or perhaps the waving-flag tail of a mutton snapper.

A flight down from Miami is even more dramatic. Following the Keys south, then west, at 5,000 feet you imagine that you can see the great sweep of the tide shifting from the Atlantic to the Gulf and back again. And the passing of the tidal thrust through so many configurations of land masses and small mangrove keys creates rivers. It occurs to you that you are not fishing a series of mangrove islands and their adjoining flats at all but twenty or so rivers whose courses may be seen only from the air.

Rivers or flats, the Keys are a wilderness of water, and a stranger could fish for a long time without even seeing any of the vaunted species that make angling here such a quantum experience. There is simply too much water: close to 750 square miles between Bahia Honda down through Key West with a slight crook southwesterly out to Boca Grande and the Marquesas beyond.

The stranger will waste his time blundering around from flat to channel with his nose in a series of imprecise charts and an inscrutable tide book. He will get lost, or at least run his boat aground. So the only sensible thing to do in order to save time and grief and raw nerves, stove-in hulls and gouged bottoms—and ultimately to catch fish—is to book a guide. In this vast stretch of country there are perhaps a dozen good ones, not to be confused with the backwoods handyman retards he might have encountered on other sporting ventures.

The skiff floats far out on the Gulf side of Jack Bank; it is still very early but there is a good tide. The light is bad, however, with thunderheads piling up, pushed by a fifteen-knot wind out of the south. The thunderheads reflect the sun and form a sheen on the water that is almost impossible to penetrate; though the water is only three feet deep, a 100-pound tarpon can pass by unnoticed. These are scarcely good conditions for the neophyte but he realizes he needs them to excuse his ineptitudes.

The guide, Woody Sexton, stands on the deck of the skiff holding a long push pole at midpoint so that is balanced in his hand. He is breathing hard because he has just finished chasing a pod of tarpon upwind and uptide but they stayed out of range.

"I see more fish," he says.

"Where?" The customer's voice quavers.

"About twelve o'clock straight off the transom about a hundred yards, moving from left to right."

"I don't see anything." The customer is staring, rather than scanning the water as he should. He checks his fly line to make sure that the wind hasn't whipped it around the motor or the console.

"They're turning toward us." The guide gives several hard pushes on the pole. "Get ready."

The customer begins to false cast, ready to throw to the fish. He sees only waves and their small darkened troughs. "I don't see anything."

"You're not looking. Coming at us a hundred feet. Ten tarpon. Shoot off the lead fish."

"I still don't see them."

"Cast!"

The customer casts and begins stripping his line. He thinks he has seen a shadow or at least a movement.

"You spooked them," Sexton says. "You dropped your line on the lead fish and they spooked."

The customer slumps in his seat. First-day blues. A few hundred yards away Cal Cochran, another guide, is pointing out something to his customer, Mead Johnson. Johnson casts and is on to a fifty-pounder. The first-day blues deepen.

Sexton decides to make the four-mile run over to Big Spanish Key, where we will have a slight lee from the wind. He is being sweet and generous, assuring that though the cast was in the wrong direction it was good. But Big Spanish only extends the comic possibilities of the day. The customer strikes a fish so hard with his brand new Great Equalizer, the largest tarpon fly rod available, that the tip touches the reel seat. The leader snaps. "You really crossed his eyes," Sexton says, starting the motor.

That night the customer sees the fish over and over again as he tries to sleep; he is like a bridge player reliving almost grand slams in his dreams. His mind moves like a badminton bird between the desire to punch his guide, to catch a record fish, to be back home playing in the snow, to know enough about Keys fishing to do it by himself. Where no one could watch.

Sexton is to saltwater fly-fishing what an astronaut is to the space program—super technocrat. With his short gray hair and mesomorph physique, he reminds one of a retired NCO who has refused to go soft. He can be irritatingly humorless. Guides can kill the charm of a day's fishing by becoming screaming drill sergeants. It is, after all, a sport, and most notions of sport include the idea of entertainment. No customer likes to sit in the gun seat all day with the general feeling that he is a hopeless incompetent.

Though he has a certain honest charm, Sexton watches with absolute disgust when, after a day's fishing, the customer goes to an oyster house and loads up on quantities of shellfish and beer. Sexton worries aloud like an old lady about the dangers of alcohol and hepatitis. A disease lurks in every cherrystone. He does not like fish. He tells how, when he trained with weights, he would break a dozen eggs every day into a malted milk. And the customer knows that these finicky attitudes are carried to great ends. An errant cigarette ash in the Sexton skiff is quickly wiped up with a wet towel.

All of Sexton's equipment, however old, looks brand-new. The customer's dog leaps up for a peek into Sexton's new camper. Horrors. A dog can scratch a car. Everything on earth threatens decay and one maintains oneself only with a devotion to discipline that makes many of Sexton's friends reach for a big drink.

As the customer draws nearer to sleep he feels more warm and less nit-picky about Sexton. So what if a man devotes to fishing the same kind of energy Lee Iacocca devoted to the Mustang. A day with Sexton isn't as terrifying as fishing with Stu Apte, for instance, who gives the impression of overbearing faultlessness. Perhaps too overbearing—another guide once went after him with a kill gaff. And unlike Cal Cochran, Sexton often acts puzzled and doubting. Cal Cochran has a macho routine on the waterfront that Marlon Brando should study.

When he is not enervated by bad weather, Woody Sexton gives the appearance of tremendous strength and vitality. He constitutes some sort of classic in conservative guiding; while most guides have turned to larger skiffs—Fiber Craft or Hewes—for the comfort of their customers, Sexton keeps his light Nova Scotia. The skiff was bought from a Hamiltonian Republican who named it *Amagiri* years ago after the Japanese destroyer that sank PT-109. The name is still on the skiff and has been known to vex some of the Navy personnel on the Keys. Sexton still spends a lot of time on his push pole, a diminishing practice which on a heavy skiff is absolutely brutal. A 1,000-pound skiff with a 135-hp outboard does not glide across a flat easily. Sexton, however, is willing to chase tarpon upwind and uptide, and the amount of power he gets into the pole is appalling. The skiff leaves a wake and if you are standing you maintain your balance with difficulty. This requires the kind of physique and conditioning that leaves the joggers and exercise buffs hiding in any available closet. (At home in the evenings, Sexton exercises his casting arm—which looks like an oak club—by going through all the motions with a twelve-pound sledgehammer with a foreshortened handle.)

Sexton divides his year in half, moving to the West Coast in early July and back to Big Pine usually in February. Typically, he spends much of his vacation time in the West, fishing steelhead and hunting ducks and chukars. During World War II he was a physical fitness instructor in the Navy. Up until 1966 he cut big trees during the winter on a freelance basis for the timber industry. Sexton gives the impression of being hyperintelligent, cranky and totally physical. One cannot imagine a more stylish or powerful fly caster, or anyone more capable at hooking and fighting fish.

At noon you are staked out in the Snipes and it is very hot and still. You hear the outgoing water gurgling through a tidal cut in the mangroves and you are tempted to throw yourself in to wash away the sweat that is dripping into your eyes and down your chest and legs. There are few tarpon around so you have decided to try the barracuda fly Ray Donnersberger has devised. One version has been called Red Death, a name that deserves to be hooted. But the fly, unlike many flies you have used on barracuda before, works. It is at least a foot long and evidently imitates the needlefish, a favorite food of the barracuda. Donnersberger claims the fly casts "nicely" and you agree, assuming you can stuff it down the barrel of a shotgun. But there are those who wouldn't need a gun. You remember an early morning at Vista Linda marina when Cal Cochran decided to cancel; the sky was dark and the wind was running over thirty miles per hour. A few guides were standing around taking turns casting. Cochran threw the whole line and leader about 100 feet across the marina lagoon into the wind.

This sort of act can cause a great deal of difficulty and misunderstanding between guide and customer. The guide might have logged twenty years on the water and his devotion to angling is all-consuming. The customer has been making money so that, among other things, he can afford the $90-a-day guide fee. Although the customer most often is not one of the great anglers of the world, a few guides have been known to get very hot over a blown cast. Even to the point of running a customer back to shore if the errors are numerous.

Most guides are fairly tolerant and affable, however, especially if a customer's interest is sincere. Even in the frenzy and exoticism of the sport, the good guides remember that their purpose is to enable a customer to catch fish.

The names of guides most frequently heard are Cecil Keith Jr., George Hommel Jr., Stu Apte, Roy Lowe, Bill Curtis, Harry Snow Jr., Eddy Wightman, Jack Brothers, Jimmy Albright, Arlin Leiby, Bob Montgomery, Jim Brewer, Steve Huff and Cal Cochran. A mixture of the great, the good and some retired. Albright, for example, has been famous for a very long time; Huff, who is only twenty-seven, will be famous for a very long time. A few are extremely versatile—you suspect that Bill Curtis, who works out of Key Biscayne, or Cal Cochran would gladly trailer their skiffs to the moon if they thought the fishing was worthwhile. Cochran tackles his job with the belligerence of a pro defensive end. Stu Apte has retired from guiding and become a copilot on a 747, which reveals something about the type of person who becomes obsessed with this sport. In his spare time Apte is making a movie about fly-fishing for tarpon from a canoe. One wishes him well. It is said he does not know how to swim.

Harry Snow Jr. is a justly famous guide as was his father before him. His family came originally from Nantucket to Saint Augustine, and later his father moved to the Keys to work on the railroad; he stuck around because he liked the fishing, ending up guiding such notables as Herbert Hoover. The other guides admit that on bonefish Junior is probably in a class by himself and have stories to illustrate. As an instance, Snow can place a customer on the deck, spinning rod in hand, and tell him to cast. Snow invariably can get a cast off first though he has to reach in the rod holder for his equipment. He also has the ability to find fish in the vilest of weather. One morning, sitting over breakfast at the Half and Half up on Big Pine with Woody Sexton and Steve Huff, Harry Snow Jr. looked particularly happy. Though he is booked much of the year he had received a paid cancellation and he and Woody were going to spend the day fishing for pleasure. You look closely into his sun-weathered face for traces of madness; how can he guide for maybe 300 days a year in the heat of the Florida Keys only to go fishing on a day off? He excuses his obsession by saying he wants to relax.

A stretch of bad weather translates into unpaid cancellations and a loss of income for the guides. High winds and clouds can pose additional dangers if a customer on a short vacation insists on going out. A Hewes skiff can streak across the flats at about forty-five knots and if bad light hides the configurations of the bottom it is easy to run aground. Sometimes bad weather pays off, though. Permit are less wary and take a fly better. And tarpon, if you can see them, are more prone to strike when it's choppy.

There are problems involving etiquette and secrecy. Many good spots have code names to conceal their locations: Animal Farm, the Eccentrics, Monster Point and others. Some areas are named after guides: Hommel's or Woody's Corner. Some secrecy is understandable; it is a guide's livelihood and he probably spent a great deal of time and gas money doping out the fishery. And though the area is huge, a dozen skiffs can make it appear crowded. But even if a bungling initiate, or a dread spy from Miami or Islamorada, had the chart name of the area, the precise slot the tarpon or permit tend to travel on a certain tide would be difficult to unravel.

But the biggest problem is when a guide cannot find fish during good conditions. Say there is a big tide and a fly-fishing customer wants to take a mutton snapper, a currently fashionable fish. The guide goes out from Key West, across an area called "the lakes," to Woman Key and Boca Grande, expecting to see snappers behind the rays that move up on the flats with the tide.

But while in two hours spent poling the very best water he sees many rays, no snappers are feeding behind them. All of the good signs are there, including cormorants feeding behind the rays. Even the flat smells fishy. So what has happened? He decides it might be too bumpy along the reef line — a brisk southeast wind has raised a moderate surf. Maybe the snappers don't like it. There aren't many permit around either, though ordinary permit aren't disturbed by the weather. He is flatly boggled. The week before under similar conditions he saw thirteen snappers. Also the rare sight of five permit, two snappers and a cormorant following a single mudding ray. Maybe the way the waves draw in upon themselves along the reef, the shallow trough, make the fish think there is less water than there really is. If fish think. Or the weather has been cooler and the change in water temperature might have affected the feeding habits. Both guide and client are upset; the guide is perplexed, the client irritated. A guide is forced to think. If he is not prepared to think technically, to become a master strategist, it is unlikely he will survive, since the core of his livelihood is return business.

World War II proved to be very good for the offshore fishing around Key West, though no one realized it at the time. There were German subs in the area and they knocked off a few of our ships. These wrecks provide the prey with shelter from the predator; the wreck is a giant restaurant for a wide spectrum of sea creatures that ranges from the tiny crustaceans that plaster themselves on the steel to huge sharks and 300-pound jewfish. Some of the wrecks are extremely difficult to find and some are too far from Key West for any but the fastest boats. But Bob Montgomery has mastered both the finding of them and the light-tackle approach to fishing their bounty.

Montgomery was a flight engineer for twelve years in the Navy before he decided that the Navy was not "what it used to be." He was raised on Mondongo Island off the west coast of Florida where his father was a fishing guide. He docks two boats at Garrison Bight, Key West, both of which he custom-built: a nineteen-foot Carey for the flats and a twenty-three-foot Formula for offshore wreck fishing. Montgomery is an aggressive though very pleasant human. He likes the idea of versatility in fishing, and owning two boats gives him a wide range of options.

There is a touch of the blond Ernest Borgnine to Montgomery. He is jovial but with a firm sense of what he is on earth—he smiles a lot but only on his own terms. He is of average height but with massive chest and shoulders, and could easily be mistaken for a bricklayer or a retired jock who has become a beer salesman. And he would not be out of place in a deputy's uniform in one of those movies that highlight the powder-keg versatility for mayhem of the Deep South.

You wonder about a football-coach syndrome you find in the guides, Montgomery included. Everyone in the sporting world has remarked on particular types who are absolutely incapable of abandoning their obsessiveness for any occasion. And guides, whether at breakfast or a social dinner, are going to drill you into a corner about fishing or boats or the threat to business posed by a new guide in town. After a long day on the water it can drive you limp with boredom. You suddenly want to tour geriatrics boutiques with your maiden aunt. It's fun to bring up another subject—farming, or Watergate—and see how fast they can get back to fishing. Only sex competes. A sweet young thing in a bikini can disarm the most insistent sports freak, if only momentarily. "Yum yum wow gurgle. But you know those ole tarpon are stacked in the channel like cordwood." Actually, if you are paying, it is an obsession you learn to appreciate.

Early one morning we left Garrison Bight in the Formula for a destroyer wreck out on the edge of the Gulf Stream. Montgomery's brother Gene, also a guide, was at the dock with a long face and two clients who looked like a guaranteed pain in the neck. Days can be long. We went around the tip of the island, then headed out in a fairly heavy chop. But the Formula has a V hull and is powered by two OMC 165s, so there was no real discomfort. We deep jigged when the Fathometer showed the destroyer and the schools of fish above it, but the wind made it too difficult to stay on target.

Around noon the weather abruptly changed and the water calmed down. We decided to fly-fish for dolphin along the weed lines that had begun to appear. We trolled until we hooked a dolphin, then cut the engine and began to cast. We caught several and they proved to be fine fighters on fly tackle. We noticed several sharks massing themselves under another bed of weeds, almost peering out, the water so clear that you could see them eye the pilchards we were throwing as chum. A large fly was cast and quickly taken but the leader popped. Another fly and a good hookup on the lip. Half an hour later and you have your first shark on fly, 100 pounds or so but a not very dramatic fighter.

Montgomery fishes about half-a-dozen wrecks in addition to taking customers out on the flats for permit and tarpon. He has an elaborate Vexilar Recording Fathometer mounted on the Formula console, and without such an instrument wreck fishing is out of the question, especially when you're going a long way to a little-known site. The wreck of the *Luckenback* is twenty-four minutes, twenty seconds at 3,400 rpm off Smith Shoals at 004 degrees on the compass. A long run. Shortly before you reach the spot, a few hundred square yards in all of that ocean empty of markings, you turn on the Fathometer and wait for the wreck and the fish to show. If you miss the wreck, you throw over a buoy, and circle until you find it. This all might strike some as excessively technical until they see the profligate number of fish: cobia, amberjack, yellowtail, snapper, barracuda, among others. Often giant jewfish rise up to take a hooked fish. After a moderate amount of chumming most fish take readily to the fly. You become selective in order not to exhaust yourself.

Montgomery gets very angry when spies attempt to follow him to the *Luckenback*, assuming they have a fast enough boat—the Formula does close to fifty. He once led a Miami boat thirty miles in the wrong direction before turning back, an expensive act of deception in terms of time and gasoline, but if the spot were widely known it could be cleaned out by fish hogs. All good guides release fish except for a record or a mount or an occasional fish dinner. But some guides hang fish to attract customers. The tarpon and permit end up in trash barrels.

Another unfortunate practice designed to entertain anglers who might better be tied to bar stools or TV sets is the daylong fishing contest to see which "club" can kill the most fish. Often long lines of shriveled barracuda and snapper are stretched out in the hot parking lot next to Garrison Bight. Intelligent guides have long since given up the idea that the ocean's bounty is endless. The decrease in number of game fish is obvious to anyone who has been in the business for a few years. The fishing is still good and with a little sense on the part of even the most bovine angler it can be kept that way.

After fishing in the Florida Keys for a number of years it becomes obvious that guides do not make a lot of money despite their high daily fee, and certainly not much commensurate with their abilities as men. A fully equipped skiff with motor costs at least $5,000, there are the many blown-out charters, and the rigor of the job equals that of a jackhammer operator. But there is a dignity and grace in the profession unavailable in all but a very few areas to very few men. You have to be good or you don't eat. Few of the guides could imagine doing anything else. At least until they simply wear out.

And there is the rapport that the guide, no matter the repetition, shares with his customer: the sheer fun and excitement of the sport. It is most palpable early in the morning. At dockside the customers are talking with strenuously subdued giddiness, trying to act offhanded and experienced. The guides gas up the boats and double-check the gear. They are wary and gruff, concealing their nervousness in all the details of preparation. But the nearly crazy unvoiced hope of all is that it might be one of those special days to be talked of with awe through all the boozy nights to come; say jumping twenty tarpon or a first permit on fly or a dozen bonefish. Or even the unmentionable—breaking Apte's record of a 154-pound tarpon on a fly. No wonder he's arrogant. And no matter that the boats will probably return in eight hours with the guides grim with uneven success and the customers looking as though they had just spent eight hours in a sauna under a sun lamp. When it is bad for some and good for others the anger of the losers is nearly primitive. The guides shuffle and grimace around the dock in the late afternoon sun wondering why they aren't doing something sensible for

God's sake. The unsuccessful anglers lunge for their cars, which have heated up like ovens. But the lucky ones—and luck is always a factor, along with skill and good guiding—don't want to leave just yet. They move around the boat slips in sort of a peacock trance, talking to anyone who will listen for even a moment about their experience, certainly among the top few that angling—or life—has to offer.

1973

Canada

Among the strangest customs of fishermen in northern Michigan are frequent trips to Canada. I say strange because the fishing has been so good right here for the past few years, especially in Lake Michigan, which is only a mile or so from my farm. One cold evening in May, casting from shore, I caught an eight-pound brown trout and a twelve-pound lake trout. I fished for a total of twenty minutes. Not that this happens every evening, but limits occur with regularity. And Lake Leelanau is only a mile in the other direction. It yields good catches of brown and rainbow trout and smallmouth bass. If you like to troll in the big lake, chinook and coho salmon are available in late summer, and fall brings some sturdy steelhead runs. I can also name three reasonably good brown-trout streams within an hour's drive.

So why go to Canada? It's not just to escape the Indiana farmers and arc welders from Detroit who clutter up northern Michigan to fish in the summer. Some of my friends even go to Canada in the dead of winter to ice-fish, if that can be imagined.

I think, rather, that in going to Canada you recapture a sense of what the sporting life was in northern Michigan (or Wisconsin, New York, Minnesota) from the late forties to the mid-fifties: a sweet peacefulness with fairly abundant fish and game, threadbare cabins and kerosene lamps, war-surplus sleeping bags and musty tents. And even more pleasant, you bring back a time when woods, lakesides and riverbanks weren't littered with Day-Glo "No Trespassing" signs, when campsites weren't on the verge of computerization, when the big tract owners and farmers didn't care if you pitched a tent, under the entirely reasonable assumption you wouldn't muck up the land.

So in Canada is this sense of something we have largely lost. Like tourists in England, you are shocked by the politeness and affability of the people.

And in all the roadhouse stops that seem to accompany sporting trips, you don't feel that cold, ozone-tinged sense of violence so common now in American bars. This may sound like propaganda but it isn't. It's simply a reaction to a fine surprise.

Driving north in late May, as I did with three friends last spring, you see spring gradually disappear into the tentative beginnings of a few weeks past. The darker greens around your farm fade into paler greens until at the end of 400 miles you see only buds a few days old, and in the total landscape earth colors predominate. The last leg of the trip, from Thesalon, Ontario up toward Chapleau, is a sort of Appalachian feast, only without people— sheer rock faces, hills on the verge of becoming small mountains, fast-moving creeks—until you round another corner and see the great Missis-sagi River. Your trance is disturbed by the knowledge that the Mississagi is dammed at Aubrey Falls, which has diminished the fine fishing. But the Aubinadong River just up the road isn't dammed and you mean to have a go at the large brook trout it's rumored to hold.

When we reach a sign announcing Alvin Armstrong's Mashagama Lodge, we learn that we have to walk the last two miles—the rough trail won't accommodate our low-slung car. A Jeep is sent to pick up our gear, and the four of us (four fatties) are a little embarrassed as Alvin stares at the vast load of food and drink we've brought along for our week's stay, in-cluding cases of wine and ale. Though we have assured each other that we will eat fish all of the time, we have brought along chickens, a whole filet, an eight-pound chuck for chili, pastrami, lots of asparagus—just for start-ers. Too many of my camping trips have been marred by lack of protein, by fish that stay in the water unwilling to be eaten.

At first in the gathering dark Mashagama Lake looked small, but quick reference to a map showed that it is irregularly shaped, with only part of it visible from any single point. That first evening I was surprised to see a family of common loons swim by the dock less than a hundred feet out. Male, female and six little ones in gliding tow. I had not seen loons so close since my childhood. Later we heard their long tremulous wails far out in the lake, surely the strangest of all bird songs. I decided before sleep that if there was a bird living on the moon, that was the sound it would make.

The next morning we were all grumpy. We had announced to each other that we would begin fishing at dawn and we had barely finished breakfast by noon. No one had gotten up to stoke the fire and it had been cold.

But this was only an initial awkwardness, as was the slow fishing. It took two days to change our methods. For instance, there was no point in dry-fly fishing when there wasn't an active insect within a hundred miles because of the cold. The other three switched to trolling with light tackle using small Mepps spinners and a variety of spoons. I switched from my fancy dry-fly patterns to streamers but without much luck. The others caught enough lake trout between two and five pounds to keep us in wonderful breakfasts. Mashagama Lake trout were much better tasting than those we were accustomed to from Lake Michigan. They were fine-fleshed, virtually fatless, and their flavor resembled that of the Rocky Mountain cutthroat. Lake Michigan trout feed heavily on smelt and alewives, and though they're beginning to reach a grand size they lack that pure trout flavor.

After a few days of concern bordering on depression I began to catch both lake and brook trout on a large Spuddler Streamer. No matter how often one insists that fly-fishing is not properly a competitive sport it rankles to be outdone by spin fishermen. Despite the obvious grace of the sport, how can you proselytize for fly-fishing when you are a failure? Thus I was close to ecstasy when I went out alone and returned with a three-pound brook trout, flopped it on the table beneath cynical eyes and walked out the back door to get yet another ale from the cases we stored in the burbling spring behind the cabin. My pleasure was leavened a bit when I found out the others had brought back half a dozen brook trout from their trolling expedition. I wanted to be critical of the béarnaise sauce that accompanied the roasted filet that evening but it was perfect. I sniffed the cork and was studious about the wine but that, too, was flawless. We were humble cabin dwellers in the vast north. Alvin had mentioned that he often heard the howling of wolves in the winter while tending his trapline.

Oddly enough I nearly lost the brook trout—out of general pessimism I had neglected to bring a landing net with me. But when my sloppy, diffident casting finally was rewarded, I tailed the fish after three successive lunges with my frantic hand. For some reason my luck changed after that afternoon, probably because the weather broke and spring finally arrived in the far north.

In addition to fishing, the area offered some fine walking terrain and a profligate amount of birdlife. We counted eight different types of warblers in a single afternoon and stalked a loon that slid from its nest like a plump feathered otter. The local grouse were evidently unused to people. I chased several in circles and was unable to get them to flush. They were the kind of grouse I prayed for in my youth when weeks would pass without a single flying bird in the bag.

Only one other of the lodge's twelve cabins was in use during the week we were there. It was occupied by some hunters from Colorado who had come all that way for the spring bear season. One day they struck a mildly discordant note by bringing in a bear that appeared definitely cubbish to me—it was not all that much larger than my Airedale. I'm no real enemy of mammal hunting, but the black bear, as opposed to the grizzly, has always appealed to me as a huge, reasonably docile form of my daughter's teddy bear and not a fit thing to shoot at.

On our last evening, staring down at the bony remnants of a fine trout dinner, we noisily agreed we would come again. Canada was a ready-made time capsule into our sporting past—gentle, affable and not all that far away. No matter that we were tired and fly-bitten, our dinner tinctured with the odor of kerosene and mosquito dope. I walked down to the dock and watched the northern lights, experiencing if only for a moment that great flow of wilderness, the peopleless territory ranging thousands of miles from the dock to the North Pole, full of rivers, forests and fish.

1974

Night Games

The picture on our calendar this month is Ghidrah, a three-headed, winged dragon busy tromping a small Japanese village into bits and pieces. The calendar is there at the insistence of my preschool daughter. It frightens her over breakfast. She likes to be frightened. I envy the purity of her fright, mindful that adult monsters are weapons, institutions, neuroses, that lack the visceral beauty and immediacy of Ghidrah. The tonic reality of an actual Ghidrah entering Leelanau County trumpeting screams and celluloid groans and spewing fire is a bit too distant to be tasty, like a fantasy of catching and releasing a sperm whale on a streamer fly.

On the outside, though, I know what I will do for a little fright, what I have done to reach the nexus of feeling surrounding this emotion, what dubious adventures I've conceived that have sent me reeling around the world mostly in the name of consciousness to get that familiar jolt of awe and wonderment. But mostly I just use night. It's far easier and obviously cheaper than jumping from a plane. And up near my small farm in northern Michigan there's some interesting night fishing to do from May until October, not to speak of ghostly winter walks under a full moon.

Night fishing. In *The Snow Walker* Farley Mowat says the Eskimos have over a hundred compound words to describe variations in the condition of snow. The conditions of night own as many variations but there's never been a call for the thesaurus. Night is just night, not certainly for most a time to be walking around in the woods looking for a river that you were sure abutted the end of a particular path. Your ears strain for the sound of rushing water. Nothing. You turn around and the path doesn't look like a path anymore. Above the whine of mosquitoes you hear your heart beating. If you pause long enough the owls will begin again. You make another careful tack into the woods, steaming from the exertion in your waders. Your sweat mixed with mosquito repellent stings your eyes. Your fly rod catches in the tag alders and bends dangerously. But then you spot a land-mark clump of yellow birch and stop long enough to hear the river just beyond.

There is a strange fragrance to a river at night that I've never been able to identify, some water-washed mixture of fern, rotting poplar, cedar, and the earthen odor of logjams. If you fish long enough at night alone and are a trifle unstable anyway the moon that guides your casts across the river smells vaguely metallic just as the sun that burns the first dew off after dawn smells copperish. This will sound farfetched only to those who haven't been there. I knew a young Ojibwa Indian once who demonstrated to me how he could find deer by their scent. Then he got drunk one day and went to Vietnam and hasn't been heard from since.

Night fishing is best, though, with friends, barring those times obvious to anyone when you want to be alone and clean out your head. I fish mostly with a friend I used to work for, Pat Paton, who is a carpenter and block layer. He is very good at starting fires and it's a solace to sit looking at a fire when the fishing is slow. If we're camping and the night is particularly dark and impenetrable we drink a lot of whiskey. If either of us is in a violently hasty retreat from what is popularly known as the "real" world we cook a steak in the middle of the night. This is an unabashedly primitive coolant to a troubled mind—to eat steak and drink too much whiskey out in the woods in the middle of the night. But it works in the same way as anyone's psychiatrist, I suspect. Maybe even better, assuming you stay out in the woods.

One night I caught a bat. The bat swallowed my fly and under the shaft of my penlight the bat was clearly suffering from the hook. The booze made it even more garish. I couldn't put a bat in the creel with my trout. I couldn't call Pat who as a hardened country boy is afraid of bats and snakes. Luckily another friend was with us that night. This friend is somewhat of a gun nut and he was packing a .357 sidearm for no real reason other than he enjoyed doing so. Everyone knows that a .357 will blow a hole through an engine block and that police use the weapon in some cities because it shoots for keeps. It is good for close-range whale and grizzly attacks and for cutting down trees if you've forgotten your axe.

"Put this miserable bat away. He's swallowed a number eight muddler minnow."

"Hold the light and stand back," my friend said.

There was a billowing blue flash and the kind of roar associated with a thunderstorm a foot away. We were covered with riverbank mud. The bat had vaporized. At least we couldn't find him.

"That's a handy piece you got there."

"Sure is," he said.

If you get enough trout it's best to cook them immediately. We usually take along a little fat and an iron skillet and salt. The only better way to cook a fresh trout is *au bleu*, poaching the fish with a little vinegar in the water and serving it with cucumber mayonnaise, watercress, French bread, and white wine.

Night fishing for lake trout on the shores of Lake Michigan is even more susceptible to hard-core buffoonery. It's best to have a driftwood fire because the water can be very cold. In this sort of fishing you get a definite release from the refinements of your sport, and that's one of the best things about night fishing. You can forget the long, delicate casts with a $200 bamboo rod, the minuscule fly drifting toward the water on a pound-test leader like the bug it's supposed to imitate. The sophisticated trappings disappear and you're young again with a spinning rod and plug, on some elemental but fun gathering mission. The legal limit is now three but a few years back it was five and the trout often average over ten pounds. We caught ten one night, over a hundred pounds of lake trout, then discovered that my old station wagon had lost its brake fluid a half-dozen miles from the nearest house. It was fine caroming off trees on the logging road on the way out. The main thing was to make the blows glancing rather than direct. You return to the yellow light of the tavern or home like a blinking creature wakened from a sleep in which he has been given back his health.

We forget our ears or only use them casually except while listening to music. My first memory of night fishing was as a boy in 1946 on a small lake we shared with a half-dozen other cabins. One of the cabins owned a small war-surplus diesel generator, while the rest were lit by kerosene. I would row my father around at night while he plug-casted for bass. After the doctor turned off his generator our ears would slowly attune to the plop of the bass plug hitting the water, the creak of oars, perhaps a loon's cry and the frogs and crickets along the shore. Denied one sense, another is enlivened until you can hear the fish strike and know when to strike back. Without sight the world becomes almost unbearably tactile. The clownishness that creeps in is a reaction to a near embarrassment over how deeply the experience is felt, an escape from muddiness into clear water.

I stood one night in the Bechler Meadows in the southwest section of Yellowstone Park. There were no people for miles and in the moonlight I heard thousands of migrating herons calling. I had a bad toothache, the best toothache I ever had. My friends were asleep and despite a mixture of codeine and whiskey sleep escaped me. I tried to fish on a branch of the Bechler River but my attention was overwhelmed by the sheen of thousands of acres of marsh grass in the moonlight, my throbbing jaw, the noise of the herons and imaginary grizzlies. I was a night creature as surely as I was a few years later in a boat with a broken-down motor out in Lake Okeechobee. There is a very particular "I don't care" abandonment mixed with a raising of the hairs on the neck that Matthew Arnold described as the test of good poetry. This contrasts with dipping smelt off creeks emptying into Lake Michigan with mobs of other mostly drunk men filling tubs with the small fish which we sometimes cook without cleaning. The coldness of the water makes you think of night fishing off Little Torch Key in Florida. You stand in the water which seems to approximate body temperature, feeling on your bare legs the subtle pull of tide. The fish cast phosphorescent wakes. You are a pure sense mechanism with the easy arc of your fly line repeated so often that it has entered the realm of the instinctive. You are so far "out of your mind" that you are rather surprised, and not necessarily pleasantly, when you return. But that's what sport is supposed to do, and night fishing is a sport with an umbilical connection called play that colors all your other movements. The boy catching bass at night to the man repeating the gesture three decades later is an inexhaustibly sensible step through time.

1976

Okeechobee

An hour before dawn it was unseasonably warm, with the wind out of the southeast pushing a bank of thunderheads in the moonlight. It was indolent weather, the sort one associates with the morning hatch on a trout stream in July. It was mid-December but there were mosquitoes in the air at the marina. I swatted at them while my friend finished loading the skiff with decoys and shotguns and attempted to coax his yellow Labrador, Rain, into the boat.

Rain is a wonderful dog. When you are around people and call out to her, everyone looks up in the air. If you shout "Rain" angrily, the people are likely to look askance at both you and the sky, and feel sorry for the dog. On this morning Rain was acting put upon and, when called, lay on the dock with her feet in the air. She didn't want to go for a boat ride in the dark for as yet unrevealed reasons. I lifted the dog gently into the boat as the motor started.

Lake Okeechobee proved to be the strangest body of water I've ever been on. Leaving the marina we traveled down a long canal, still in total darkness. The canal abuts a huge dike built during the Depression to control Okeechobee's floodwaters. The lake level is thus higher than the canal, so your boat must go through a small lock that opens at 5:30 A.M. for duck hunters, bass fishermen, commercial catfish long-liners and other odd citizens who might want to be out on the lake as the world wisely sleeps. The lock was strangely thrilling to an outsider. As the skiff rose a foot under the arc lights, the attendant yelled down for our boat's identification number and the operator's name. I learned later that our goings and comings were recorded, in part to keep us from staying lost if we got lost. Okeechobee is an immense lake, and the swamps of palmetto, saw grass and cane are a navigational nightmare that takes years to solve. To the inexperienced Northerner, Okeechobee looks like the "green hell" of stories and motion pictures; a sense of insecurity mixes with breakfast in the pit of the stomach.

It was a half-hour run to our spot, and our speed in the dark was appalling, nearly forty knots, with bugs stinging against the face so powerfully that I tried to keep my head down. The speed seemed senseless, but we wanted to set out our decoys before dawn broke. One consolation was that Okeechobee lacks the logs and deadheads that plague northern lakes. I signaled happily to my friend as our boat kicked up large rafts of ducks. He shook his head and yelled, "Coots!" over the roar of the big outboard motor. A coot is a daffy, unwary member of the rail family. In sporting terms shooting a coot is akin to shooting a parked car.

Phobias are clearly understood only by those who share them. My wife's vertigo I find quietly amusing, though she hid in the backseat in terror on a day when we drove over the Bighorn Mountains. Mice and spiders can crawl over me if they choose. And on airliners I often sleep during takeoffs and landings. However, snakes drive me up—and over—the wall with a visceral kick of adrenaline. Thus, when we reached our spot and I stepped off the bow of the boat into a large truck inner tube with a sling in the middle, my heart pounded at the thought of water moccasins. The inner tube is unquestionably a wonderful device for warm-water duck shooting, but within moments, sitting in one, you feel a terrible sort of vulnerability. Your wadered legs hang down treading water—an obvious alligator meal—and though the top of the tube is six inches above the water, you are sure this is no barrier for the feisty moccasins that slither around in search of Michigan hunters dumb enough to challenge Okeechobee.

I pulled myself through the reeds to where my friend stood on a ladder in the chest-deep water. Rain sat on her platform looking utterly bored, her eyes peeking out from the camouflage covering. She was glad to see me and wriggled precariously on her narrow seat. I explained my fears. My friend shooed me away.

"Nonsense! We can't hunt this close together. We'll make an outline, and the ducks won't come into the decoys."

"I'm not sure I like you anymore," I said, pushing back towards my spot. "I don't see any ducks around anyhow."

"Ssshhhh!" he hissed, pointing out into the lake, now gray with dawn.

I could see a large raft of ducks about 200 yards away that he seemed to know weren't coot. My fears were not really allayed, though. I had heard a probably apocryphal story about a water skier who had fallen into an Alabama lake and been attacked by hordes of moccasins. But then a giddy resignation began to come over me. How noble to die a truly "natural" death. It was the same feeling I have had in grizzly territory in Montana or at sea when the motor fails. Or in Africa once when we lost our transmission near a pride of lions.

This utter irrationality is peculiar to phobias. I have never had an accurate intuition in my life, but a few days before, while snipe hunting near Palm Beach, I had envisioned one of the particular, very individual giant eastern diamondbacks striking the back of my knee as I stepped over a log. As I fell mortally wounded, after blasting the snake, I knew what I would say to my friend: "Looks like you'll have to clean the birds." This mood had ruined my shooting for the first hour; it is difficult to lead a bird properly when you are staring at the ground in front of your feet. But, avoiding the nonexistent logs, I had begun hitting birds, and we soon had our limit. On the way back to the car my friend said, "Think about it this way. You're never going to see the one that gets you." Wonderful.

By midmorning on Okeechobee, nothing duckwise, as they might say on Madison Avenue, had occurred. My interest had long since turned from the inanely bobbing decoys to the overwhelming life in the reeds behind me. In a lifetime as an amateur bird watcher, I had never eyeballed warblers so closely, and there was a profligate amount of other bird life. The birds would bathe, then stand on lily pads to dry, all within a startling few feet of my camouflaged mound in the water. The warblers saved the lives of the three ring bills that did fly over. Before I recognized the sound—the staccato huff and sigh of low-flying ducks—they were well past range.

By noon we decided to make the run back to the lodge for lunch. My skepticism about Okeechobee duck life was noted, so we made a short detour out into the lake. We flushed great rafts of ring bills. Hordes of ducks. Thousands of them, in fact. I had never seen so many ducks, and the whole purpose of the trip returned in main strength. The trouble was it was so hot and clear and calm that there was nothing to urge the birds in toward the sheltered water of the reed beds. The fact that I had leaned forward too far to study warblers and had filled my waders didn't matter. The warmth of the water was tropical. There were plenty of bass there in the weeds; a rod would have served me better than a shotgun. At one point a bass fisherman had passed quietly in a boat with an electric motor and cast a plug near me. I had considered shooting the jitterbug as a practical joke but instead had raised my camouflage net and grinned. The fisherman had widened his eyes, then pretended indifference. I should have shot the plug.

At lunch we ate a big basket of catfish freshly caught from the lake and drank a copious amount of beer to counter the heat. The bass mounted on the lodge wall were immense; any of the hundred would have been a trophy in Michigan. My thoughts went back to all the warblers I had seen just after dawn; they had enough sense to leave Michigan for the winter while I turned my home into a hibernating cave. If you wanted to hunt our late blue bill season in December you would likely tear your waders on the ice. And as a night person who can't really sleep before 3 A.M., I found the classical shooting of Okeechobee most improbable. Dawn in a duck blind back home would require a tailored polar-bear skin for comfort. People do it by the thousands, but I don't have to admire them for it. A leisurely breakfast at midmorning perfectly suits the grouse hunter.

After a nap we returned to the lake with revived interest. We covered a crazy-quilt forty miles on a scouting trip and again saw thousands of ducks, but few within less than mortar range of shore. I explained the highly dangerous cut-shell method to my friend. With a jackknife you make number six bird shot shoot like a slug. You fire over distant rafts of ducks and, you hope, flush them toward your blind. I leave out the technical explanation here to avoid poisoning young minds.

On our scouting expedition I shot a particularly low-flying duck—a cripple, in fact—that we had seen swimming in circles before its wobbly take-off. Crippled game is the most unsavory aspect of hunting. It makes any aware hunter queasy, but most know that it can be largely avoided by not taking the long shot known as "sky busting." It is a disgusting practice. While grouse can fall with a single pellet, a duck is a sturdier creature and any grace the sport possesses demands the etiquette of a surer shot.

We finally found a likely spot near a point. While putting out the decoys, I saw a large animal swimming in the water some fifty yards away. It was plainly an alligator. We motored over to get some idea of its size. Measured against the skiff the alligator was around thirteen feet long, and girthy. It submerged and came up another thirty yards or so away, but not really very far from where my legs were going to be hanging down through the inner tube. My friend was nonchalant and I tried to ape his attitude of indifference. Now I had something new to fret about, compared to which a moccasin would look as puny as a tadpole.

Oddly, I was soon able to push the alligator from my mind. It has taken me too many years to learn that when you are hunting you can think of nothing else. There is nothing more painful than wandering through a clearing thinking about lunch and flushing half-a-dozen grouse. This had happened to me one October, and I had blown the only truly easy shots of the season.

But within an hour my attentiveness began to dissipate. Again the ducks were out there on the horizon, sitting still and comfortable like tiny floating Buddhas. A bald eagle passed high above us. Hundreds of swallows flew in from the lake; they were barely higher than our heads.

"Ducks! A single coming in from your right," my friend hissed.

By the time I shot, the duck had spread its wings to settle with the decoys. Rain burst from her platform and retrieved the bird. I gave a few whoops to honor our change in luck.

"It's a redhead," my friend yelled. "A female."

I slumped in my inner tube low enough to fill my waders. Redheads are protected in Florida. Each redhead shot represents seventy points of an allowable 100 points for a day's shooting. I now had a cripple and a seventy-point duck to my spurious credit.

Another hour passed. Rain sneezed and I whirled and screamed, thinking the sneeze was the attack cry of the bull alligator. There was nothing behind me but darkening swamp.

We loaded our gear and picked up the decoys. The long-suffering Rain huddled in the boat demanding a tummy rub. The motor wouldn't start; the battery was dead. I held the light in the gathering dark while my friend dismantled the cowl and tried to start the motor by hand with a piece of rope. It was some fifteen miles back to the lodge. Short of lassoing and riding the alligator, how could we make it? Then part of the cowl fell into the black water. My friend, who works out daily in a karate dojo, stamped and yelled. I feared he might kick the boat to pieces. Finally the motor started, and we made our way haltingly back in the dark.

At the lodge our hunting friends, a young couple from Palm Beach who shared our two-room cabin, listened sympathetically. They slyly admitted that they had shot their limit. After several drinks we cooked a meal of venison chops and went over to the main lodge to play Bingo. I hadn't played

Bingo in twenty years and looked forward to it, but when we entered the hall, a local wise guy asked, "How many ducks?"

"Forty-seven redheads," I yelled to the assembled Bingo players. It was a showstopper.

Dawn again—a butter-thick, damp dark full of bugs. During our sleepy wait at the lock, the keeper called down to say that the week before a crew of vacationing Miami homicide detectives had shot their limit every day. Then he said that it was too warm and still for duck hunting and that we should have stayed in bed. Or gone bass fishing. As a trout fisherman, I look at bass as a variety of hyperexcitable carp.

After the usual long run, we chose a spot with no real confidence. As the sky lightened, some high-flying ducks passed over but did not pause at our decoys. Then we heard shooting from well behind us, perhaps a mile into the swamp. More shooting came from down the lakeshore a few hundred yards, but also well into the swamp. Our irritation grew as we watched high flights pass over, followed by more shooting. As the shots became intermittent my friend left me to do a little spying down the lake. After fifteen minutes he returned looking happy. He had hidden in the rushes and had seen a small skiff emerge from a channel so narrow that it was invisible from the lake proper. We loaded up and went for a look with a conspiratorial air.

We passed through a long reedy cut into a small pond but could find no blind. Then we found yet another small channel, and now we had to get out in our waders and push the skiff. The going was obnoxious and oozy, the surroundings resembling an aquatic viper farm. Rain watched us from the stern of the boat with modest curiosity. Eureka! We emerged into another pond that held, smack in the middle, a lovely little duck blind built of palmetto fronds.

We sped back for lunch and a quick nap. At the lock we joined another boat, in which my friend recognized the builder of the blind. He asked us about our luck, and we said zilch. He said, "Got a few myself." Which meant his limit, if the number of shots we had heard was any indication. Back at the marina, it was apparent that he was packing for the trip home.

There was no nap this day. We had another catfish lunch. The radio promised a northern front, and back out on the lake we could see the clouds coming on the far horizon with the wind picking up and the lake developing a stiff chop. The temperature began to drop, and the lake was clearing of the ubiquitous bass fishermen.

We eased rather strenuously back into our discovered spot and hastily set out the decoys. The blind was small and the shooting would be close. My friend returned the boat to the channel for hiding and to discourage anyone else's entry. We were barely situated when the ring bills began to come in. I was pleased when the ducks wouldn't decoy but instead would come over for a look at full speed—perhaps twenty yards in the air, right or left. This made for the most demanding sort of pass shooting. Rain was so pleased that she was hard to restrain on her perch during the frequent misses. She only resumed her true character when, upon retrieving a bird, she delivered, then quickly turned to Silly Putty in the water. I had to lift her back on the platform with the water running down under my sleeves. Then I arranged her limbs, turned my face while she shook off the water, and rearranged the camouflage.

We limited out well before dusk, feeling inordinately proud of our shooting and sleuth work. The next day we had equally good luck and became even more careful about taking reasonable shots. Still, we lost several cripples, and it was disturbing to watch the dog swim in narrowing circles around the scent of duck. Ring bills, blue bills and other diving ducks that are wounded will go under, grab a strand of weed and stay there until they drown. This singular fact keeps me from ever becoming an ardent duck hunter, no matter how delightful the sport can be.

I finally got a moderately difficult double. Despite more than a decade of hard-core shooting, I am still a C-plus shot. During our lazy moments we discussed the menu we intended to cook for twenty people when we got back to Palm Beach. My friend mentioned that in the seven years we have fished and hunted together we have talked about our weight and diets on an hourly basis to no visible effect. We ended up serving a feast that reflected our figures: courses of crab fingers, *moules marinière*, snipe broiled and flamed in calvados, then chilled, sautéed duck breasts in a vermouth cream sauce, venison stew and a country ham. It is fun to cook something you can't find in even the best restaurants on earth.

On our way into the lodge that last afternoon we were lucky enough to be granted the kind of grace note given only to those who spend a great deal of time outdoors. First the sun went blood red from the smoke caused by farmers burning off cane. Then that red sun was caught in the froth at the wave tips as the promised rough weather started to chop up the lake. Rafts of coots skittered out of the way, and above, the first southward flock of teal wheeled in a swift-moving cloud.

1976

A Day in May

Without having flown over this particular stretch of water southwest of Key West, I can still envision it topographically: the infinite shadings of blue over the tidal flats—azure, indigo and the predominant light turquoise of the shallows with the paler striations of white sand. Then the brown turtle grass, the dark outlines of coral outcroppings or tidal cuts that game fish use to reach the feeding grounds, and the darker green random splotches of mangrove keys. Farther to the south is a sometimes garish penumbra of purple, that imaginary point where the Gulf and the Atlantic meet in a great ocean river, the Gulf Stream.

This vision is open to errant civilian pilots, gulls, frigate or man-o'-war birds at the edge of their northern cycle, and Navy pilots on practice bombing runs off the Marquesas. I saw it most poignantly last May, reflected off a motel wall in Hollywood after a month of butting my head into the movie industry with the kind of nondirectional energy that characterizes boobs from the Midwest.

One evening I drove back to the room in a borrowed car, going eighty miles per hour, in wet underpants from the sort of poolside party I will refuse to remember on my deathbed. In no time at all I was on the red-eye flight from L.A. to Miami, where a friend picked me up at dawn. Before noon we reached Key West and launched the boat. Just a clean, bare skiff with no equipment save a saltwater fly rod and a box of tarpon flies. Already the baggage of the clumsy Hollywood hustle was fading; we pulled out of Garrison Bight, ran at thirty knots past Christmas Island, then slowed for the heavy riptide of the ship channel. It was hot, but I was somehow shivering. Off Mule Key, not an hour into it, the first tarpon was hooked, a single stray lying along a dark bank of turtle grass in cloudy light. It was a sloppy cast, but the hookup was good, with perhaps eighty pounds of fish thrashing upward in three shattering jumps before breaking off. The break off was fine because it was the beauty of the jumps I was looking for, and we let all the tarpon free anyway.

Afterward I noticed my forearm was twitching from the electric strength of the fish. With the sun and heat and wave-lap against the boat, thinking became oddly cellular, not cranial. I'd learned again how badly the body wants to feel good.

On the way back to Key West we paused near the wreckage of a shrimp trawler. Here, a few years back, we saw an explosion up on the flat and checked it out. It was a hammerhead shark, nearly as long as the seventeen-foot skiff, chasing tarpon in the shallow water. He paused to investigate us and we teased him with the push pole. The shark circled the skiff with one goggle eye raised and tried to figure out if we were a meal. There was a stiff wind, and the sun focused him in brilliant flashes under the swiftly fleeting clouds. The water only intermittently covered him, and his long, thick, gray body glistened in a bulbous wake. Aside from a mostly imaginary threat, I could no more kill one of these creatures than I would a house pet. He belongs where he is and we are only visitors.

The next day was a long relaxing blank after the harsh, grisly nightlife that Key West specializes in—or that I seem to specialize in when I go to Key West. At dawn you always study the palm trees out the window. If they're merely rustling, the weather will be fine for fishing. If the palms are wild and bending in the wind, you check to see if anyone's in bed with you and, if not, you usually decide to make the run in bad weather. Once I fished thirty days in a row, celebrated God knows what most of every night, and took a whole month in Michigan to recover from the "vacation."

But a blank day on the flats can be a wonderful thing. The long hot hours of nothing are alleviated symmetrically by long hours of talking about food and other pleasures. It is a natural sauna that soothes the muscles and makes you grasp neurotically for the memory of whatever it was that drove you batty. Sometimes we dive into a reef to gig lobsters for dinner. Or stalk Cottrell Key, a strange combine rookery of frigate birds and brown pelicans, hundreds of each filling the sky while the females stick glaring and restive to their nests. The air and still water of the lee are permeated by a hot low-tide smell of bird dung and the unearthly noise of the birds getting used to your presence. Later, you tie long gaudy flies to wire leaders and play with the barracuda off Cottrell, the tarpon having evidently fled to Tibet for the afternoon.

Now, there's a little panic associated with the slow fishing. After a month of it, I'm always stuck with an Andersonville or Russian Front sort of homesickness that swells in the throat and can only be handled by getting there. On a final trip, in contempt of our luck, we made the long, thirty-mile run to the Marquesas, and found a kind of tarpon epiphany. We saw nearly two hundred fish drifting in from the west, from the direction of the Dry Tortugas—a dozen schools, darkish torpedo shapes against white sand. On the flight home I still heard the gill plates rattling from the tarpon that jumped lithely over the bow of the boat, his six-foot silvery length seeming to hang freeze-framed a few feet away.

And at home, finally, in northern Michigan, the world was full of the cool green pastels of spring. On the first morning back, I went mushroom hunting with my four-year-old daughter and noted that the shades of green equaled the multifoliate blues of the tidal flats I'd just left. I looked for morel mushrooms among the first fiddleheads and wild leeks. Anna is as good at mushroom hunting as I am, perhaps because she's three feet closer to the earth and not daydreaming.

At the local bar, Dick's Tavern, I watch Anna at the weekly ritual of her pinball game. She disregards the flippers to lean on her elbows and watch the flashing lights. I would like to get that much out of a pinball game. I think of a recipe I have modestly devised that uses sweetbreads, leeks and morels, with a dash of white wine to deglaze the pan. I discuss the local fishing with Richard, the bartender. A few hours later we are standing close to shore in our waders in the cold serene waters of Lake Michigan, looking out at the Manitou Islands, their piney humps bathed in evening mist. Unlike tarpon, you don't let the lake trout go. You eat them. Sometimes your wife fillets and broils the trout and sometimes a neighbor farmer smokes them for you with apple wood. It is all part of an embarrassingly ardent cycle of fishing and hunting that keeps you alive the rest of the year during the enervating pursuits that are life in this century.

1976

A Sporting Life

It begins very young up in the country, whether you are raised on a farm or in one of the small villages which, though they often double as county seats, rarely number more than a thousand souls. There is a lumber mill down by the river that manufactures crossties for the railroad, and the creosote the ties are treated with pervades the air. It is the smell of the town, depending on the wind: fresh-cut pine and creosote. In the center of the town there's a rather ugly yellow brick courthouse, plain Depression architecture. The village is in northern Michigan and does not share the quaintness of villages in New England or the deep South, being essentially history-less. There are three baronial, rococo houses left over from the hasty passing of the lumber era, but most dwellings are characterized by their drabness, simply a place for the shopkeepers to hide at night.

In the spring and summer the boys in the town carry either baseball mitts or fish poles on their bicycles. Two different types are being formed and though they might merge and vary at times, most often they have set themselves up for life. During the endless five months of winter one boy will spend his evenings poring over the fishing-tackle sections of the Sears Roebuck and Montgomery Ward catalogs while the other boy will be looking at the mitts, bats and balls. One tinkers with a reel while the other sits in a chair plopping a baseball over and over into his glove just recently oiled with neat's-foot. One reads about the Detroit Tigers while the other reads *Outdoor Life* and fantasizes about the time when he will be allowed his first shotgun. He already has an old .22 Remington single-shot, but he knows it is an interim weapon before the shotgun and later yet, a .30-.30 deer rifle.

The village is surrounded by woods and lakes, rivers and swamps and some not very successful farms. The boy wanders around among them with a World War II surplus canteen and a machete he keeps hidden in the garage from his mother's prying eyes. His family owns a one-room cabin a dozen

miles from town, where they spend the summer. He shoots at deer with a
weak bow and arrow. On many dawns he accompanies his father trout fishing on a nearby river; he is forced to fish the same hole all day to avoid getting lost. The same evening he will row his father around the lake until midnight, bass fishing. The boy and a friend sit in a swamp despite the slime
and snakes and mosquitoes. They pot two sitting grouse with a .22 and
roast them until they are black. The boys think they are Indians and sneak
up on a cabin where some secretaries are vacationing. A few feet behind the
window in the lamplight a secretary is naked. A true wonder to discuss
while walking around in the woods and gullies or while diving for mud turtles or while watching a blue heron in her nest in a white pine.

Two decades later. Wars. Marches. Riots. Flirtations with politics, teaching, marriage, a pleasant love affair with alcohol. Our boy, now presumably
a man, is standing in a skiff near the Marquesas thirty miles out in the Gulf
from Key West. He's still fishing with a fly rod, only for tarpon now instead
of bass, bluegills or trout. He wants to catch a tarpon over 100 pounds on
a fly rod. Then let it go and watch it swim away. Today, being an open-
minded soul, he's totally blown away on a triple hit of psilocybin. A few
numbers rolled out of Colombian buds add to the sweet stew. It's blissful
except for an occasional football-field-sized red hole in the sky and for the
fact that there are no tarpon in the neighborhood. A friend is rubbing himself with an overripe mango. Then he rubs a girl who is fixing a lunch of
white wine, yogurt and strawberries. Where are the tarpon today? Maybe
in China. They want to hear the gill plates rattle when the tarpon jumps.
The overripe mango feels suspiciously familiar. Peach jokes should be
changed to mango jokes.

An osprey struggles overhead with a too-large fish. Ospreys can drown
that way, not being able to free their talons in the water. The flight slows
painfully. Between the great bird's shrieks we can hear the creak and flap of
wings and the tidal rush through the mangroves. Lunar. The bird reaches
the nest and within minutes has torn the houndfish to pieces. A meal. We
watch each other across a deep-blue channel.

Barracuda begin passing the skiff with regularity on the incoming tide,
but no tarpon. We rig a fly rod with a wire leader for the barracuda's sharp
teeth. And a long wonderfully red fly that matches the red holes that pe-

riodically reappear in the sky. The fish love the fly and the strike is violent, so similar to touching an electric fence it brings a shudder. The barracuda dashes off across the shallow water of the flat, is fought to the boat and released.

The midafternoon sun is brilliantly hot, so we move the boat some fifteen miles to a key that doubles as a rookery for cormorants, pelicans and man-o'-war or frigate birds. We watch the birds for hours, and the sand sharks, rays, bait fish and barracuda that slide past the boat.

Why get freaked or trip while you're fishing? Why not? You only do so rarely. You're fishing in the first place to avoid boredom, the habitual, and you intend to vary it enough to escape the lassitude attached to most of our activities. If you carry to sport a businesslike consciousness, it's not sport at all. Only an extension of your livelihood, which you are presumably trying to escape.

But how did we get from there to here across two decades? In sport there is a distinct accounting for taste. That corn pone about going through life with a diminishing portfolio of enthusiasms is awesomely true. We largely do what we do, and are what we are, by excluding those things we find distasteful. You reduce your life to those few things that you know are never going to quit. And when you reach thirty-five, your interest in these few things can verge on the hysteric: a freshly arrived single white hair in a sideburn can get a book written or instigate a trip to Africa. What energy you have left becomes obsessive and single-minded. When I am not writing poetry or novels I want to fish or, to a slightly lesser degree, hunt grouse and woodcock.

But this is to be an ideologue about something that is totally a sensuous, often sensual, experience. We scarcely want a frozen tract by Jerry Garcia on just why he likes "brown-eyed women and red grenadine." Visceral is visceral. Always slightly comic, man at play in America has John Calvin tapping him on the shoulder and telling him to please be serious. For beginners, you have to learn to tell John to fuck off. And if you're a writer, many of your friends in the arts look at you with an "Oh, the Hemingway bit" tolerance, as if that stunningly arrogant doctor's son had forever preempted hunting and fishing. They might better ask why someone who wanted to paint like Cézanne would find so much that is memorable and durable in fishing and hunting. My own life is so largely an act of language, I've found that I survive only by seeking an opposite field when not actually writing. When it feels as if you're typing with sixteen-ounce gloves, you have to get out of the house, sometimes for months at a time.

Twenty miles off the coast of Ecuador, near the confluence of el Niño and the Humboldt current, it's not all that far after dawn and already the equatorial sun is shimmering down waves of heat. I count it lucky that when you skip bait for marlin the boat is moving at eight to ten knots, thus creating a breeze. The port diesel is fluttering, then is silent. We rock gently in the prop wash, then are caught in a graceful Pacific swell. It wasn't the port engine. Or the starboard engine. It was the only engine. The pulse quickens. My friend smiles and continues photographing a great circle of man-o'-war birds hovering far above us, far more than we have ever seen in the Florida Keys. It must be hundreds of miles to the closest pesticide. The birds follow schools of bait as do the striped marlin, and are considered a good sign. The captain looks at me and shrugs, the universal language of incompetence. He speaks no English and I no Spanish.

My friend, who is a French count, pretends he speaks Spanish, but in a week down here has yet to make any significant contact except with some Braniff stewardesses who speak fluent English. My room overlooks the pool and I saw him flat on his back with camera poised: he had arranged a circle of stewardesses around him with the prettiest in her bikini directly over his head. The magic of photography. Either a camera or a guitar works, but you never point a typewriter at a girl. I ran down to the pool hoping to catch the camera's aura of snazz.

I stretch out along the gunwale trying to convince myself that I am relaxed, but paranoia comes in surges. They'll never get the engine started and we'll drift to Australia, missing the Galápagos in the night by a helpless few miles. I can't even see land. We don't have any water, which anyway is undrinkable hereabouts. A lot of foul-tasting Chilean soda pop. In a shrugging fit, one of the two mates hands me a plate of fresh pineapple. It is ripe, cool and delicious. Feed the fearful bear. I toss a chunk at three passing sea snakes, who look terribly yellow in the blue water. They are related to the cobra and extremely venomous though not very aggressive. They scatter, then one swirls around to check out the pineapple. I've been assured that they never bother anyone but the wretchedly poor Peruvian fishermen who deep-jig from cork rafts. Good ole swimming hole. Sharks. Snakes. Even whales. Often in nature you get the deep feeling you don't belong. This is especially true of the Pacific and the Serengeti.

Hours pass, and they are still tinkering with the engine. I glance into its guts and regret not knowing anything about them. The day before the engine had quit while I was fighting a striped marlin. It is a difficult and exhausting job from a dead boat, especially after the spectacular jumps are over and the fish bulldogs. You can't follow the marlin on its long runs. You have to pump him back. And I had hooked the fish out of vanity on twenty-pound test. It took over two hours in the ninety-degree sun and I felt murderous. Now I was pretending the boat had a marine radio, which I knew it didn't.

But it had been a fine week's fishing so far, though we had failed to catch a striped marlin on fly rod, something that had only been done twice before. My friend had teased a marlin to within forty feet of the boat before the marlin rose up and slashed with his bill, then took the fly firmly in the corner of his mouth. I was thinking numbly about how beautifully blue his body was and how from the side his eye appeared to be staring at us. Perhaps it was. But it only lasted a few seconds while he twisted his head and sped off in a flume of water. The leader popped. It was like fly-fishing for Dick Butkus or a Harley Davidson, I thought while trying to sleep on a sunburn that night. We had been getting a lot of sleep, having been warned by the hotel manager of the endemic shanker problem in the local villages.

I have a great deal of time to think between fish, and I wonder why I am never bored. My friend the novelist Tom McGuane has fished for months in a row in the Keys, particularly when he was learning saltwater fly casting. When I was learning from him there were moments of doubt until I had my first big tarpon in the air. Before that I had been quite pleased with a two-pound rainbow. And still am, though the true maniac deserves a tarpon. Such sport is a succession of brutally electric moments spaced widely apart. Someone with McGuane's quantum energy level quite naturally applies the same effort to fishing.

There is doubtless the edge of a lunatic here. In Ecuador, the crew was enormously alarmed when my friend went overboard to get underwater photos of a fighting marlin. Billfish have been known to charge a boat out of generalized ire. I was supposed to control the fish. I was sure my stomach wall would burst and spill its contents—an even quart of Añejo. But dangers in nature are vastly overrated, though while backpacking I tend to think of grizzlies as 700-pound Dobermans that don't respond to voice commands. In Africa, you are more likely to get bit by a snake than attacked by a mammal. Comforting thought.

There are unquestioned flops. We try to see the brighter side of our flops, telling ourselves we haven't wasted our time. And we are dolts if we aren't comfortable in a world outside our immediate preoccupations. A sports bore is far more deadly than a krait or a Gaboon viper. A true NFL freak can make a more casual fan pine for opera. A real quadra or stereo buff makes you want that Victrola the big white dog was listening to.

One of the reasons I wanted to go to Russia was to scout the possibility of an extended trip for fishing and hunting. How splendid to shoot grouse where Ivan Turgenev had hunted, and I had heard that there was good steelhead and salmon fishing on the Pacific coast of Siberia. As a poet, I have a tendency to imagine conditions and pleasures without precedent on earth. When fishing is bad, you can't tell but that just around the next green island there might be a nude fashion model on a mohair chair on the water.

Once reaching Russia, my ideas seemed clearly impossible except for an important official visitor or someone on an established tour, a loathsome prospect. Red tape is a euphemism. And my first morning in Moscow had been encouraging, watching old men fish the broad Moscow River, which runs through the middle of the capital. They were sitting on an embankment below the faded red walls of the Kremlin, the mid-October sun catching the gold of the minarets as a backdrop. But I never saw anyone catch a fish, just as I had gazed at other fishless afternoons on the Seine in Paris. It is enough to have a river in a city.

After several days of badgering I managed to get to a horse race. But the weather had turned bad and the horses passed all but invisibly in what must be called a howling blizzard. The tote board said that Iron Beauty beats out Good Hoe, our plump female guide translated. Her pleasure was to wander aimlessly in great halls filled with the machinery of progress. It's hard to explain to someone so adamantly political that you see enough progress at home, and that to you, progress meant motors that quit rather captiously far out in the ocean. Or the shotgun that misfired when you had a good chance at a double in grouse. No matter that it was the first time in your life that a shotgun misfired. It brutishly picked the wrong time.

The climate of inquiry was pleasanter in Leningrad, where a black market is active and there are more creature pleasures. I found a sporting goods store on the Nevsky Prospect where the clerks were affable. An electrical engineer I met there joined me for a number of drinks and explained that fishing in Siberia would be difficult. Permissions were necessary. Bird hunting would be difficult but not impossible. Since I find even mild queues a torment, I checked Russia off my list. It was sad, as I had visions of sitting at the edge of a swale taking a break from grouse with a chilled bottle of Stolichnaya and some blinis on which I would spread large amounts of beluga caviar, rolling them up like miraculous tacos.

I had another interesting failure down in Killarney, with wet May weather, on the banks of not even a secondary Atlantic salmon river, with a gillie whose language, ostensibly English, I couldn't understand. In the ceaseless rain I became convinced that he had been invented by someone who taught Irish literature. I admit I was dizzy from the dehydration brought on by a raging case of *turista*, an infirmity I pick up on the road, even in Tucson, Arizona. On one of my frequent trips to the bushes a lovely lady rode by on a horse, but in my position I didn't feel up to greeting her. So the gillie and I sat under a tree, mumbling and watching the rain. Then a hotel waiter appeared in a parka and asked what I wanted for lunch. The shock was so sweet that I ordered a six-pack of Guiness Stout and a bottle of Jameson. And watercress sandwiches in honor of the water. Booze is a sure tonic for any colitic problem. You can always get well when you get home and don't have anything else to do. Anyway, the language barrier dropped and the gillie invited me to go fox hunting with clubs. But I got up too late the next morning and missed the show. I could imagine them out there on a rainy hillside, a hundred fictional characters trying to club a real fox to death in the mud.

Outdoor sport has proven fatally susceptible to vulgarization based mostly on our acquisitiveness. Fishing becomes the mechanics of acquiring fish, bird hunting a process of "bagging a limit." Most sportsmen have become mad Germans with closets full of arcane death equipment. To some, an ultimate sport would be chasing coyotes with a 650cc snowmobile armed with an M-16. And some have found that baseball bats work as well, as a coyote can't run more than twenty miles and a snowmobile has a superior range.

You suspect that the further hunting and fishing get away from our ancient heritage of hunting and gathering, the better. And I don't mean the Native Americans, the Indians, who had the mother wit to understand that "the predator husbands his prey." Hunger causes the purest form of acquisitiveness, but our tradition always overstepped hunger into the fields of hoarding and unmitigated slaughter. The saddest book printed in our time is Peter Matthiessen's *Wildlife in America*, where the diminishing and disappearance of many species are minutely traced to our greed and game hoggery. Sporting magazines still publish those obscene photos of piles of trout, though there does seem to be a change in the air. The dolt who stands smiling before the 100 crows he shot should be forced at gunpoint to eat them, feathers, beaks, feet and offal. The excuse is that crows eat duck eggs, as if crows were supposed to abandon a million-year food source because some clown has taken Saturday morning off for a duck hunt.

Any sense of refinement steps slowly into the mind of the sportsman, and every advance made to improve the ethics of sport by organizations such as Trout Unlimited or the Grouse Society is countered by thousands of examples of boobery, murder and exploitation. Each state has a professional natural resource staff, but so often their efforts are countered by what are called the beer-bottle biologists in the legislatures, who think of hunting and fishing as some sort of patriotic birthright, something they know intimately by osmosis. You see the same thing out west with townspeople who've never been on a horse assuming they are all-knowing because they are Westerners.

I know a plain of about 500 acres near the Manistee River. We often begin a day's hunt there, and my image of grouse and woodcock shooting is inextricably tied up with this great, flat pasture, cut near the river by a half-dozen gullies choked with thorn apple and cedar trees. On our long walk to the grouse cover near the river, we hunt a small marsh that invariably yields a few woodcock and snipe. You are lucky if you connect with one shot out of five. It is always early in the morning: cold, often wet, with the shotgun barrels icy to the fingers. The same location means nothing to me in the summer before the frost has muted the boring greenness.

Part of the pleasure of bird hunting is that it comes after the torpor of summer: beaches, the continuous sound of motorboats, the bleached air of August, a tendency to go to too many parties and to experiment with drinks an honest bourbon addict finds abominable in the winter. (A drink of my own devising I call the Hunter Thompson Special: take juice left over from stewed figs, add ground lime rind, a jigger of bitters and eight ounces of cheap tequila, one gram of hash, powder from three Dexamyl spansules and a cherry bomb for decoration to an iced mug; stir vigorously with either end of a cue stick. This is the only aphrodisiac I've ever discovered. It will also remove warts and give you an interior suntan.)

And there is the color, the hardwoods sinking their juices into the ground before the horror of a Michigan winter. This stunning transformation of leaves creates colors that would look vulgar on a woman. It looks good on trees, and with the first cool days of autumn you find yourself hunting grouse and woodcock. You have given up duck hunting as too sedentary. Besides, you have to get up at dawn, while mid-morning is plenty early for grouse. So you walk around in the woods for a month and a half. Unfortunately, the steelhead fishing is good during the same period, but you can't afford to divide your attention. An obvious boon in a writer's life is that he can concentrate his work into the months when no suitable sport is available. Surely it is a dream world; the nearly thundering flush and the always difficult shot. Grouse are very fast and the cover is heavy. If your shooting isn't trained as a gut reaction you simply miss, and when you miss a grouse you lose a very good meal. I suppose I especially value this form of shooting because I lost an eye in an accident and it has taken me years to reach even average competence.

The symptoms of all the vaunted instabilities of artists tend to occur in interim periods. It is the mental exhaustion of having just finished a work, and the even more exhausting time of waiting for another set of ideas to take shape. Poetry and the literary novel are a desperate profession nowadays—they probably always were—and any satisfying release seems to be desperately energetic. You tend to look for something as intricately demanding as your calling so you can forget yourself and let it rest.

Fly-fishing for trout offers an ideal match of the exacting and the aes-thetically pleasant: to sit by a stream during the evening hatch and watch what trout are feeding on, then to draw from the hundreds of variations in your fly boxes a close approximation and catch a few trout. It's easily the most hypnotic of the outdoor sports. Once we began fishing in the Middle Branch of the Ontanagon at dawn. I was numbly depressed from having finished my second book of poems and had been sleepwalking and drinking for weeks. My friend, who is equally maniacal and has no pain threshold that is noticeable, insisted we eat a pound of bacon, refried beans and a dozen eggs for strength. We fished nonstop then from dawn to dark at ten in the evening. It was a fine day, cool with intermittent light rains and enough breeze to keep the mosquitoes away. I remember catching and re-leasing a half-dozen good brook trout from a pool where a small creek en-tered the river. We saw deer and many conical piles of bear shit that gave us pause, but then our local bears are harmless. We watched the rare and over-whelming sight of two adult bald eagles flying down the river course just above our heads, shrieking that we didn't belong there.

To perhaps lessen the purity of the day, I admit at nightfall we drove 100 miles to a whorehouse across the Wisconsin border. The next night a local bumpkin of the *Deliverance* sort was waving an axe around at the edge of our fire, warning us not to steal any of his logs. We felt at ease—rather than a bow and arrows, we had a rifle along.

This is a peculiarity of trout fishing—you can lose yourself completely for days at a time. If you feel your interest in women and the not-so-ordinary simplicities of sex waning, try getting on a horse and spending a week or two fishing up in the Absaroka Mountains of Montana. There are no women up there. Not even a little one. When you get back down to Liv-ingston, a barroom tart invariably reminds you of the Queen of Sheba or Lauren Hutton. Unless you're careful, you can manage to get into a lot of pointless trouble. Of course, the same conditions can be imitated by going off to war, but it's not as much fun.

There is something about eating game that resists the homogeneity of taste found in even the best of our restaurants. A few years back when we were quite poor, lower-class by all the charts, we had a game dinner at our house. There were about twelve people contributing food, and with a check for a long poem I bought two cases of a white bordeaux. We ate, fixed in a number of ways, venison, duck, trout, woodcock, snipe, grouse, rabbit, and drank both cases of wine. I doubt you could buy the meal on earth.

The French, however, are marvelous at game cookery. Two years ago I spent a week up in Normandy covering a stag hunt at the invitation of a friend, Guy de la Valdène. His family has a château near St. George and a breeding farm for racehorses. You do not go to Russia to eat, and I had just returned from a hungry trip to Moscow and Leningrad. Other than the notion that stag hunting seemed to me the pinnacle of stylishness in mammal hunting, the memorable part of the week was the eating, a vulgar word for what took place nightly in a local *auberge*. Despite my humble background I found I enjoyed saddle of wild boar, or a 1928 Anjou with fresh pâté de foie gras in slabs, trout laced with truffles, *côtelettes* of loin from a small forest deer called a *chevreuil*, pheasant baked under clay with wild mushrooms. It all reminded me of the bust of Balzac by Rodin at the Metropolitan in New York, the evidence in his immense, bulbous face of his legendary interest in food and wine. But moderation only makes sense to those whom such food is continually available. The stag hunt itself began after dawn, and the animal was brought to bay by the hounds at twilight, when the master of the hunt dispatched the stag with a silver dagger after the manner of some six centuries. All day we had been sipping Château Margaux straight from the bottle and not feeling even vaguely boorish.

I suspect that many of the misunderstandings of sport are caused by those who write for the outdoor magazines, not the best of the writers, but by the generally venal texture of the majority of the work. Most of it is simply dead, full of fibs and outright lies repeated in hundreds of variations of the same story. There is the usual tale of the grizzly hunt where we are led to assume that the bear had spent its entire life hell-bent on murdering the author, rather than merely walking around in the woods looking for lunch. And no matter that the animal is shot at 200 yards, before it can see the hunter. I can remember an account when the grizzly was asleep, something to the effect that "I poured hot lead into Mister Dozin' Bruin. It was the surprise of his life!" Certain macho aspects can be funny—a story titled "Bulls of the Midnight Pond" conceals an inflated account of an ordinary frog hunt.

149

The best outdoor writing is on the periphery of sport, in such writers as Edward Abbey, Peter Matthiessen, Ed Hoagland, John McPhee and a very few others. These writers are first of all artists and they deliberately avoid even a tinge of fakery. You learn slowly that to the extent that there is any pretension of expertise you don't own, or willful snobbishness, you lose it all and are simply another of millions of incompetents whose outdoor activities are very probably an extension of their sexual neuroses. It seems odd, but I know only one good writer who is truly a first-rate angler and wing shot, Tom McGuane. I hear Vance Bourjaily is good but have never met him.

After I'd read about African hunting for twenty years, it took a trip to Kenya and Tanzania to cure me permanently of any notion that I might hunt there except for duck and grouse. And it's not that a great deal of the hunting there by outsiders lacks validity, excepting the endangered and diminishing species.

It's simply that my time there more closely resembled a religious rather than a travel experience. In the Serengeti you get an eerie conviction of what the American West was like before we got off the boat. Perhaps I could have hunted there in the twenties or thirties, before it became apparent that the natural world was shrinking in direct proportion to our insults against it; almost as if this world were a great beast herself and she had demonstrably passed the midpoint of her life and needed the most extreme and intense care not to further accelerate her doom.

The problems of East Africa have been talked about and publicized to the saturation point, which has not in the least slowed the unnatural predation of new farms, overgrazing, poaching for skins, the tide of population, ivory smuggling for jewelers and to the Orientals who have the silly notion that ground ivory gives them hard-ons. Think of the boggling sexual vanity involved in killing a seven-ton beast for hard-ons. And it is not at all sure how long we can expect native populations who smarted under colonization to maintain game parks for wealthy Westerners, no matter how beneficial.

I came to the point rather early when I realized I was not much interested in shooting mammals. This does not mean I disapprove of others doing so. Maybe it's my squeamishness over gutting and cleaning a large animal, though I suspect my qualms would disappear if I needed the animal to feed my family. And deer hunting as opposed to bird hunting is difficult to do cleanly. We mammals are more sturdy than we assume. While a single pellet can bring a grouse tumbling down, both man and deer can crawl on for hours after Claymore mines, .357s, a half-dozen badly placed rifle shots. When they were butchering, it took seven unlucky shots for my neighbors to bring down their Holstein cow.

Last Thanksgiving Day during deer season we heard loud bleating, then barking, from up behind our barn. Our horses were frantic and stared in the direction of the woodlot like pointing dogs. The bleating was from a deer dragging itself through the snow by its forelegs. The deer had been wounded in the spine and a hind leg had been shot nearly off, barely hanging by a tendon. A large collie had been harrying the deer and had torn much of the deer's ass off. It was red as a baboon's. The game warden came and put it away. The deer was a young buck and lacked legal horns. Someone had shot the deer, then discovered it lacked legal horns. Before the game warden dispatched it, the deer in deep shock stared at us, seemingly well past caring, some kind of runaway slave that had fallen victim to our fatal hobbies.

It is finally a mystery what keeps you so profoundly interested over so many years. The sum is far more than simply adding those separate parts. In the restorative quality there is the idea that as humans we get our power from the beauty we love most. And the sheer, unremittent physicality makes you lose for a while those fuzzy interior quarrels your head is addicted to, sitting as it does on the top of a Western man. It is also the degree of difficulty: to outwit a good brown trout with a lure less than the size and weight of a housefly or mosquito, to boat and release a 100-pound tarpon on a twelve-pound test leader, to hit a grouse on that long shot between the poplar trees. It could be very sporting to hunt a lion if you had the balls to do it as the Masai do—with a spear.

The beauty and sensuosity of the natural world is so direct and open you often forget it: the tactility of standing in the river in your waders with the rush of water around your legs, whether deep in a cedar swamp in Michigan, or in Montana where you have the mountains to look at when the fishing is slow. With all of the senses at full play and the delicious absence of thought, each occasion recalls others in the past. It is a continuous present. You began at seven rowing your father around the lake at night, hearing in the dark the whirr of his reel as he cast for bass, the creak and dip of the oars and the whine of clouds of mosquitoes around your head. You might have been lucky enough to hear a loon, surely the most unique birdcall on earth, and see heat lightning silhouette the tips of the white pines and birch.

You think of this thirty years later in Anconcito, a small, shabby village on the coast of Ecuador. You're taking the day off from fishing, with heat weakness, vertigo, sore hands and the fear of death that being sick in a foreign country brings. You are sitting on a cliff next to a pile of refuse and a small goat. The goat is pure black and when it stumbles close you see that it can't be more than a few days old. The goat nuzzles you. Not thirty feet away a very large vulture sits and stares at you both. You stare back, idly listening to the Latin music from the tin-shed café in the background. A piglet scurries by. You, the goat and the vulture watch the piglet, and the goat takes chase. Far below you, so far that they are toys, there are fishing boats in the harbor powered anciently by sail. It is the hottest day you can remember. Beyond the harbor is all the vast, cool, deep-blue plenitude of the Pacific.

1976

The Last Good Country

It all began quite accidentally. I wanted to go farther north than my northern Michigan home for a few days of rest from nothing, a condition of torpor that is the most exhausting of all human activities. So I loaded my old yellow Chevy pickup with gear and headed out for the Straits of Mackinac, deciding at the last moment to avoid the freeway by passing through Charlevoix and Petoskey. Just beyond Charlevoix I swerved by impulse onto a side road to drive over to Horton's Bay and Walloon Lake.

These place names are particularly resonant to anyone who cares about Ernest Hemingway because they are the locus for most of the Nick Adams stories, the author having spent the summers of his youth vacationing in the area. Despite the closeness I have only been in the locale once before in my adult life.

The area is still beautiful, green and hilly with a vernal juiciness that reminds one of the Lake Country in England. But it's hard to identify the landscape with the woods, swamps and rivers where Nick Adams played Injun, and endured the *rites de passage* that Hemingway wrote so cleanly about. Not, anyway, when you see a million-dollar condominium peeking through the woods like some sort of fey Rotarian Xanadu. This is not to quibble about progress, merely to say that the place no longer resonates of the literature that put it on the map, in the same way that if you are looking for the golden Colorado of the fifties you'll only find it in Montana. How quickly mass tourism subsumes the indigenous culture, converting it to its own pursuits. For three months of the year northern Michigan is a vast summer suburb of Detroit, Chicago, Indianapolis, in the same manner that Aspen, a former mining town, is a winter haven where businessmen, movie people, the disaffected children of orthodontists may rub souls to the porcine, blissed-out strains of John Denver.

Farther north I crossed the Mackinac Bridge and my thoroughly predictable snit dissipated. Several times a year I use the Upper Peninsula as a tonic, its vast, not particularly distinguished forests and rivers as a retreat from the summer eyesore of a Rolls Royce pulling into a local filling station. You can even find a wee trace of Hemingway along the Fox River where he fished brook trout after World War I. But then the brook trout, which are the pimps of the trout world, are mostly gone now. Instead of turning left into the Upper Peninsula I continued on straight north into Canada, up the Ontario coast of Lake Superior until I stopped at an unlikely little town called Wawa.

Late that first night after eating fried steak and onions I lay on my motel bed looking at two girlie magazines which had the collective sexual impact of a dozen sleeping pills. I spread out a large map of Ontario wondering at the rivers I had crossed that day and how they bisected groups of hills that formed a humble but somehow impressive coastal range. The road had offered a seventy-mile section without a sign or gas station. Lake Superior had a Bahamas-like clarity when I stopped along the shore to look at some Ojibwa petroglyphs, a sea monster accompanied by three wriggling serpents. It seemed strange that we had, with the Indians, desolated a kingdom, murdered a civilization, that had not thought it important to build monuments to itself. And I knew that in the backcountry the lakes and small streams that fed the rivers held good brook trout for those who cared to walk. Then I remembered a long but only partially finished story of Hemingway's called "The Last Good Country," in essence a boyish fairy tale of escape with his little sister into the woods from a charge of poaching a deer. In texture it is not far from Robin Hood with a nearly mythic sense of the young outlaw.

I poured a glass of bourbon and wondered why I had always in my own youth preferred the dank lushness of Faulkner to Hemingway's cool but utterly romantic precision. But I had grown up in northern Michigan and at a certain age you tend to find your own concerns closely rendered in prose embarrassing and suffocating. And there was that pickup truck full of fishing equipment out in front of the motel. All my sporting obsessions verge on anachronisms, the ready assumption that everything used to be better in the outdoors to the narrowing point of the present, where you may as well fall in love with Germaine Greer and forget about the whole thing. Ah, how mournful. It was this fatal but necessary penchant for self-dramatization that was so cruel to Hemingway. And it was clearly born in the Indian-outlaw-cowboy fancies and confusions of his youthful summers in the woods, the enchantment with a backcountry peopleless enough, pristine enough, impersonal, cold but beautiful enough, to bear for a lifetime a warrior's code so intractable as to oftentimes be comic in its pretensions.

But also somehow courageous even if he did have to sometimes chop off the horse's legs to make him fit in the stall. An image of a man standing out in a field yelling MORE! The brook trout, deer and grouse of his youth in Michigan accelerated to elk and grizzly in Montana. In Key West he began with bonefish, then the violence of tarpon. The obsession with the huge marlin of the Gulf Stream and the Straits of Cuba was inevitable. Live pigeon shoots in Spain, innumerable quail and duck. He had to be among the very best and clearly was with a vengeance often embarrassing to his companions.

Then Africa. A few years back I was sitting at dawn in a small cabin at Keekoruk in Kenya sipping tea. Keekoruk is the stepping-off point into the justly fabled Serengeti. There was a large herd of Cape buffalo nibbling at the tender shoots of grass of the airstrip a very few yards away. They tend to get pissed off when you shoot at them, I reflected. By and large, the greater part of African hunting has been the rich sportsman's hoax on his gullible fraternity of hunters back home. The blockhead who shoots a lion at three hundred yards does not like to be reminded that a Masai warrior dispatches the same cat at smelling distance with a spear. The point is that there's not more than an off chance at finding your balls by pulling a trigger.

And of course the ultimate arena of the gun is war. Hemingway was involved with honor in three of them. And he wrote just about as beautifully as any man in our century when he didn't allow his purposefully fabricated public personality to get in the way. It was a mockery of the warrior code that had actually been repeatedly called upon to keep him alive.

This is not to say that a great man can't be a preposterous asshole, information easily got from any of the pork-and-bean critics with a liberal arts degree in psychologizing. To say that Faulkner was a garden-variety drunk scarcely dismisses twenty or so novels. Maybe it's the idea that by the time you let your personality start killing fish, animals, men, you have blown it, removed yourself from the arena of sport or hunger, from the adrenaline of fatal play. It becomes a public act of wanton attrition, a singular blasphemy to the last good country you have looked for all your life but have been sidetracked from for reasons of vanity, no matter how understandable.

As a matter of simple fact, the shark and hyena own the lion's majesty, are breathing beasts not put here as anthropomorphic reservoirs of our hate. If you can't understand a shark or hyena you probably don't have a shot at understanding yourself. If the next good country doesn't exist it's because we pillaged the last one we so stridently walked through. The old horse outside my granary door is autumnal without knowing it. It is more interesting to be absorbed enough in your life cycle not to have opinions about it. Witless Thoreau understood that you couldn't really "know" anything unless you started with the forty acres out behind the barn and the brain that perceived it.

"Il faut, (d'abord) durer," Hemingway liked to think and say, with an animal tact. Melville wrote a book about incomprehension which gives him the edge. You can't parse the furrow in the grizzly's brow by shooting him. But then Hemingway was a great man, too, with a transparent power in both his virtues and vices, occasionally an absurdist samurai insisting that the world's edges be as sharp and clean and durable as his youthful visions. It was a thing of beauty that within his embittered code, *hari-kari* was much the more graceful act than senescence.

Meanwhile back in Ontario: out beyond Hawk Junction, far off the road, I have found a stream that has become a beaver pond for a hundred yards, then a stream again. Mosquitoes and flies form so dense a nimbus around my head they might be mistaken for a cloud. Out in the middle of the pond a large brook trout is rising. I am in the water to the tip-top of my waders and I still can't reach the fish with my light, split-bamboo rod. I return to the truck for a heavier fiberglass fly rod. The fish is perhaps a hundred and twenty feet away and I still can't reach it. The rocks are slippery under my feet. I am not going to drown to catch the fish. I'm not even going to get wet. I am going to sit on the bank until dark and watch it feed, also watch the loon at the far end of the pond watch me.

1977

The Preparation of
Thomas Hearns

P olarities are rarely solved by guitars, I thought. I looked at my pistol, a Ruger Magnum, lying on the railing of the deck which broaches the Sucker River in Grand Marais, Michigan, some five hundred miles north of Detroit. The pistol was bought this spring not to defend myself against people, but porcupines: porcupines can eat through the walls of a cabin and when you return after a long winter the whole cabin is literally full of shit. The other creature I shoot at is the sea lamprey when it comes wriggling upriver like a short, fat snake. Lampreys are so ugly they're not even Freudian. They arrived in the Great Lakes after a major ecological fuck-up during the building of the Saint Lawrence Seaway. Lampreys destroyed the native lake trout population so I shoot at them, rarely killing them, only rolling them over a few times.

But polarities and guitars: there is a Lou Reed tape on the car stereo (no electricity in the cabin except that provided by an old Kohler generator in the evening). Nothing made me quite so happy as when the bourgeoisie forgot about folk music. I remember black college students watching, say, a white pre-med type from Scarsdale sing a ditty, "Dis train I gwine ride carryin' one thousand ton de waddymelon back to mammy. . . . " That was thirteen years ago when I taught at a university. I try to avoid universities now, thinking of them as producing bung fodder for a strung-out economy.

T his morning while I was grouse hunting a big coyote crossed diagonally in front of me; well-muscled, rippling fur, he pretended I wasn't there. The coyote reminded me of Thomas Hearns, a great fighter who blew it in the fourteenth round the other night in Vegas. I lost the price of a used Subaru on the match, but felt oddly unmoved. The damage didn't equal that of a previous venture into a charter boat in Key West, English gambling stock, Australian oil stock. If you get the idea I'm a financial moron you've stuck the bandelero in the ass of the donkey.

But Thomas Hearns. And Detroit. Hearns wanted to win one for himself and Detroit, which has been on a very bad roll for a decade. The city looks like a bad roll—worse even than a lamprey's mouth, a vast cold suburb of Moscow, so bleak and tormented that citizens shoot each other out of boredom. Of course there is the usual array of high-medium restaurants and the town is ringed by snazzy homes inhabited by vastly overpaid auto executives who precipitated the slump by being outsmarted by the Japanese. And there are four professional sports teams (the Lions, Tigers, Pistons and Red Wings) with collective records that have matched their city's long ugly economic slump. A Hearns victory would have provided at least a Pyrrhic boost. Now there will be a cold winter's wait for the next move while the melting pot continues to leak and we open the Detroit *Free Press* to read of shoot-outs between dozens of different minorities.

In August Thomas Hearns trained at a ski resort, with the titillating name of Sugarloaf, in my home area, Leelanau County. The curious thing about Hearns training in Leelanau County is that there are no blacks up here. You must think of Michigan as your hand: up past the palm where the fingers begin is the northern lower peninsula. Your little finger is the Leelanau Peninsula, a country of rolling hills, fruit orchards, magnificent beaches. The closest town to the Hearns camp was the former fishing village of Leland which plays host to a rather fungoid summer aristocracy based on the periphery of Midwestern capitalism: non-addictive glue, the insides of car-seats, holeless donut-makers, and glass jars with or without lids. The Leland area is a sort of Republican Key West packed full of Reaganite bliss-ninnies smirking over the recent tax cuts. It's smack dab on the 45th parallel and is perhaps too far north to be seriously considered by blacks and gays as it is a region climatically unsuited for either vice or good food. As in Aspen, certain nitwits make much of how long they've been coming to the area. The real charm in living here, outside of the natural beauty, is the grace of the residents (many French Canadians, Scandinavians, WASPs who don't know they are WASPs), the respect for privacy, the lack of any cloying moral majority. You have to eat at home but there are a few good bars. You can even drink with some particularly decent cops who will gladly bust you if you do something wrong. There have been two murders in twenty years. The hunting and fishing is pretty good. That has to be enough. Thomas Hearns chose the largest local resort, Sugarloaf, to train at not because the resort had filed for Chapter Eleven bankruptcy, but because it had a large tennis barn in which to set up a ring, a golf course to run on, and some good local trout fishing. Hearns is a fishing addict, sleeps with teddy bears, and belongs to a police auxiliary.

So Thomas Hearns and the Kronk boxing team trained up here on the 45th parallel for two weeks, and thousands came to watch, partly because it was free and partly because it was so bizarre. The lack of admission is important in that the whole state is an economic garage sale with everyone buying each other's used mitre boxes, chain saws, hunting boots, Robert Hall sportcoats, plastic dinnerware and legless dolls.

The camp was a wonderful nonevent, something akin to a Chinese puppet show. The whites watched and the blacks boxed. Everyone in the county was polite and the blacks endured not a single racist slur in two weeks. Thomas Hearns looks like a cobra, a little like a pissed-off Miles Davis at four in the morning, but the man invited local kids into the ring for a lesson. He likes kids and understands adults are a waste of time while training for the big one, especially adult journalists.

At the training camp the media posed the only problem. This was true, too, in Las Vegas. I despise the word "vibration" but the media always exudes a sourness, a negative energy. They live and work in a voyeuristic space where they're always outside jacking off while watching life taking place on the other side of the window. The New York group, particularly, bites like Dobermans on quaaludes. They didn't like Hearns because he's not a "show nigger" like Sugar Ray, and they didn't get a chance to help in the hype and build-up for Hearns.

It really never occurred to me that Hearns could lose, though my feelings about boxing as a sport are ambivalent: say, similar to my best friend making an obscene phone call to my wife. Boxers, like novelists and poets, begin on an incorrigible trajectory that comes to nothing for all but a few. The wounds and scar tissue run so deep they go all through the body and out the other side. Note that Ali isn't sounding so well lately; the speech patterns, the badinage, lack the precision of a few years back. Joe Louis, the last Michigan boxing hero until Hearns, went to his grave speaking a language that only a few friends and relatives could truly comprehend. Maybe it was worth it for Louis, arguably the greatest of all heavyweights. With Hearns we'll have to wait and see. Boxing fans resemble the wives of fighter pilots. I haven't been in a fight in ten years but I still remember poignantly how ugly it is to be hit hard. It's worse than a whole pile of bad reviews.

Heraclitus said that "the moon is the width of a woman's thigh." This is to draw us back to the earth herself; not necessarily a gentler earth, but at least an earth far from the place where two men beat the shit out of each other for money. It's a solace that only a minority really cares about such things. In newspapers the food page always exceeds the sports page in readership. Much of the news is media news read by others in the media and of little concern to anyone else. On TV we are led to believe that the news itself is less important than what baritone fop reads it from the prompter. In Hollywood there is a certain wonderment over the idea that the rest of the country doesn't care about the process, but wants a story not necessarily about what some schizoid technocrat thinks about the history of show business.

Meanwhile, in the little village of Lake Leelanau, seven hundred Plamondons are having a family reunion. First they drink and eat and dance, then they drink and eat and dance again. At mid-afternoon they march through the village (population 400) led by an assortment of Traverse City bagpipers. The bagpipers seem a trifle out of place in that the Plamondons are French Canadian, but that is carping. I retire to Dick's Pour House (owned by Richard Plamondon and formerly owned by Ralph "Dick" Plamondon) to sort out this spectacle. I am informed that it is the *Tricentenaire de la famille Plamondon en Amerique du Nord, 1680–1980*. None of the local Plamondons speak French, but that doesn't interfere with the common language of food, drink, and dancing. Early in this century 200 local Plamondons went out to Alberta and founded a town called Plamondon. The only really newsworthy Plamondon in the history of the family is the infamous

Weatherman saboteur, Pun Plamondon, who did time for blowing up a government building in Ann Arbor.

Then there are two more events in rapid succession, though they do not leave one breathless. There is the magnificent Heavyweight Championship Horse Pulling Contest at the Grand Traverse County Fair. At the fair there are no blacks but a lot of people who are classifiably poor by government standards. The horse pulling is a big annual event for me, and if I'm lucky this year out in Glitzville, I hope to field a team next summer. I inquire about the price of a gelding, part of the winning team and weighing 2600 pounds. I tickle his ear. They want $25,000 for the horse. You can't deduct geldings. The government again. The prize for the winner here was $250, a lot less than the upcoming fight in Vegas. The team pulled the equivalent of a moving weight of eighty cars.

Another short event: our Labor Day beef roast with a whole side of rare beef, plus two roasts, a barrel of sweet corn, beans, kegs of beer, cases of whiskey, sponsored by Richard Plamondon. To say it was a hog show is to give the finger improperly to the pigs. People danced, sometimes rolling on the ground. There was a fistfight over the twin questions of cherry farming and deer hunting. So much brave irreverence, and hormones, spilling over wantonly.

Now I am back in Grand Marais, out on the river, and I've just found out Hearns lost. If I'd been home the loss would have meant more, both for the money and the sympathy for a fighter with so implacable a sense of dignity that he does not quite seem to belong to us. In the two weeks I spent around him I never saw a small move, only a feline grace like some black Mifume preparing for the first big test. He'll be back.

Meanwhile there is the night, and tonight it is a cold saturating of stars— García Lorca described "the enormous night straining her waist against the Milky Way." Sometimes up here I have seen the northern lights shoot with a green twinkling hiss across the sky. No TV or radio, just your own questionable skull. I'm up here bird hunting and have six weeks of walking around the woods in search of grouse and woodcock to look forward to.

My bird dog looks out into the impenetrable dark and begins a deep growling; my scalp prickles and I think of the pistol and shotguns in the cabin, or my fists, as simpleminded men will do out of fear, or for fame, or for money.

1980

Bird Hunting

Many of our life-giving rituals are deeply private, whether their nature is sexual, religious, or involved in far simpler pleasures. I like, in May—perhaps love is a better word—to stand in a clearing near dark and watch the mating flight of the male woodcock, the sweeping contorted spiral, then the whirl back to earth. Not incidentally, this dance tells you where the birds will be in the fall during hunting season as they mate and breed in the vicinity of their singing grounds. And when migratory groups gather and accumulate they tend to favor these same clearings. The French philosopher Bachelard ascribed a peculiar magic to certain things and locations—attics, haylofts, seashells, a cabin in the dark with a window square of yellow light. Since the age of seven, when I began hunting, I've favored the bottoms of rivers and lakes and forest clearings.

Five months later, in early October, four men stand in such a clearing, perhaps fifteen miles from any human settlement. The October sun is thin and weak at this latitude in Michigan's Upper Peninsula, an area remote and charmless except to a few. The four men are planning the evening's menu and staring at the five bird dogs sprawled in a pool of sunlight. There are two yellow Labrador bitches, one owned by myself and the other by a French count I've been hunting with more than a dozen years. My neighbor, whom I think of as "Dogman," has a German shorthair, an English setter and an English pointer. This lovely pile of animals would make a flawless painting if my bitch Sand, bred from the English Sandringham line, weren't making love to the males with punishing force. It is her way of celebrating the hunt and they cry out as she smothers them. It is hopeless to try to call her off—there is apparently no obedience training when it comes to sheer lust. The fourth hunter among us, an artist from Montana, is especially amused. He is unable to own a bird dog for reasons of temperament.

"Like me, she is a generic love," the artist says. He is the most focused menu planner of the group. During the hunt he stops and stares a lot because he is fat, but also because he is an artist and likes to study the sere umbers, the siennas, the subdued Tuscan riot that is a Michigan October. He suggests for dinner that he quickly do some Hunanese pork backribs for an appetizer, then we can marinate chunks of grouse and sweetbreads in cream and Tabasco in order to stretch the grouse. After we've browned these chunks we'll add a cup of vastly reduced game stock and a cup of the marinade. We would have had more grouse but no one had the energy to brave the densest thickets where they seemed to be that day. Meanwhile the Dogman would grill ten of the plucked woodcock over a wood fire until medium rare, basting them with butter, lemon and pepper. The more elegant *salmis de bécasses* would be made by the Count later when we traveled south to my farmhouse. This evening as a last course the Count would offer two racks of lamb with some garlicky flageolet and a salad to tamp it all down. Three Montrachets and four Châteauneuf du Pape would be the rinse. I can't be disturbing my remaining great wines by travel. They would come later.

A minor regional novelist recently said that "*cuisine minceur* is the moral equivalent of the fox-trot." Perhaps. In any event you simply can't hike through rugged territory for eight hours and be satisfied with three poached mussels and an asparagus mousse. It is another ritual, though never talked about as such, that the food go as well as the hunting, with each occasionally making up deficiencies in the other. When we're on the road together, say on the way to Montana to fish brown trout, the Count will polish off a plate of bad restaurant food, then hiss "filth" for anyone who cares to hear or not. This is also, not incidentally, his response to any political discussion.

The hunt had gone well for a day that had begun too warm for the dogs, but by late morning the wind had swung around to the northwest off Lake Superior. The artist and I formed the "B" team, in that Sand must be kept separate from the others as she tries to hog the good cover. There is something marvelous about a dog with a sure sense of function, and an intelligent, experienced animal recognizes cover. Good cover for grouse and woodcock, though not identical, is a practical matter of finding their main eating areas. In short, they both hang out where they eat: patches of aspen in clearings, edges of the forest with berry-bearing bushes, tag-alder swales along creeks, near pin cherry, chokecherry, thorn apple, beechnut, red and white dogwood. In other areas abandoned farms are good for reasons of fertility of undergrowth. In my region of the U.P. there are not abandoned farms because farms themselves are scarce—there's one about thirty miles south of here. The main local livelihood is logging, a positive influence on game quantity; as opposed to what most people think, a fully mature forest is relatively sterile in terms of mammalian and game-bird life.

The artist and I are never disturbed over the idea that the others will over-shoot us. To be good at bird hunting you need a combination of excellent dog work, an ability to shoot well, and a knowledge of cover. The Dog-man's shorthair could find birds in a busy roller rink. I once saw this dog, Cochise by name, crawl beneath a brush pile in search of a wounded grouse, his tail pointing up at the heavens through a mat of cedar brush. I am mindful that the fine novelist, Hemingway, wasted an entire African hunt brooding over the idea that his partner was doing better. Frankly, everyone in his secret heart must know who is the best. I'm not letting Gabriel García Márquez and Saul Bellow ruin my life as a novelist because they're better at it. If the Count and Dogman return garlanded with birds we will rejoice at the table.

We do have one advantage and that rests in the fact that I spend a lot of the summer locating birds, driving hundreds of miles on forest two-tracks. In the past five years I have pretty much covered a strip of land a hundred and fifty miles long by thirty miles wide bordering Lake Superior. Sand is upset that I don't shoot the birds off-season but if she finds a covey of grouse she'll become affectionate back in the car. I fight her off, telling her, "I'm not of your kind, I'm an American Poet."

The artist has new boots and his feet hurt after the first half-hour aspen walk with two flushed birds and no hits. We drive to a tag-alder swale only a mile or so from the village. We are excited enough by this area to stop talking about food and love for a short while. Even the dog is beside herself when we pull to a stop beside the marsh. We each take a side with Sand casting back and forth in the improbably dark tag-alder thicket. Educated luck! Within a half hour a dozen woodcock have burst from cover and we have bagged five. The artist is beside himself and throws himself on the ground laughing and necking with the dog. "Sand, we are American Sportsmen," he yells to the blue sky and a red-tailed hawk a thousand feet above us. On the way back to the car Sand flushes a grouse from a clump of goldenrod. The grouse falls to the artist's long shot. To maintain this state of grace we go to the bar for a few drinks then back to the cabin for lunch and a short midday nap. We envision the Count and Dogman on a forced march to bag the number of birds we have done effortlessly. We discuss the merits of a pasta dish I had devised in May with a sauce of wild leeks and morels, sweetbreads and cream. I have some dried morels and domestic leeks at the cabin. It will make a serviceable lunch, adding some julienned prosciutto.

In the state of post-nap grogginess our victories seem less specific. We jounce over a dozen miles of logging road to rendezvous with the Count and Dogman at a bend in the river. We are somewhat disappointed to see that they are drinking on the riverbank, and eating a pâté the Count had in his cooler made out of Hungarian grouse and teal he had shot in Montana. They have seven woodcock and two grouse. They are pleasantly surprised at our bag and head off to hunt another hour. When they're gone we finish the pâté and head off lazily down the road with neither of us willing to break brush. We shoot only one of five flushed birds, destroying the morning's invulnerability. Even the dog seems disappointed in us. Hearing distant shooting I climb to a bare hillock and look through my monocular (I'm blind in one eye so in a moment of brilliance gave up binoculars after thirty years). The Dogman and Count approach a swale perhaps a thousand yards distant. My monocular is a small round movie screen focused on the three pointers on tightly honored point. There is a flush and the Count swings left and right and two birds fall. Unlike the artist and I the Count and Dogman take turns. Now I see my own dog, Sand, streaking toward the real action as the Count's retriever fetches the birds. I turn with the monocular and focus on the artist dozing under an oak tree, his left hand brushing acorns from beneath his ample bottom. I am not exactly "one with the earth" but I'm feeling good. Simultaneous visions of a fashion model and a duck I had cooked with marrow and exactly thirty-three cloves of garlic sweep through my mind. It is our first day of hunting together, much like the Glorious Twelfth in England. I can feel my happiness emanating in bands to the hunters in the distance.

Back at the cabin, while the artist is preparing his fiery ribs of the Orient, I inoculate the cracks of the log walls using a large marinade hypodermic and a solution of Tabasco and Canadian whiskey. This drives away bats which have been using the walls as both bedroom and toilet. They fly around drunkenly like poets on grants. I sip this concoction to feel life even more strongly. I am quickly losing the self-absorption that made me all the money in the first place, a self-absorption that paradoxically only regains its value after you lose it for a while. I am wearing a Texas tailored camouflage jump suit with which I sneak up on snowshoe rabbits for illegal summertime French fricassees. I have also seen a curious female coyote five times but never before she has seen me first, wondering perhaps at this burly man creeping through the swamp in clumsy imitation of other beasts.

I turn from my bat chores and look at my friends busy in the kitchen, feeding dogs, dressing after a shower. We in the Midwest have to face up to the idea that no one on America's dream coasts will visit us except for very special occasions. True, we have the Great Lakes but they have the Atlantic and the Pacific. They also have restaurants. Tom McGuane, the novelist, said to me about the Midwest, "Mortimer Snerd must have bred five thousand times a day to build that heartland race." True, but the land as I find it, and daily walk it, is virtually peopleless, with vast undifferentiated swamps, ridges, old circular logging roads; a region of cold fogs, monstrous weather changes, third-growth forests devoid of charm, models, and actresses, or ballerinas, but somehow superbly likable.

After the meal and a goblet of calvados we sit before the fire and watch the Count tease his teeth and upper lip with a thumb, a small piece of blanket on his shoulder. Technically speaking he is *not* "sucking his thumb." He has reminded me that for years I have preferred to watch television through the tiny squares of an afghan thrown over my head. *Pourquoi?* Beats me. The artist becomes morose, commenting that after years of experience in the nearby village he is sure that if he wore a Dolly Parton wig he would be the most attractive woman in town. He has offered local ladies paintings for their favors and the paintings are worth thousands.

"They don't want paintings, they want a husband," says the Dogman. "Besides, you're as ugly as we all are. I drink because I'm ugly. You don't try hard enough. Romania wasn't built in a day."

It is easy to tire of this masculine nonsense, and after a week, when the supply of good wine runs out, we head south to my farm in Leelanau County, a rather spectacular area itself; a hilly landscape of cherry orchards jutting out as a peninsula into Lake Michigan. With a northern front the weather has turned cold and somber which will drive the woodcock south on their migratory route. For years we have found them arriving in our favorite areas between October sixth and tenth.

A Native American myth insists that the Great Spirit made the woodcock up last out of the leftover parts of other birds. *Philohela minor* is colored in shades of brown, black, and gray which says nothing until you envision the mottled shades of autumn—foliage burned by frost, wet leaves, bare earth. They smell musky and their breasts are plumper than a quail's. The French prefer their flavor over all other game birds, spreading their entrails on large croutons. Jeanne Moreau told me that as a young actress she would save a month to buy a brace of woodcock. The Count doesn't know yet but I've purchased two cases of Echêzeaux, his favorite. Childish surprises are still the best.

My farmhouse owns the still ample remains of my Warner Bros. Memorial Wine Cellar, though my oldest daughter has hidden a '49 Latour and some '61 Lafites against my excesses. She has made and brought from New York a goose *confit*. My agent has sent a pound of caviar. A bow-hunter friend has sent over a half of venison. I have ordered a quarter of prime veal and a freshly killed local lamb. The Dogman is taking a few days off from grouse and woodcock to get some wild ducks, hopefully teal and mallard. A farmer drops off the dozen barnyard chickens and ducks we called about in August. It's too early to get any fresh truffles from New York but we'll have to make do. We'll poach two local salmon for dinner to lighten up a bit, and I'll make gravlax out of a third. I bought seven pounds of garlic, my favorite number!

And so it goes. We hunt hard during the short Indian summer days and cook hard during the long evenings. I suspect this will strike some as primitive. Years ago we had to hunt much harder and the Count reminds me of how my wife and two daughters would hear the car and run out of the house to see the bag. One day, the best ever, we came home with nine grouse, seven woodcock, and a few rabbits. He says that ten years later whenever he sees a girl wearing braces he thinks of my daughter at thirteen, peering at the game birds with utter delight. Then she would set about plucking enough birds for dinner, and we would hang the others a few days, a desirable practice for flavor.

A week of the local hunting leaves us with a caloric load that we can't quite walk off in our daily hunting. I would like to say that somehow our genes are issuing messages to store up for the coming winter but this is ardent nonsense. In times past certain of the deadly sins achieved a certain spirituality when taken far enough. I resolve to make notes on the spirituality of gluttony but the idea is a bit too remote to attract anything more than thoughts of Rasputin's talents for sex and drink, Nixon's for fibbing, Rabelais's, Toulouse-Lautrec's, and Curnonsky's for food. Before we leave for the austerity of the north we watch the Count working deep into the night. He is assembling a rough pâté in a clear glass tureen made out of gorgeous layers of ground veal flavored with apples and calvados, duck, venison, woodcock and grouse. This little dish is being made as a precaution against our living too simply back in the U.P. That evening the Count had made an enormous *salmis de bécasses*, the most exacting of woodcock dishes, and one would think exhaustion would have driven him to bed, but he lacks our very American cheap resolve to eat nothing to purge too much. During eating, the French discuss future eating. After the dinner we had decided that Sand should lick the platter, a traditional reward for a dog that has done well in the field. When the platter was put down on the rug with its dark freight of extra sauce she had approached wiggling, her eyes closed in pleasure, and limping with fatigue. After two long, tentative laps the hunger became generalized and she flopped on the platter, rolling in the juices. It was comic and touching. A dog is entitled to a favorite time of year just as we are.

Once I fell down just as a dog came on point in thick cover. I was a little worried as years before I had spent a month in traction from a fall during bird season. Two setters honored the first dog's point, skidding to full attention behind the first dog. It was a rainy day in late season and I watched it all from ground level, having come suddenly to the point where I didn't want to shoot any more birds that year. The grouse wild-flushed off into the mist, free to die during the harsh winter, or live another year.

The season is over and my heart is as full as Neruda's interminable artichoke. Everyone is gone and I draft a novel, further taxing my overused system. I go to a Mexican health farm for two weeks but am terribly embarrassed when I catch a few local workers staring at me at some exercises. Twenty years ago I was a laborer building small buildings as they are now. We were very poor then and a half a venison meant a great deal. I skip the exercises and walk alone every day in the mountains. I hunt rattlesnakes without harming them. After flushing coveys of quail I begin to devise ways of snaring a few to enhance the expensive vegetarian diet at the spa. In New York and Los Angeles, or anywhere in the world, I mostly hunt good restaurants.

My own hunting and fishing are largely misunderstood activities cataloged under the banal notion of "macho," whereas I tend to view them as a continuation of my birthright. The forest, after all, isn't my Louvre. The Louvre is my Louvre. I walk there from my rooms at the Lotti. There are ideas currently afoot about the positive effects of "male bonding," inferring there might be something to such activities as they have had a regular place in the male life since prehistory. There is a studied silliness in responding to old ideas brought up in new dime store frocks by newspaper feature editors. Hemingway went for record kudu and marlin in public, while Faulkner in self-designed obscurity hunted and fished with friends, played polo, chased foxes, sailed, and drank a bit.

Just the other night, in the middle of August while I was writing this, I went calling coyotes with a friend. In the right mood coyotes will respond to our imitation of their call, also to a loon's call which is more difficult to imitate. Despite what taxonomists say, these creatures are related, if only spiritually. To the east the moon was full and enormous at midnight; to the north there was the pale green fluttering sheen of aurora borealis, the northern lights; in the west a large thunderstorm and line squall was forming and bolts of lightning cracked the sky in the forms of undersea coral. We were in a thousand-acre clearing with a thousand huge, gray white pine stumps, cut a century ago. My friend called and the coyotes responded in this mythological landscape with breathless abandon intermingled with the thunder. On the long ride back in the rain one sensed the sky was full of black anti-rainbows. Around a puddle in the trail three woodcock preened and fed. I eased out of the car and stooped quite close to them, their eyes fiery and blinded by the headlights. I spoke to the birds a few minutes, then watched them flush through the glittery beads of rain into the darkness. A wonderful hunt.

1985

Log of the Earthtoy Drifthumper

A few summers ago in Michigan's Upper Peninsula I walked out of my cabin well after midnight, took off my clothes, and dove buck-naked into the river, swimming and drifting downstream in the darkness, clambering over several logjams. It was pleasant, if eerie, until it was time to make my way back through the unpeopled forest and swamp. Then it became clear why shoes and clothing had been devised.

This is not generally recommended behavior, but then we like to think that life is usually lived between the lines, when we surprise ourselves, or lived while others are making plans and appointments. Mostly, though, I had to take the swim because I needed to know what it was like in order to conclude the novel *Sundog*.

This January I was having trouble with another book, because I am just another alpha manic-depressive who spends too much time in the air, with a dozen or so not very meaningful trips a year to either of America's dream coasts: to New York which is really Europe, and to Los Angeles which is an enticing, sunburned void. I needed to know what the Great Plains were like in the winter, and the kind of information I wanted could not be extrapolated from the vantage point of 37,000 feet or from trips to the library.

At the outset you should know that I am not a car freak or maven. This disinterest can be attributed to a childhood trauma. At sixteen I bought a 1929 Model A, covered with birdshit, out of a barn and received a ghastly electric shock from something under the hood that my father described as a "magneto." Other young folks have been bitten by horses and turned to cars, but I was bitten by both, as it were. That summer I rode a balloon-tire Schwinn 128 miles in one day in reaction to horses and cars.

As a consequence I have gone through life at forty-nine miles an hour—if I were a boat, I'd be a tug. I have never run out of gas (for fear that the car won't start again), and I haven't washed a car since my teens, when I washed too many of them for quarters. Not that I am a totally slow-track guy—through the kindness and misapprehension of friends I have driven Porsches, a Ferrari, a Maserati, a 600 Mercedes, even my wife's Saab. Also a Daimler limousine in London when the chauffeur was drunker than I was. Curiously, I have never met anyone who thinks I drive well.

Late on the eve of my departure from Lake Leelanau, Michigan, I am having a heavy nightcap to steady my nerves, and listening to the wind howl. The snowdrifts have collected against the lower tiers of the window-panes. Dimly under the yard light I can see the fully packed 1986 Subaru four-wheel drive Turbo station wagon with manufacturer's plates. Parked next to it is my own 1981 Subaru four-wheel drive station wagon, only mine has a skidplate, a cowcatcher, and a winch. There is a temptation to take "old reliable" and leave the new one at home. All I want in a car is re-liability, just as in boats I prefer one that floats. The tempting factor is the turbo, though my wife quipped earlier in the evening that I don't know what "turbo" means. If it sounds good, you don't need to know what it means, I replied, remembering Paris, where I invariably order unknown items from the menu. Much of life seems to be a blind date.

Soon after daylight—actually, a few hours—I was on my way, double-checking for the shovel, the sleeping bag, and the big, white candles that were to save me if I became stranded—I'd read that if you light a few can-dles in your car, they give enough heat to keep you from freezing to death. I headed northward to the Straits of Mackinac with the snow coming down so hard I only averaged 38.5 miles per hour in the first four hours, or so said the elaborate trip computer. The trip computer was to be virtually my only sore point about the car. I was reminded of what Garrison Keillor, Lake Wobegon's celebrity, had said: "People in the Midwest don't take trips, they compute mileage and distance." I wanted my land voyage to be taken on house-cat time, with no attention paid to anything but the essentials of what I was seeing. Do you want to remember that you climbed a 10,000-foot mountain or what happened to you on the way up or down? But then I couldn't use my heel or Magnum on the trip computer because it wasn't my car. I've always felt those nitwits on the annual coast-to-coast race should be beaten across the gums.

I began to cool off approaching the Mackinac Bridge. There's no real point in getting angry while driving solo, when you can only yell into your dictaphone. There are racers, and there are those who tour. Meanwhile, the bridge was swaying visibly in the gale-force winds. I began to have thoughts about mechanical mortality; just as a car grows old and dies, with gray hairs hanging from its mud flaps, so also must a bridge die. I just don't want to be there when it happens, when it finally gives up its bridge ghost and plummets into the bottomless straits. A few years ago, I missed by a mere seven months plunging off the bridge that collapsed between Tampa and Sarasota.

My spirits picked up when the weather cleared enough for me to see that there was barely any traffic. This was a signal thrill that was to follow me for the next twenty-eight days. By summertime standards, the progress was unimpeded by other cars. To be sure, there were trucks, but then they are somewhat predictable and reliable. There must be folks heading south to Florida, I thought, drawn there for the vermin-ridden night flowers, and for the clothing and pharmaceuticals on display in *Miami Vice*. I punched on cruise control and opened the sunroof, standing on the seat and steering with my fingertips.

I was headed west on Route 2, and now the sun glistened off the storm-tormented northern Lake Michigan. It was like driving a two-ton motorcycle without a wind visor. An oncoming car beeped, suggesting perhaps that my method was reprehensible. I forced myself into a more serious, mechanical mood. My 1981 Subaru, with four forward gears, required 3300 rpm to go fifty-eight miles per hour, while the 1986 Subaru in fifth gear required only 2400 rpm to maintain the same speed. Any fool could figure out that if you were a skater or a dancer, 900 fewer twirls per minute would make a big difference.

I had planned my first night's stop for the House of Ludington in Escanaba, my favorite Midwestern hostelry. When I got out, I gave the car a friendly pat for a good day's work. Despite some harrowing moments, I felt much better than I would have arriving at La Guardia, or on a jam-packed flight at Los Angeles International with a dead woman and bizarre but friendly Siamese twins connected at the head, as had happened in December. Besides, no terrorist or member of the criminal element was likely to stick a bomb in the car. And I didn't have to pull up at this wonderful hotel and restaurant at 170 miles per hour, which has always been an enervating way to retouch earth.

Not knowing where the next good meal might come from in the hinterlands, I treated myself to fresh oysters and soup and a bottle of Graves. I was torn between the roast duck and the roast smoked pork loin, so I ordered them both, accompanied by a Châteauneuf-du-Pape. This normally might have put me to sleep, but I walked a mile up the street to see the kindly dancing girls at Orphan Annie's, somewhat as a soldier might do on the eve of battle, or a sailor before a voyage that might very well take him off the edge of the earth. The Great Plains were not known for nude dancing girls, and it would be best to take a look now. There were to be no flesh colors in future landscapes, or so I thought.

At daylight, or soon after, I adopted a slightly higher sense of purpose. At the current rate, what could I discover through red eyes and 10,000 lost dollars, a bilious stomach in a land without rest stops? I had worked the bugs out to the point where I comprehended the entire, intricate instrument panel of the car—except, of course, the trip computer. There were a few bugs left in my head, but they would presumably pass with the miles.

The trip through Wisconsin and Minnesota (the weather was nasty, but it was a garden-variety nasty) illustrated the central weather fraud current in America: Everyone brags about his bad weather. I've even had Texans tell me that I had "never lived through a Texas winter," a winter so severe that most northern Michiganders wouldn't bother putting on their winter coats. The fact is, the Leelanau peninsula had 108 inches of snow by New Year's, and much of the Upper Peninsula had half again as much. In Michigan I had humped through drifts about the size of a low-slung ranch house. Naturally you pause to check for oncoming traffic before you crank up toward the redline.

Route 64 through northern Wisconsin was a good choice, an improbably beautiful landscape with frozen forests and clearings, Scandinavian barns with frozen white, shimmering haystacks, an immense field with thousands of bright, frozen thorn apples catching the morning sun, the breath of Holsteins rising in steamy wisps in the still air. Hooking to the left on 73 and 95, you descend into the upper Mississippi River basin, moving down toward La Crosse through a rural landscape pretty much unequaled, somewhat like the hills of Kentucky. A well-tended hill farm owns a pure but functional beauty. Nearing a town or city of any size, you are reminded again of the implausible junkiness of mankind—I don't mean, in the anal-compulsive sense, that everything should be beautiful, but that ninety-nine percent of our artifacts are ugly, and strewn around so haphazardly that we are forever pausing to figure out why we feel so badly about what we are seeing.

At a service station near Sioux Valley, Minnesota, I flipped out my dictaphone, determined to get at some troublesome questions concerning the average weight of heartland ladies, also whether any of the assembled had ever named their vehicles. The consensus was 150 for the ladies (the respondents were truly big ole boys, upward of 200 apiece). All of the men admitted to having named cars and trucks anything from Bullet to Bob to Fireball to Myrna (after a girlfriend). They liked the idea that I was going no place in particular for as long as cash and credit cards lasted.

"How long would that be?"

"About thirty days west of here," I answered.

"Too bad you can't drive to Hawaii. You should go to Vegas." (Everyone in the Midwest wants to go to Vegas or Hawaii.)

"I'm going to end up in Arizona to track mountain lions and track a Mexican wolf known as a white lobo. I might shoot some quail to eat, too."

There were long faces at the station when I pulled out. Everyone wants to go someplace and the comparatively rare idea of a trip without a plan was even more attractive. As the days passed, I came to think that the finest thing about a long solo car trip is that you get to forget who you are, if anything celebrated or negotiable beyond the normal bounds of ego. Every place you stay is a place you never stayed before. Everyone you talk to is new, and no one can get you on the phone unless you call home. The bottom line is that you are free, however temporarily, and you return to the exhilaration of those childhood myths of Robin Hood or the lone cowpoke.

I'm heading through a hellish Minnesota storm toward a corner of Iowa, and the closest thing I have to a destination, Nebraska. The radio announces that all local schools will close because of the storm. I come upon the aftermath of a truly nasty truck–snowplow collision. I feel like I'm driving in a dentist's chair during an unsuccessful root canal. This weather is why I've had two Subarus for a total of seven years—there was only one trip to the garage, and that was caused by a caroming trip down a steep hill through the woods. Suddenly there's a bit of ugliness caused by a jackknifing semi that overshot an exit. I'm forced over a bank onto a cloverleaf in a split second. In another split second I think, "I'm not getting stuck here this close to lunch," punch the four-wheel-drive button, downshift to second, and fishtail in big circles to gain speed, throwing a rooster tail of snow that I pass through before leaping a bank back onto the shoulder.

I am rewarded by a grotesque pork fritter and canned gravy at a truck stop where the assembled Knights of the Road all look like they need a resident nutritionist. On the road, breakfast is the most reliable meal. When I'm settled into my motel in the early evening, I invariably call the local radio station for a hot dinner tip. I figure disc jockeys are layabouts like writers and they would likely know the best place to eat. This works pretty well if you're willing to settle for a little less and can develop the uncritical state of mind that is required if you're ever going to get out of bed in the first place. In Alliance, Nebraska, I had a fabulous two-pound rib steak, watched a soft-core porn film on TV, and went to an American Legion country dance, where I jumped around like a plump kangaroo to work off the protein rush, or whatever.

I suppose if the country I had been driving through held anything in common from state to state it was that it had changed less as time had slipped by than it would have anywhere else in the United States. I mean outside the cities of Sioux City or Omaha or Lincoln. Iowa owns a charming lack of differentiation. If you lived there, you would seek out the extraordinary tuft of grass or mudhole, the most beautiful pig. Only one bird nests in all of Iowa, and it is called, simply enough, "brown bird." Iowa has a fifty-by-fifty-foot national park called Wild Thicket. The Iowa Writers' Workshop visits this place every year to write an annual nature poem— "how thick the thicket / where Brer Rabbit lies." There are no Sierra Club–type articles called "Hiking Across Iowa."

I spent a number of days wandering around Nebraska. At one point, the January head wind was so strong my car seemed to hold in one place, a land Cessna passed by crows. Not incidentally, the sunroof is a splendid vantage for the roadside bird watcher, just as in Kenya and Tanzania; birds, especially hawks, and coyotes are less disturbed if you stay in the car. Near the Wyoming border I was able to study at close range a golden eagle on a fence post and, one morning just after dawn, a big coyote with a blood-wet muzzle settling down for a stint of car watching. We exchanged deeply meaningless glances, the same as one does with a porpoise at sea. Much of the Great Plains will return to being a sea of grass when we stop overproducing beef, and when the Bureau of Land Management decides to stop disastrous overgrazing. The Sandhills themselves, an area of some 150 by 100 miles between Broken Bow and Alliance, Merriman and Lemoyne, will be largely abandoned by agriculture because they share the same diminishing Ogallala aquifer as Houston, Texas, far to the south.

Without question the best place to begin exploring Nebraska is the Stuhr Museum of the Prairie Pioneer, in Grand Island. I spent a full day there and will return this summer to finish my research. It isn't a place readily admired by yuppie nitwits, but it will deeply satisfy anyone with an interest in how we used to live and, consequently, why we live the way we do now. I was mostly studying the lay of the land, the windbreaks and shelterbelts, the possible soul history of the Dismal, the Middle Loup, and the Niobrara rivers. I am reminded that these concerns are not everyone's and shouldn't be. I'd like New York better if I could see it with the spirit of George and Ira Gershwin. I imagine if I lived out here, I would have to take R and R in Omaha every few months. For inscrutable reasons, there are some very good Chinese restaurants in Omaha.

One evening up near Whitman I had an urge to frighten myself. The moon was nearly full, and I had stopped along the creek bed after a large bird had swooped across the road. I was sure it was a great horned owl, so I walked up the creek bed in the direction the owl had taken. I circled up and over a hill with the air icy and metallic and the moon visibly moving as I walked. Far off I could see a small herd of ghost buffalo, though they were probably cattle. Now I could hear the owl from the creek bed, and he showed his lack of curiosity about me by staying there. I felt fine and undramatic, though a little lightheaded. Unlike the train I heard in the middle distance, I could make a right turn and do something different.

And I continued doing so. I woke up in the morning in Alliance after the kangaroo country hop and watched the news on CNN, which was dismal, unlike the Dismal River. I had finished my research in Nebraska and felt it was an even bet that I'd end up living there, because I like to live at the end of the road. Despite the fact that it was zero outside—the car gives the handy exterior temperature—I spread the map against the steering wheel while listening to Aretha Franklin sing "Spanish Harlem." I would hook a left outside of Alliance and reach Colorado Springs in time to watch the Super Bowl. Then on south through Taos, where my Zen master, Kobun Chino Sensei, owned a blue 1984 Subaru four-wheel drive. He liked my turbo but was no help on the unruly trip computer, which he gazed at serenely. Then south to Tucson and Patagonia for a week, turning left to drive three days to Point Clear, Alabama, for sailing on Mobile Bay and quail hunting in Baldwin County with my friend Tom McGuane. Another left turn and it was north toward home with a day's stop in Oxford, Mississippi, to visit Rowan Oak, the home of my dead mentor, William Faulkner.

I liked being home for the first forty-eight hours; then the urge to drive returned. May seemed like a good possibility. A little green would be a nice alternative to black trees, white snow, the brown frozen prairie grass. I would call Lincoln, Nebraska, and get a set of county maps and log a couple of thousand miles on gravel roads. Maybe rig some foot pedals so that I could steer while standing through the sunroof of my motorized prairie schooner.

Suddenly I have decided to admit that I came within a few inches of losing the car on a two-track in Arivaca Canyon in Arizona. As the car slid toward the precipice on the frost-slick dirt, I undid the seat belt and opened the door, under the assumption that a car is easier to replace than a novelist. Perhaps I'll order another Subaru this summer, if only because the car is foolproof.

1986

Going Places

Everyone remembers those kindergarten or first-grade jigsaw puzzles of the forty-eight states, not including Hawaii or Alaska, which weren't states when I was a child and perhaps for that reason are permanently beyond my sphere of interest. I'm not at all sure at what age a child begins to comprehend the abstractions of maps—Arthur Rimbaud's line about the "child crazed with maps" strikes home. Contiguous states in the puzzle were of different colors, establishing the notion that states are more different from one another than they really are. The world grows larger with the child's mind, but each new step doesn't abolish the previous steps, so it's not much more than a big child who finally gets a driver's license, certainly equivalent to losing your virginity in the list of life's prime events.

It is at this point the pathology enters; out of a hundred drivers the great majority find cars pleasant enough, and some will be obsessed with them in mechanical terms, but two or three out of the hundred will be obsessed with going places, pure and simple, for the sake of movement, anywhere and practically anytime.

"You haven't been anywhere until you've taken Route 2 through the Sandhills of Nebraska," they're liable to say, late at night.

"Or Route 191 in Montana, 35 in Wisconsin, 90 in West Texas, 28 in the Upper Peninsula of Michigan, 120 in Wyoming, 62 in Arkansas, 83 in Kansas, 14 in Louisiana," I reply, after agreeing that 2 in Nebraska is one of my favorites. To handle Route 2 properly, you should first give a few hours to the Stuhr Museum in Grand Island to check on the human and natural history of the Great Plains. If you don't care all that much about what you're seeing, you should stay home, or if you're just trying to get someplace, take a plane.

There is, of course, a hesitation to make any rules for the road; the main reason you're out there is to escape any confinement other than that of change and motion. But certain precepts and theories should be kept in mind:

Don't compute time and distance. Computing time and distance vitiates the benefits to be gotten from aimlessness. Leave that sort of thing to civilians with their specious categories of birthdays, average wage, height and weight, the number of steps to second floors. If you get into this acquisitive mood, make two ninety-degree turns and backtrack for a while. Or stop the car and run around in a big circle in a field. Climbing a tree or going swimming also helps. Remember that habit is a form of gravity that strangulates.

Leave your reason, your logic, at home. A few years ago I flew all the way from northern Michigan to Palm Beach, Florida, in order to drive to Livingston, Montana, with a friend. Earlier in life I hitchhiked 4,000 miles round-trip to see the Pacific Ocean. Last year I needed to do some research in Nebraska. Good sense and the fact that it was January told me to drive south, then west by way of Chicago, spend a few days, and drive home. Instead I headed due north into a blizzard and made a three-day back-road circle to La Crosse, Wisconsin, one of my favorite hideouts. When I finished in Nebraska, I went to Wyoming, pulled a left for Colorado and New Mexico, a right for Arizona, headed east across Texas and Louisiana to Alabama, then north toward home. My spirit was lightened by the thirty-five days and 8,000 or so miles. The car was a loaner, and on deserted back roads I could drive on cruise control, standing on the seat with shoulders and head through the sunroof.

Spend as little time as possible thinking about the equipment. Assuming you are not a mechanic, and even if you are, it's better not to think too much about the car over and above minimum service details. I've had a succession of three four-wheel-drive Subaru station wagons, each equipped with a power winch, although recently I've had doubts about this auto. I like to take the car as far as I can go up a two-track, then get out and walk until the road disappears. This is the only solution to the neurotic pang that you might be missing something. High-performance cars don't have the clearance for back roads, and orthodox four-wheel drives are too jouncy for long trips. An ideal car might be a Saab turbo four-wheel-drive station wagon, but it has not as yet been built by that dour land without sunshine and garlic. A Range Rover is a pleasant, albeit expensive, idea, but you could very well find yourself a thousand miles from a spare part.

A little research during downtime helps. This is the place for the lost art of reading. The sort of driving I'm talking about is a religious impulse, a craving for the unknown. You can, however, add to any trip immeasurably by knowing something about the history of the area or location. For instance, if you're driving through Chadron, Nebraska, on Route 20, it doesn't hurt to know that Crazy Horse, He Dog, American Horse, Little Big Man, and Sitting Bull took the same route when it was still a buffalo path.

Be careful about who you are with. Whiners aren't appropriate. There can be tremendous inconveniences and long stretches of boredom. It takes a specific amount of optimism to be on the road, and anything less means misery. A nominal Buddhist who knows that "the goal is the path" is at an advantage. The essential silence of the highway can allow couples to turn the road into a domestic mudbath by letting their petty grievances preoccupy them. Marriages survive by garden-variety etiquette, and when my wife and I travel together we forget the often suffocating flotsam and jetsam of marriage.

If you're driving solo, another enemy can be the radio or tape deck. This is an eccentric observation, but anyone under fifty in America has likely dissipated a goodly share of his life listening to music. Music frequently draws you out of where you belong. It is hard work to be attentive, but it's the only game in town. D. H. Lawrence said that "the only true aristocracy is consciousness," which doesn't mean you can't listen to music; just don't do it all the time. Make your own road tapes: start with cuts of Del Shannon, Merle Haggard, Stravinsky, Aretha Franklin, Bob Seger, Mozart, Buffett, Monteverdi, Woody Guthrie, Jim Reeves, B. B. King, George Jones, Esther Lammandier, Ray Charles, Bob Wills, and Nicholas Thorne. That sort of thing.

If you're lucky, you can find a perfect companion. During a time of mutual stress I drove around Arizona with the grizzly bear expert Douglas Peacock, who knows every piece of flora, fauna, and Native American history in that state. In such company, the most unassertive mesa becomes verdant with possibility.

Pretend you don't care about good food. This is intensely difficult if you are a professional pig, gourmand, and trencherman like I am. If you're going to drive around America you have to adopt the bliss-ninny notion that less is more. Pack a cooler full of disgusting health snacks. I am assuming you know enough to stay off the interstates with their sneeze shields and rainbow jellos, the dinner specials that include the legendary "fried, fried," a substantial meal spun out of hot fat by the deep-fry cook. It could be anything from a shoe box full of oxygen to a cow plot to a dime-store wig. In honor of my own precepts I have given up routing designed to hit my favorite restaurants in Escanaba, Duluth, St. Cloud (Ivan's in the Park), Mandan, Miles City, and so on. The quasi-food revolution hasn't hit the countryside; I've had good luck calling disc jockeys for advice. You generally do much better in the South, particularly at barbecue places with hand-painted road signs. Along with food you might also consider amusements: If you stop at local bars or American Legion country dances don't offer underage girls hard drugs and that sort of thing. But unless you're a total asshole, *Easy Rider* paranoia is unwarranted. You are technically safer on the road than you are in your own bathroom or eating a dinner of unrecognizable leftovers with your mother.

Avoid irony, cynicism, and self-judgement. If you were really smart, you probably wouldn't be doing this. You would be in an office or club acting nifty, but you're in a car and no one knows you, and no one calls you because they don't know where you are. Moving targets are hard to hit. You are doing what you want, rather than what someone else wants. This is not the time to examine your shortcomings, which will certainly surface when you get home. Your spiritual fathers range from Marco Polo to Arthur Rimbaud, from Richard Halliburton to Jack Kerouac. Kerouac was the first actual novelist I ever met, back in 1957 or 1958 at the Five Spot, a jazz club in New York City. I saw him several times, and this great soul did not swell on self-criticism, though, of course, there is an obvious downside to this behavior.

Do not scorn day trips. You can use them to avoid nervous collapse. They are akin to the ardent sailor and his small sailboat. You needn't travel very far unless you live in one of our major urban centers, strewn across the land like immense canker sores. Outside this sort of urban concentration, county maps are available at any courthouse. One summer in Michigan's Upper Peninsula, after a tour in Hollywood had driven me ditzy, I logged more than 5,000 miles in four counties on gravel roads and two-tracks, lifting my sodden spirits and looking for good grouse and woodcock cover (game birds literally prefer to live in their restaurants, their prime feeding areas). This also served to keep me out of bars and away from drinking, because I don't drink while driving.

Plan a real big one—perhaps hemispheric, or at least national. Atrophy is the problem. If you're not expanding, you're growing smaller. As a poet and novelist I have to get out of the study and collect some brand-new memories, and many of our more memorable events are of the childish, the daffy and irrational. "How do you know but that every bird that cuts the airy way is an immense world of delight closed to your senses five?" asked Blake. If you're currently trapped, your best move is to imagine the next road voyage.

I'm planning a trip when I finish my current novel, for which I had to make an intense study of the years 1865 to 1900 in our history, also the history of Native Americans. I intend to check out locations where I sensed a particular magic in the past: certain culverts in western Minnesota, nondescript gullies in Kansas, invisible graveyards in New Mexico, moonbeam targets in Nebraska, buffalo jumps in Montana, melted ice palaces in the Dakotas, deserted but well-stocked wine warehouses in California. Maybe I'll discover a new bird or animal. Maybe I'll drive up a gravel road that winnows into a two-track that stops at an immense swale, in the center of which is a dense woodlot. I'll wade through the bog into the woods, where I'll find an old, gray farmhouse. In this farmhouse I'll find all my beloved dead dogs and cats in perfect health, tended by the heroines in my novels. I'll make a map of this trip on thin buckskin that I'll gradually cut up and add to stews. Everyone must find their own places.

1987

Don't Fence Me In

You must picture two middle-aged men in the Best Western Inn parking lot on a hot July evening in Des Moines. (Best Westerns are scarcely elegant, but they make up for it by being ubiquitous and also nonuniform, unlike the other chains.) My friend, whom I'll refer to as Teacher, and who for twenty years has tried to keep me connected with reality, flips a coin between the 8th Street Seafood Bar & Grill and Jimmy's American Café. A rare sense of choice is in the air. Fish wins tonight, though we will hit Jimmy's on the return. I order everything laden with garlic and drink two bottles of fine white wine to fight the heat. When you're heading out at dawn for the backcountry of Nebraska, South Dakota, and Montana, it's best to load up on fresh garlic, which civilized people regard as a vegetable rather than an herb. At the outset you must accept the fact that the northern Midwest and points west provide the kind of dining that only a Muscovite could adore.

It's a tad eccentric, but I would choose a place like Des Moines, Iowa, to begin. I suggest this in order to experience the transition from the immensely fertile heartland to the prairies and to the Great Plains. You will also own the cachet of being the only one you know who is starting a vacation in Des Moines. The state of Iowa, and to a greater extent Nebraska, are the only states that actually remind you of what America thinks she is like.

We are in a new four-wheel drive which is clearly the ultimate touring car for road comfort coupled with rough-country accessibility. It is packed tight with camping equipment and emergency gear, including an espresso machine that works off the cigarette lighter. One of the gravest problems when traveling away from our dream coasts is getting a cup of coffee in which you can't see a dime on the bottom. We've planned our trip around a dawdling pace, making the drive to Jordan—the epicenter of the Big

Open—in a graceful three days, to be followed by three days in the area, plus visits elsewhere in Montana, and three days home. In many respects Montana is the most worthy of our least traveled states, so after the Big Open you could profitably drive around Montana for several weeks, depending on the length of your vacation.

Why drive? Because short of walking it's the only way to really see the country, which anyway is not serviced by readily available airports. If you fly a great deal, which many of us do, you forget that flying is a tyranny with despotic capitals known as airports, allowing you little more freedom than a feeder calf or a school sardine. Those who spend their time east of the Mississippi also forget that driving can be a pleasure when there's no traffic to speak of. We were leaving on the Fourth of July weekend, the supposed height of the tourist season, and on many of the paved roads of our route I clocked only three or four cars per hour.

This sort of driving can be a fabulous restorative. Unlike in an airplane, you can stop, turn right or left, on a whim. Driving into emptiness keeps you at least a few miles ahead of your neuroses, and by the time they catch up to you when you bed down in the evening, you are too tired to pay any attention to them. This past year I had a great deal of leisure time, so I drove 42,000 miles around the United States, avoiding the interstates whenever possible. Driving offers peace, solitude, inaccessibility, and the freedom and adventure that allow me to think up new novels and rest from the last one. Your whimsicality returns; you've already driven to Arizona—why not continue on down to San Carlos, Mexico and hike out the Seri Indian territory on the coast of the Sea of Cortés? And there, camped out on a mountain ridge under a glorious full moon, you throw the wrong kind of porous log on the fire and then dance a new tune as a dozen angry scorpions shoot out, a fresh brand of reality pudding. The trip was a mere seven thousand miles but without a single moment of boredom, the brain once again rippling like a smooth underground river.

It is important to get up at dawn without benefit of the newspaper or a peek at CNN. Head west on I-80, taking the Omaha bypass and crossing the Missouri to Nebraska Route 75, where you turn north. Outside Sioux City you head west on Route 12. Now you're entering wonderful country, with the rolling prairie stretched endlessly out before you, a dulcet greenish brown folding in on itself, surely a sea of grass.

On a bluff outside the village of Niobrara you can see the confluence of the Niobrara River and the Missouri, with the feeder stream's braided path mixing its beige water with the Missouri's green tide. The state of Nebraska has built some new rental cabins on the breathtaking site, and I make a note to spend a November week here with my bird dogs, hunting and river-staring. Lewis and Clark also liked this spot.

A few hours down Route 12 the land grows even emptier. I carry along Van Bruggen's *Wildflowers, Grasses and Other Plants of the Northern Plains and Black Hills*, several bird books, *Nebraskaland Magazine*, and the dozen volumes in the Montana Geographic Series, in addition to Thomas Mails's *The Mystic Warriors of the Plains* and Carl Waldman's *Atlas of the North American Indian*. Knowledge informs, gives shape to scenery, whether it's the names of birds or flora, or that you know the Sauk prophet Black Hawk was there before Iowa's cornfields drowned the landscape, or that Route 12 belonged to the Ponca and Pawnee and, farther west, to the Santee Sioux, who tended to wander. It's a melancholy thought indeed that General Philip Sheridan said that to destroy the Sioux you must destroy his commissary, the buffalo: "Only then will the great prairies be safe for the speckled cattle and festive cowboy." It is somehow unimaginable that we slew eighty million of these great beasts out of greed and stupidity.

Farther down the road is the cow town of Valentine, the county seat of Cherry County, which is ten thousand square miles, twice the size of Connecticut, with barely over seven thousand people. I'm hesitant to mention Cherry County, as it's one of my favorite places on earth, but it is also safely remote. Southwest of Valentine is the Samuel R. McKelvie National Forest, which doesn't own all that many trees but is nonetheless grand. We stopped along the road to look at a few rattlesnakes, then at an eastern hognose snake, which likes to pretend it is a rattler. On being prodded, the hognose flops over and affects death—a splendid tactic during war and bar fights. Just east of Valentine is the Fort Niobrara National Wildlife Refuge, where we watched two bull buffalo having a thunderous argument through a fence. Other spectators were a group of bored female buffalo, a red-tailed hawk on a fence post, and several quizzical antelope. At dusk we recrossed the Niobrara, which, near Valentine, is as luminous, sparkling, and clear as an eastern trout stream.

At either dawn or evening on the prairie or the Great Plains you understand the quality of light as you do in East Africa. What might be a dullish, flammable vista in the midday July sun becomes vibrant, so that the land seems to roll in shadows toward the eye.

That second evening out, in the motel in Valentine, a few sore points tried to emerge, the first under the heading of "gizmo guilt." Why were we in a motel with a car choked with camping gear? It is more fun to buy equipment than to use it. The Teacher wisely suggested we could drag the gear behind the car for a mile on a dirt road so our wives would think we used it. A brilliant idea, I thought. It was a hot night and, unlike the natural world, the motel room was air-conditioned and held none of the plump rattlers we noted along the road. Our cots were only two feet high and my sleeping hand might have dropped to the ground smack dab on a rabid bull rattler. The newly discovered immediate cure was to use jumper cables and administer electric shock to the bitten area. I could imagine the singed flesh and shower of sparks on a moonless night. No thank you. Perhaps five-foot-high cots were available.

I had become bored with Art and People, cities and politics, and was obsessed with emptiness, and Valentine was one of the centers of this obsession. The indigenous grasses we stared at, from little bluestem, Indiangrass, switchgrass, prairie sandreed, and sand lovegrass, to hairy gramma and blowout penstemon—a wildflower—had become more interesting to me than New York City. A single meadowlark beat out Los Angeles, and two young antelope playing twilight tag held a solace not found on recent bookstore trips.

The next day there was an obligatory stop at the site of Wounded Knee, northeast of Pine Ridge in South Dakota. A genuflection was in order, also the questions to an unknown god of how we could have done such a thing, and are we still capable of doing so?

We felt an emotional crunch back on the interstate (interstates tend to resemble the banality of television) near Rapid City, though we used it only for the thirty miles to Sturgis. I had recently read the galleys of Dan O'Brien's *The Rites of Autumn*, the story of how he made a four-month trip from Montana to Texas teaching an orphaned peregrine falcon how to hunt. I wanted to meet the bird in question, and when I approached her large cage, Dolly let out a threatening shriek that redefined my notion of the feral as does a grizzly bear. I felt the sound up and down my backbone. I looked off in the near distance at Bear Butte, a mountain sacred to the Sioux, and thought of Rilke's verse: "With all its eyes the creature world beholds the open."

Up past Belle Fourche on Route 212 we found new dimensions to emptiness, turning north on 323 at Alzada on the gravel road that leads to Ekalaka, the county seat of Carter County, and the only county seat I know of whose main approach in one direction is a gravel road. Ekalaka has a wonderful museum with a collection of dinosaur bones rivaling those of the great museums of the East. The bones are local and were gathered by the high-school science teacher, Marshall Lambert.

Now we were nearing Miles City, the cow capital of Montana, and the Big Open itself, about which definitions vary. In your *Rand McNally* you might draw a vertical line between the Fort Peck Reservoir (the overdammed Missouri) and Miles City, and a horizontal between Winnett and Brockway. This is a little limiting, as the drive between Lewistown (a wonderful place) and Sidney is five hours, and the largest town of the first three-hours' drive is Jordan, with a population of 485. The stretch between Winnett and Brockway is an absolutely empty 130 miles, except for Jordan. I realize this is not everyone's cup of tea, but I draw enormous solace from this expanse. Those who think of the area as desolate are ignorant of earth herself. The redoubtable state senator from Jordan, Cecil Weeding, sent out a campaign brochure that said, "We don't have people standing at our elbow everyplace we go. We've learned to fend for ourselves and enjoy the solitude isolation brings. Crime isn't even a real problem . . . neither are crowds . . . gouging . . . pushing . . . shoving." This is a reflection from Garfield County, with nearly 3 million acres and a population of 1800.

Early the next morning (we had a choice of 5 A.M. and 7 A.M., before or after his morning chores; we chose the latter) we met with Art Larson, who ranches south of Cohagen (population twelve) with his wife, Nancy, and son, Carl. The Larsons ranch about thirty sections (a section is 640 acres) of their own and an additional forty in partnership. Art, a third-generation Swede, is the owner of the property and possesses all the misunderstood characteristics of the cattle-bound Westerner: laconic, shy, almost absurdly independent, loathes government control, loves horses, and is deeply suspicious of sheep ranchers and wheat farmers. I was a little startled to learn that Nancy had been a member of the San Antonio Symphony and reads the outlandish novels of Tom McGuane, who had initiated this introduction, and that their son was off at a rock concert in Billings. After half a day with them I had a distinct feeling that here was a life being lived well.

We spoke of the violent windstorm of the evening before, during our first night in Jordan. The Teacher and I had been dining in the QD Cafe there when a cowboy ran in and hollered he had "outdrove a storm down the creek bed." Then the building began to shudder and garbage cans flew across the parking lot, where cars and cattle trucks wobbled in the wind. Everyone in the café was silent, waiting for the rain that might abate the drought, one of the worst since the 1930s, but no rain came. After dinner (a fine rib steak) we drove into the nothingness as the wind subsided a tad. The air was pink from the dust against the setting sun, and great bolts of lightning drove earthward in the black sky to the south. It was so Wagnerian that the Teacher slipped a Wagner tape into the car deck.

Art and Nancy looked a little tired, and we learned that those selfsame *Gotterdammerung* lightning strokes had kept them and their neighbors up all night fighting range fires. Despite his fatigue, Art drove us around the ranch checking the windmill-driven water wells. The ranch feeds eighteen hundred yearling cattle, which are driven, as in the old days, down to Miles City in the fall. After checking the water tank, we looked over a herd of cutting horses that the family breeds, raises, and trains. Cutting horses are an elegant hobby indulged in by solvent ranchers, and for many of them the contests provide their major social occasions.

It is a comfort to the Larsons that there are only two neighbors within twenty miles, and then the next is fifty miles to the west. There is also a mildly grim note in that near the turn of the century, soon after Art's grandfather arrived, the countryside was covered with homesteaders. The average rainfall in the area is between twelve and thirteen inches, but averages reflect a thirty-five-year cycle and, as such, can be—and are—killing statistics. You might get a few years of twenty inches followed by half a dozen years of half a dozen inches, at which point the final homesteaders would leave by the thousands, which they did in the Great Depression. As in western Nebraska and Kansas in the 1870s and 1880s, the railroads and their robber barons, the dominant force in homestead expansion, tended to fib about the amount of rainfall past the ninety-eighth meridian. Even now, Deborah and Frank Popper, of the Rutgers University geography and urban studies departments, respectively, have predicted that economics and climate will force most of the region—especially its most rural areas, including much of the western Dakotas—to return to its native state.

Incidentally, there is a specific etiquette that should be followed in visiting remote places. You don't ask, "How could you live here?" which implicitly questions the value of someone's entire life. There's an amusing sign in the café-store-bar in the tiny village of Shell, Wyoming: "Welcome to Wyoming. Frankly, I don't give a —— how you do it back home."

Art sent us off on back roads to Ingomar to have a bowl of beans at a bar called Jersey Lilly's. This added a mere 150 miles to a round-trip back to Jordan. We saw great numbers of antelope and the rare, brief sight of a songbird astride a flying hawk's back, pecking away in foolhardy rage. We swerved off the road, thinking we saw a yellow balloon with a basket of passengers, but it was a golden globe of tumbleweed a few hundred feet up, catching the sun and drifting along in the wind currents.

Ingomar turned out to be a near ghost town and the bar the only functioning business. There were rails out front where you could tether your horse, and two footloose lambs gave us a hard look. We had a good bowl of spicy pinto beans with the proprietor of Jersey Lilly's, Billy "the Horseman" Seward, a prominent lightweight boxer of the late thirties and early forties. World War II saved Billy from becoming punchy, and he runs his unintentionally period-piece bar and café with verve. We looked at his boxing scrapbooks, and I noted a photo of a ballerina from Chicago that he didn't care to talk about. For a moment I was back inside a novel, some western version of Sherwood Anderson. I asked about a sign advertising the Ingomar Rodeo and Fondue Party. The idea was that you had a big scalding potful of boiling oil and folks stuck chunks of beef in on pitchforks so they could cook it to taste. Sauces were also provided.

On the long way back to the Garfield Motel, the Teacher mentioned that at our current rate of expenditure a month in the Big Open would cost far less than our four days in April in New York City. I agreed with pleasure, though a great deal can be said for room-service breakfasts at the Carlyle, lunch at Lutèce, and the simple fact, at this point, that I would pay a cool fifty bucks for a slice of pizza from Ray's.

Before dinner at the QD (the only game in town, but quite pleasant) I stopped at Jordan's two saloons, because I like taverns and, not incidentally,

I like a few drinks. How can you experience the rich fabric of life in a locale without visiting bars? The answer is, you can't. On this particular evening I wangled invitations to bird hunt on a couple of ranches. This wasn't difficult, as reasonably behaved strangers are met with curiosity and friendliness in Jordan. Then I met a peculiar lout, a stranger from Bozeman, who bragged that he had shot 2,200 gophers that summer and was aiming for the "record" of 4,700. He wasn't amused when I asked him how he cooked the critters. Did he lie? I get to ask such questions because I am not a shy, retiring shrimp of a fellow. The air was cleared when the Teacher came into the saloon to fetch me for dinner.

On this trip I chose not to visit the Charles M. Russell National Wildlife Refuge, which encircles Fort Peck Reservoir. I made this decision because I did not want to rub my nose in another piece of nasty government business—some years ago two thousand antelope starved to death here because over half the forage was consumed by cattle. The Bureau of Land Management administered a program by which refuge land was rented to ranchers, so that the very name "refuge" is a phony sop offered to environmentalists. This Bureau of Land Management mess is scarcely unique to the area (read James Conaway's *Kingdom in the Country*). On a recent trip into the Cimarron National Grasslands in southwest Kansas, I was struck by the utterly barren junkiness of the area. Over the years any number of my questions have been met by the usual bureaucratic condescension, at which point I like to answer that as a seventh-generation farmer I'm quite able to recognize raped and barren land without being chided by a nitwit slobbering at the public trough. It's probably not very amazing that the worst stewards of the land are not the so-called greedy ranchers but our careless, sprawling government itself.

That last evening we drove back north of Jordan for a stroll. A lovely girl in a mauve shirt was riding a horse across a limitless pasture in the twilight. Beyond her in the darkening landscape two coyotes were calling out to each other. It was a scene of unpardonable beauty, and as far away from everything I don't like as I could possibly get. It is there, and free for the looking if you can handle the driving. The Buddhists like to say, "The path is the way," and that is the proper mood for this trip. You can sing "Home on the

Range" at the antelope, hawks, meadowlarks, rattlers, and sharp-tailed grouse, and no one will care. And you won't have to go shopping, because there are no shops. It is the grandeur and mystery of a land in which we have only been slightly involved.

1989

LITERARY MATTERS

*Such a price the gods exact
for song, to become what we sing.*

JOHANN WOLFGANG VON GOETHE

A Natural History of Some Poems

A cage went in search of a bird.
—FRANZ KAFKA

Some lofty concepts, like space and number, involve truths remote from the category
of causation; and here we must be content, as Aristotle says, if the mere facts be
known. But natural history deals with ephemeral and accidental, not eternal or uni-
versal things; their causes and effects thrust themselves on our curiosity, and become
the ultimate relations to which our contemplation extends.
—D'ARCY W. THOMPSON

The only reason for writing a paper with the violently personal flavor of what follows is that a close inquiry into the processes of the composition of a poem by the poet himself might possibly lend to a more accurate understanding of poetry. The very real objection that anyone might have is that of honesty; papers of this sort have always had an air of the unreal to me—the temptation to pose for the picture, to exaggerate, to minimize unpleasant or embarrassing aspects, is great. The motive, the impulse in the artist to create a true harmony out of chaos does not cease when he is twice removed, or cornered by a haberdasher's three-sided mirror; the desire to be presented in a graceful literary focus generally makes him a questionable critic. I have, therefore, tried to maintain a deliberately clinical atmosphere; these are laboratory notes written by a white rat who has been mauled, forced to run warrens, prodded, shocked, and rewarded. The experience is still intense and fresh enough in mind, I think, to be closely and accurately described.

SKETCH FOR A JOB APPLICATION BLANK

My left eye is blind and jogs like
a milky sparrow in its socket;
my nose is large and never flares
in anger, the front teeth, bucked,
but not in lechery—I sucked
my thumb until the age of twelve.
O my youth was happy and I was never lonely
though my friends called me "pig eye"
and the teachers thought me loony.

    (When I bruised, my psyche kept intact:
    I fell from horses, and once a cow but never
    pigs—a neighbor lost a hand to a sow.)

But I had some fears:
the salesman of eyes,
his case was full of fishy baubles,
against black velvet, jeweled gore,
the great cocked hoof of a Belgian mare,
a nest of milk snakes by the water trough,
electric fences,
my uncle's hounds,
the pump arm of an oil well,
the chop and whirr of a combine in the sun.

From my ancestors, the Swedes,
I suppose I inherit the love of rainy woods,
kegs of herring and neat whiskey—
I remember long nights of pinochle,
the bulge of Redman in my grandpa's cheek;
the rug smelled of manure and kerosene.
They laughed loudly and didn't speak for days.

    (But on the other side, from the German Mennonites,
    their rag smoke prayers and porky daughters
    I got intolerance, an aimless diligence.)

In '51 during a revival I was saved:
I prayed on a cold register for hours

and woke up lame. I was baptized
by immersion in the tank at Williamston—
the rusty water stung my eyes.
I left off the old things of the flesh
but not for long—one night beside a pond
she dried my feet with her yellow hair.
      O actual event dead quotient
      cross become green
I still love Jubal but pity Hagar.

    (Now self is the first sacrament
    who loves not the misery and taint
    of the present tense is lost.
    I strain for a lunar arrogance.
        Light macerates
        the lamp infects
  warmth, more warmth, I cry.)

I think it was in 1960 that I first read the poems of Pablo Neruda. The discovery of a "master," of a poet of the first magnitude, is of extreme importance to a young poet—one finds his own voice finally through the
voices of others. It is a process of choosing, gradually undergoing the influence by study, and discarding the disagreeable elements. At the time I
was visiting New York City and was nearly anesthetized by its very familiar
bleakness. Every section of the city seemed to conceal some unpleasant
memory. I was impressed with Neruda's green world, his primary colors
and surrealist imagery—he seemed a christ of all fleshy things speaking in
the "out-loud" speech of the tribe. I immediately began writing a poem to
him but then, as with all of my poems of that period, I abandoned it. I realized that the poem was an intellectual exercise, an act of worship, idolatry.
Whitman's introduction to *Leaves of Grass* had made me very sensitive to
derivative art—to this day I cannot bring myself to write about a painting
or a statue or another's poem though I often have an impulse to do so.

The poem thus went underground, to be exhumed years later in Boston
during a similar period of crisis. I had been unemployed and generally at the
end of my tether for a year. My daily life had become a round of employ-

ment offices, interviews with personnel people who seemed to sense instantly that I was unsuitable, flatly unemployable. My jacket pocket was filled with application blanks for all manner of work—I seemed unable to get past my name and social security number. I was sitting on a bench on Boston Common before an appointment, wondering what someone like Neruda would answer to "biographical information and other pertinent details," when I remembered the poem. When I got back to my brother's apartment that evening—I was separated from my family—I looked through my manuscripts, all incomplete, and found the poem to Neruda. I immediately realized that rather than Neruda I had been attempting to write a poem in praise of myself—to describe what, if any, were my "pertinent details." The poem, regardless of its weaknesses, precipitated an explosion of work. I stopped worrying about being unemployable and finished, in addition to the "Sketch," thirteen poems within a month. Though some of the thirteen proved to be worthless, up until that time I had never finished a poem that was acceptable to me even in a minimal sense. I suppose I am fond of it for this reason—it made me able to function as a poet for the first time, to insist on the act of poetry as perhaps my only viable ability, to construct a complete poem, however short and clumsy.

The true matter of "Sketch" is a conscious refusal of a tradition, a rejection of what we seem to see as the "role" of a poet in a capitalist society: the poet as an economic leech, rheumy-eyed, full of vapors, a sycophant, fond of the idea of nobility and the company of the moneyed classes, vaguely elegant though threadbare, preoccupied with his ancestry, and in the United States an Eastern Seaboard education. Though I wasn't taken by Neruda's politics—he is a member of the Communist Party in Chile—I found nothing in his work to suggest the glazed decadence of most modern poets. For years I had admired and studied Yeats, Eliot, Pound, Wallace Stevens and Hart Crane—it is impossible for an American poet to reach technical maturity without reading them; but they are so mauve-tinged and seemed unable to offer any help for the life that runs counter to a young man's art. My family background was essentially Populist and it was impossible for me to become comfortably absorbed in their concerns. I was, after all, from Michigan, my youth spent in a small town in a rural area where my father was an agricultural agent. The poem's strident attitude was more in rejection of other attitudes than something that would become a fixed characteristic of my work.

DAVID

He is young. The father is dead.
Outside, a cold November night,
the mourner's cars are parked upon the lawn;
beneath the porch light three
brothers talk to three sons
and shiver without knowing it.
His mind's all black thickets
and blood; he knows
flesh slips quietly off the bone,
he knows no last looks,
that among the profusion of flowers
the lid is closed to hide
what no one could bear—
that metal rends the flesh,
he knows beneath the white pointed
creatures, stars,
that in the distant talk of brothers,
the father is dead.

"David" illustrates another aspect of the autobiographical poem; speaking through a "persona" to insure aesthetic distance. I was unable to say anything about the death of my father directly that wasn't benumbed, cloudy, constricted. When the poem finally began to "happen" it took shape through the eyes of my younger brother. Though this wasn't a conscious choice, it proved to handle the experience in a much more valid, less literary manner. This same process, even further removed, took place in the third part of "A Sequence of Women."

The girl who was once my mistress
is dead now, I learn, in childbirth.
I thought that long ago women ceased
dying this way.

To set records straight, our enmity
relaxes, I wrote a verse for her—
to dole her by pieces, ring finger
and lock of hair.

But I'm a poor Midas to turn her golden,
make a Helen, grand whore, of this graceless
girl; the sparrow that died was only
a sparrow:

Though in the dark, she doesn't sleep.
On cushions, embraced by silk, no lover
comes to her. In the first light when birds
stir she does not stir or sing. O eyes can't
focus to this dark.

Here the "lie" was doubly removed, hiding behind the artifice of modified sapphics and a "mistress" while the true subject was the death of my sister. Though this poem required a great deal of care and close attention I didn't consciously realize it was about my sister until it was finished.

While I realize that all of my poems are at least nominally autobiographical, containing events or visual images drawn from life, the above three poems show distinctly different aspects of the use of autobiography. The unanswered question is why a poet transforms experience, not so much to make it understandable, but to make it yield its aesthetic possibilities.

"What is"
hisses like a serpent
and writhes
to shed its skin.
ROBERT DUNCAN

A poet needs primarily an extreme vulnerability to his psychic moods—his trade is his "selfness." I think that the dangerous aspects of this vulnerability quite clearly illustrate the basic steps of the creative process. Earlier in my life—between the ages of eighteen and twenty-four—I had a tendency to hallucinate during periods of stress. Though I recognized later that to hallucinate is at the very least clinical, I don't remember being disturbed at the time; I was interested in being a poet and anything my mind cared to do fascinated me, especially if it seemed gratuitous like a hallucination. Here are a few of them in capsule form:

" 'Tis the good

reader that

makes the

good book. "

-Ralph Waldo
Emerson

BOOKS, MUSIC & MORE
amazon.com

More Books.
More Music.
More Fun.

Get what you want.
Find more than 3 million titles – books, CDs, DVDs, and more.

Save up to 40%.
Amazon.com is easy on your budget. Enjoy everyday savings of up to 40%.

Order with 1-Click℠.
Buy with a single click of your mouse using our 1-Click Ordering.

Find your next favorite.
Visit our Recommendation Centers and get personalized recommendations based on your mood, past purchases, and authors and artists you like.

Spread the word.
Did you find something great? Write a customer review and let people know about it.

Amazon.com
The place to search, explore, and discover is just a click away.

Everything is a perfect blackness. There is a small yellow dot in the lower left-hand corner. I move toward the yellow dot until it enlarges into a door. I pass through the door into a large bright yellow room and out through another door into a violently green landscape. Hundreds of animals are drinking milk from a great wooden bowl; wolves, snakes, lions, hyenas, cats, pigs, elephants. I see them individually, down to the small veins in their eyes and their milk-wet muzzles.

I'm walking in a large city at night and it begins to rain. I hurry down a dark alley and into a door. I am in a dimly lighted room. A man stands in the corner holding a baby which he drops to the floor where it breaks like a melon. I look up but the man is gone, then back down but the baby is no longer there. I turn to leave but the door is gone and with it the room. I try to touch myself but I no longer seem to exist.

I am walking toward a stone pile on which several huge snakes are sleeping. As I draw closer the snakes seem to shrink but then I realize I am growing larger. I kick the stone pile away and let myself down into a hole. I sink slowly, noticing the texture of earth on the way down. I pass through gradually lessening stages of red heat then descend from pink to a total whiteness.

Of course even a neophyte Freudian understands the basic processes of fantasy. I don't pretend to be able to interpret the above and I am not interested in doing so. They always occurred in periods of unrest, anxiety, a feeling of being totally out of place; they are visual, metaphorical solutions to the stress. Immediately after any single one of them took place I felt at peace for days; the world became sweet and animate, everything was endowed with personality.

The conception of a poem always has begun with a visual image during this time of unrest. The unrest may have covered a month or so or have been only an hour in duration. The first image is scarcely ever as involved or complete as those mentioned in the hallucinations, but then rarely is the stress ever as violent or clinical. For instance, the writing of this paper made me feel immoderately out of focus. At this juncture in the paper I wrote a brief, first draft of a poem, or what might become a poem after revision:

> too cold for late May, snow flurries,
> warblers tight in their trees, the air
> with winter's clearness, dull clear
> under clouds, clean clear bite
> of cold, silver maple flexing in wind,
> the sky a pale shell, luminous,

> wind rippling petals, ripped from
> flowering crab, pale pink against
> green firs, yellow green leaves,
> sky colorless, pearl cold,
> the body chilled, blood unstirred,
> blood thickened with frost. Body be snake,
> self equal self to ground heat,
> be wind cold, earth heat,
> bend with tree, whip with grass,
> move free clean and bright clear.

The inception of a poem doesn't keep hours; there is always the element of surprise. For a period of time I seemed to get most of my "beginnings" while driving; when I began to carry a notebook in anticipation nothing happened. Then I left the notebook out of the car and pretended, to whom I don't know, that I had no writing materials. But then nothing happened, nor has it since in a car. These may seem like absurd lengths but I've never met a poet who wouldn't go at least this far to be ready for a poem.

Usually I try to set aside a regular time each day for my work and part of this time is spent in "waiting." Most often it is fruitless and I revise other work or write down what prove to be mildly silly notations on art or the world at large. Sometimes I am too frenetic and force the issue, creating a dead, futureless, prosy imitation of a poem. Just as often I generate an air of expectancy, and ideas seem to rush through my head but they are simply ideas. I have described this process in "Exercise" though at the time I failed to realize exactly what I was talking about; the poem was named months after the date of composition:

EXERCISE

> Hear this touch: grass parts
> for the snake,
> in furrows
> soil curves around itself,
> a rock topples into a lake,
> roused organs,
> fur against cloth,
> arms unfold,
> at the edge of a clearing
> fire selects new wood.

One's aesthetic convictions trap the poem. Rather than consciously and rhetorically describing the poem, the subject buried itself and came up in the guise of a snake, soil, splash, sex, rubbing, and then fire.

Another rather simple poem of mine, "Complaint," expresses a different aspect of the process—that of being so weak-minded when the poem does come that you wish it would leave you alone and write itself:

COMPLAINT

Song, I am unused to you—
when you come
your voice is behind trees
calling another by my name.

So little of me comes out to you
I cannot hold your weight—
I bury you in sleep
or pour more wine, or lost in another's
music, I forget that you ever spoke.

If you come again, come with
Elias! Elias! Elias!
If only once the summons were a roar,
a pillar of light,
I would not betray you.

Often there are unpleasant qualities—your brain becomes peopled with the "a-zoological" beasts that Robert Graves spoke of in *The White Goddess*:

SHE

Who is this other
without masks, pitiless?
A bald eye in a dump,
a third rail type who loves
the touch of flesh,
the bare thigh in a cafeteria
crying mercy to the stone?
Unlyric, she coils and strikes
for the sake of striking.

Or as in the last part of "Three Night Songs" there is nothing but the imagination gone amok, when the small god in you hee-haws and thumbs his nose:

> The mask riddles itself,
> there's heat through the eye slits,
> a noise of breathing,
> the plaster around the mouth is wet;
> and the dark takes no effort,
> dark against deeper dark,
> the mask dissembled,
> a music comes to the point of horror.

The joy after the first draft is completed is very acute; there is mental exhaustion but it is similar at times to the suspended, relaxed state one feels after making love. A poem seems to condense the normal evolutionary process infinitely: There is the distressed, nonadaptive state; an unconscious moving into the darkness of the problem or irritant; a gradual surfacing, then immediate righting or balancing by metaphor, as if you tipped a buoy over by force then let it snap upwards; the sense of relief, and the casting and recasting the work into its final form. The last stage "calcifies" or kills the problem and you are open to a repetition of the process, though not necessarily willing. Though this is all rather simplified, it captures, I think, the essence of the process. There must be the understanding of time lapse though—the "gradual surfacing" may take months, the space between the first sketch and final form an even longer period of time.

The most beautiful description of this process I am familiar with was written by García Lorca in his "The Poetic Image in Don Luis de Góngora."

The poet who embarks on the creation of the poem (as I know by experience), begins with the aimless sensation of a hunter about to embark on a night hunt through the remotest of forests. Unaccountable dread stirs in his heart. To reassure himself—and it is well that he do so—he drinks a glass of clear water and inscribes senseless black flourishes with his pen point. I say black because—I say this in strictest confidence—I never use colored inks. Then the poet is off on the chase. Delicate breezes chill the lenses of his eyes. The moon, curved like a horn of soft metal, calls in the silence of the topmost branches. White stags appear in the clearing between the tree trunks. Absolute night withdraws in a curtain of whispers. Water flickers in the reeds, quiet and deep. . . . It is time to depart. It is the moment of risk for the poet. He must take out his map of the terrain into which he will move and remain calm in the presence of the thousand splendors and the thousand hideous masks of the splendid that pass before his eyes. He must stop up his ears like Ulysses before the Sirens and discharge all his arrows at living metaphors, avoiding all that is florid and false in their wake. The moment is hazardous if the poet at this point surrenders; should he do so, the poem would never emerge. The poet must press on to the hunt single-minded and serene, in virtual camouflage. He must stand firm in the presence of illusions and keep wary lookout for the quivering flesh of reality that accords with the shadowy map of the poem that he carries. At times, he will cry out loudly in the poem's solitude, to rout the evil spirits—facile ones who would betray us to popular adulation without order or beauty or aesthetic understanding. . . . It was Paul Valéry, the great French poet, who held that the state of inspiration is not the most advantageous one for the writing of poetry. As I believe in heaven-sent inspiration, I believe that Valéry is on the right track. The inspired state is a state of self-withdrawal, and not of creative dynamism. Conceptual vision must be calmed before it can be clarified. I cannot believe that any great artist works in a fever. Even mystics return to their tasks when the ineffable dove of the Holy Ghost departs from their cells and is lost in the clouds. One returns from the inspired state as one returns from a foreign country. The poem is the legend of the journey. Inspiration furnishes the image, but not the investiture. To clothe it, it is necessary to weigh the quality and sonority of each word, coolly, and without dangerous afflatus.

> *Bad poets imitate; good poets steal.*
> —T. S. ELIOT

I think there are two rather definite kinds of influence, which in turn join to make a third: a direct technical influence, a professional process of acquiring skill by studying the skilled; the influence of the totality of another poet's way of seeing, a moral impression; the rare combination where the poet's content and way of saying both hold radical interest. In the first category—one must remember that there are gradations—I place poets such as Coleridge, Eliot, Pound, Hardy, Wallace Stevens, and to a lesser extent Robert Lowell; I've admired and taken advantage of their skill at using certain stratagems, though "what" they have to say holds little interest for me.

At the other pole, artists like Christopher Smart, Blake, Whitman, Lawrence (the poetry), and among contemporaries, Patrick Kavanaugh and Robert Duncan, have had some effect on me in the moral sense though they lack technical interest. Of course some poets have seemed to me masters in both categories: Homer, Catullus, Chaucer, Villon, Shakespeare, Marlowe, Baudelaire, Rimbaud, Rilke, Yeats, and to a lesser extent, García Lorca, Neruda, Apollinaire, Char, Trakl, Pasternak, and Roethke.

An influence may not be obvious in a poet's work—when it is of a moral nature it rarely is. Influence is like a *bouquet garni* in a stew—without it the flavor would be bland and probably boring, though it cannot be confused as the main substance of the dish. I've mentioned that the third part of my "Sequence of Women" was written in modified sapphics, an ancient meter essentially foreign to our language but possessing a bittersweet, dolorous, descending rhythm appropriate to the death of a young woman. In addition, the formalism of the meter enabled me to counter directly a difficult subject; good poems simply aren't written with heart in hand.

REVERIE

He thinks of the dead. But they
appear as dead—beef-colored and torn.

There is a great dull music
in the ocean that lapses into seascape.

The girl bends slowly
from the waist. Then stoops.

In high school Brutus
died upon a rubber knife.

Lift the smock. The sun
light stripes her back. A "fado" wails.

In an alley in Cambridge. Beneath
a party's noise. Bottle caps stuck to them.

I don't think "Reverie" is a particularly good poem but it marked a significant advance in technique for me. If a modern poet views the world as horribly rended, maniacal, frenzied, death-born, he can't simply say "the times are out of joint" and make it stick. The subject has been worked over count-less times and orthodox treatments of it have become vapid and boring. I tried to express it dramatically, with rapid shifts, jerkily as if the world were being felt through a slide projector: the first couplet expresses the usual theme of violent death, then moves on into the second where we have urban man's enervation with nature to which he brings only his fatigue—driving through it at top speed in a boat or car. I wrote the poem after reading two Spanish poets, Vallejo and Otero. Though I did not compose it with them in mind I saw afterwards that I had adapted their ability to treat boredom and death as sensual objects. In a recent poem I have carried the technique even further:

NIGHT IN BOSTON

From the roof the night's the color
of a mollusc, stained with teeth and oil—
she wants to be rid of us and go to sea.

And the soot is the odor of brine
and imperishable sausages.

Beneath me from a window I hear "Blue Hawaii."
On Pontchartrain the Rex Club
dances on a houseboat in a storm—
a sot calms the water without wetting a foot.

I'd walk to Iceland, saluting trawlers.
I won't sell the rights to this miracle.

It was hot in Indiana.
The lovers sat on a porch swing, laughing;
a car passed on the gravel road,
red taillights bobbing over the ruts,
dust sweeping the house,
the scent of vetch from the pasture.

Out there the baleen nuzzles his iceberg,
monuments drown in the lava of bird shit.
I scuffle the cinders, the building doesn't shudder
they've balanced it on rock.
The Charles floats seaward, bored with history.

Night, cutting you open
I see you're full of sour air
like any rubber ball.

Here the influence, though not explicit, is a combination of technique and moral impact. I have long admired poets like Apollinaire, García Lorca and Trakl whose modernity rests in the colors of their metaphor, not stated rationally as with the poets of the academy, but a physical knowledge exuding from the emotional impact of their persons.

> *Oddly enough, it is only in poems*
> *wherein we forget that our feelings*
> *have been deliberately evoked that*
> *poetry as an art justifies itself.*
> —JAMES DICKEY

FEBRUARY SUITE

Song,
angry bush
with the thrust of your roots
deep in this icy ground,
is there a polar sun?

. . . .

Month of the frozen
goat—
La Roberta says cultivate
new friends,
                profit will
be yours with patience.
Not that stars are crossed
or light to be restored—
we die from want of velocity.

And you, longest of months
with your false springs,

you don't help or care about helping,
so splendidly ignorant of us.
Today icicles fell
but they will build downwards again.

· · · · · · ·

Who has a "fate"?
this fig tree
talks
about bad weather.

· · · · · · ·

Here is man drunk—
in the glass
his blurred innocence renewed.

· · · · · · ·

The Great Leitzel
before falling to her death
did 249 flanges on the Roman rings—
her wrist was often raw
and bloody
but she kept it hidden.

· · · · · · ·

He remembers Memorial Day—
the mother's hymn to Generals.
The American Legion fires blanks
out over the lassitude of the cemetery
in memory of sons who broke
like lightbulbs in a hoarse cry
of dust.

· · · · · · ·

Now
behind bone

in the perfect dark
the dreams of animals.

. . . .

To remember
the soft bellies of fish
the furred animals that were part of your youth
not for their novelty
but as fellow creatures.

. . . .

I look at the rifles
in their rack upon the wall:
though I know the Wars
only as history
some cellar in Europe might still
owe some of its moistness to blood.

. . . .

With my head on the table
I write,
my arm outstretched, in another field,
of richer grain.

. . . .

A red-haired doll stares
at me from a highchair,
her small pink limbs twisted about
her neck.
I salute the postures of women.

. . . .

This hammer of joy,
this is no fist
but a wonderment got by cunning.

SUITE TO FATHERS
for D. L.

I

I think that night's our balance,
our counterweight—a blind woman
we turn to for nothing but dark.

. . . .

In Val-Mont I see a slab of parchment
a black quill pen in stone.
In a sculptor's garden
there was a head made from stone,
large as a room, the eyes neatly hooded
staring out with a crazed somnolence
fond of walled gardens.

. . . .

The countesses arch like cats in châteaux.
They wake up as countesses and usually sleep with counts.
Nevertheless he writes them painful letters,
thinking of Eleanor of Aquitaine, Gaspara Stampa.
With Kappus he calls forth the stone in the rose.

. . . .

In Egypt the dhows sweep the Nile
with ancient sails. I am in Egypt,
he thinks, this Baltic Jew—It is hot,
how can I make bricks with no straw?
His own country rich with her food and slaughter,
fit only for sheep and generals.

. . . .

He thinks of the coffin of the East,
of the tiers of dead in Venice,

those countless singulars.
At lunch, the baked apple too sweet with Kirsch
becomes the tongues of convent girls at gossip,
under the drum and shadow of pigeons
the girl at promenade has almond in her hair.

* * * * * * *

From Duino, beneath the mist,
the green is so dark and green it cannot bear itself.
In the night, from black paper
I cut the silhouette of this exiled god,
finding him as the bones of a fish in stone.

II

In the cemetery the grass is pale,
fake green as if dumped from Easter baskets,
from overturned clay and the deeper marl
which sits in wet gray heaps by the creek.
There are no frogs, death drains there.
Landscape of glass, perhaps Christ
will quarry you after the worms.
The newspaper says caskets float in leaky vaults.
Above me, I feel paper birds.
The sun is a brass bell.
This is not earth I walk across
but the pages of some giant magazine.

* * * * * * *

Come song,
allow me some eloquence,
good people die.

* * * * * * *

The June after you died
I dove down into a lake,

the water turned to cold, then colder,
and ached against my ears.
I swam under a sunken log then paused,
letting my back rub against it,
like some huge fish with rib cage
and soft belly open to the bottom.
I saw the light shimmering far above
but I did not want to rise.

. . . .

It was so far up from the dark—
once it was night three days,
after that four, then six and over again.
The nest was torn from the tree,
the tree from the ground,
the ground itself sinking torn.
I envied the dead their sleep of rot.
I was a fable to myself,
a speech to become meat.

III

Once in Nevada I sat on a boulder at twilight—
I had no ride and wanted to avoid the snakes.
I watched the full moon rise a fleshy red
out of the mountains, out of a distant sandstorm.
I thought then if I might travel deep enough
I might embrace the dead as equals,
not in their separate stillnesses as dead, but in music
one with another's harmonies.
The moon became paler,
rising, floating upwards in her arc
and I with her, intermingled in her whiteness,
until at dawn again she bloodied
herself with earth.

. . . .

In the beginning I trusted in spirits,
slight things, those of the dead in procession,

the household gods in mild delirium
with their sweet round music and modest feasts.
Now I listen only to that hard black core,
a ball harsh as coal, rending for light
far back in my own sour brain.

. . . .

The tongue knots itself
a cramped fist of music,
the oracle a white-walled room of bone
which darkens now with a greater dark;
and the brain a glacier of blood,
inching forward, sliding, the bottom
silt covered but sweet,
becoming a river now
laving the skull with coolness—
the leaves on her surface
dipping against the bone.

. . . .

Voyager, the self the voyage—
dark let me open your lids.
Night stares down with her great bruised eye.

I take poetics to be the totality of the principles that guide the content and
form of a poem. In the course of a poet's life these principles never cease
evolving—their health and usefulness, in fact, depend on their ability to respond to change in his sensibilities. It is absurd to speak of poetics as a fixed
thing when it is nearly a daily "add four take away three" process. The first
poem in my book was a confession of uneasiness over the volatile nature of
poetics:

Form is the woods: the beast,
a bobcat padding through red sumac,
the pheasant in brake or goldenrod
that he stalks—both rise to the flush,

the brief low flutter and catch in air;
and trees, rich green, the moving of boughs
and the separate leaf, yield
to conclusions they do not care about
or watch—the dead, frayed bird,
the beautiful plumage,
the spoor of feathers
and slight, pink bones.

That is, form is a dynamic, alive vehicle within which the poem inseparably occurs and lives, "alive" things which happen and are given shape within the natural ecology of the poet's brain. "Form is never more than an extension or revelation of content." The dynamic quality of poetics itself comes from the idea that every poet worth the name wishes to forge a "key to a style"—a way of expressing himself equal to his vision.

When I wrote "February Suite" I was searching for a way to handle a larger body of experience without losing the intensity of the short lyric. Rilke discusses a number of times in his prose the necessity of working in forms and with subjects appropriate to the condition or degree of one's talent—no one "begins" a career with a *Duino Elegies*. I had also been impressed with the contention of the late T'ang poets that most things worth saying could be said within eight lines. But my mind had begun working in a new way and the ideas and images that presented themselves could not be expressed within the confines of a short lyric. Quite by accident I came upon the idea of a "suite" in the work of William Carlos Williams; I immediately recognized this form as a probable solution to my dilemma, though it took a number of months to become fully accustomed to its subtleties.

The impulse behind "February Suite" was that I am a seasonal creature— a characteristic I'm sure I share with others. Certain states of mind have always been peculiar to certain months with me; the month of February and at least the first half of March have always been absolute losses as far as any new work is concerned. I wanted to create this total mood, rather, make a mood insist upon itself. Each part of the poem was intended to serve as a wedge, suggesting directly the entire texture of the month—the damp, cold melancholy, the general inactiveness, the sense of being mentally impacted, each day becoming only vaguely lighter, the false starts.

After the poem was finished I returned to shorter lyrics. When the book manuscript was accepted by the publisher and I was deliberating my next move, ideas again began coming that demanded a longer form, often beginnings of poems that I had rejected in the past for lack of a proper vessel. I worked on "Suite to Fathers" over a period of five months; when it was finally finished, rather, abandoned to be published in its present form, I conceived of five more in a single evening, blocking them out as best I could in so short a time. My excitement was so intense that I later had difficulty deciphering my normally orderly handwriting.

"Suite to Fathers" seems by far my most complicated, perhaps sophisticated, poem to date. The idea that something exists which we name a father, or more exactly, the quality of "fatherness," has always troubled me. I suppose this might be psychologically transparent; it is, in fact, difficult to write such a poem being even mildly conversant with Freud. But such knowledge colors the treatment rather than paralyzes the subject; it was so urgent to me that any block was burned away in the process of composition.

In the first section I attempted to focus on the presence of Rilke and somehow dispel the power he seemed to have over me; much of what I feel about the writing of poetry had been fathered by him and this had become disturbing to me. I wanted literally to "kill him off" and gain my freedom from his powerful temperament. When I finished the section I noticed that though I had been laconic and generally sarcastic about his weaknesses, the whole thing had a Rilkean aura to it, of surfaces vaguely disturbed covering a pitchy darkness. The second part deals with the temporary insanity I felt after the death of my father; the terrible sense of freedom and loss of comfort and advice. The third part deals with the gradual sense of the self becoming its own father, of the poet as some sort of androgynous beast, constantly making his mind over in new images in order to insure his fertility as a poet.

The poem has the natural organization offered by the unity of content, assuming of course that I have forced the reader to follow me. This is a primary nightmare only removed by the sense of having done one's best, of having exhausted the equipment to make the poem work. The first two sections contain thirty-three lines, and the last, thirty-four. I set this arbitrary limit for no reason I can think of, not certainly for the trinity or in favor of any grand design.

As a poet I am conscious that I work within the skeleton of a myth for which there is no public celebration. If a poet has no particular current public importance it is because he has lost or given up his secondary or peripheral occupations—those of priest, buffoon, praiser of kings and governments and noble ladies. But he has not given up what runs through all great and good poems, his fundamental "humanness" which he holds like a public charge though with little public, his will to catch, focus and make song out of man and nature.

It is usual for the critic to worry about the continued health of the poet and poetry—somewhat in the manner that the ornithologist worries about the strange, rare ivory-billed woodpecker that has doomed itself by limiting its diet to a particular grub which in turn is being gradually destroyed by insecticides. But the act of poetry depends on what Freud called the "primary process"—I think—and is too basic to be removed by any imagined or increased neglect, much less an adverse environment. It is beefsteak, not caviar, both a way of being and a way of doing, a religious and a natural act.

The sense of play that a poet needs to make language an ally—often thought of as congenital insincerity by the public—provides the at least momentary pleasure of creation; the sense of having a foothold, if not full membership, in a guild as old as man. The child who carves a tombstone or rock out of a bar of soap knows some of this pleasure. In that language is the most commonly used medium, it is the most whorish and unyielding, the most difficult to make memorable. When we attempt to explain the processes and origins of poetry, we trip on our circular logic, on causality—if we are thus sure why can't we proceed and create at will? It is because poetry is both a dialectic and a rite, a living metaphor of the hunt, not to kill but to hold and caress. Each creature requires a new stratagem, though the stalk remains a constant. This small portion of mystery is disturbing. There is in the poet something of the magician, the arcane. He even suspects the goose might cease laying the golden eggs if he is watched, or watches himself too closely.

I have included a few selections from my notebooks to give a larger sense of background, to hint at the often vague sort of mulling that occurs before a poem is conceived. The selections are from notebooks concurrent with the writing of the poems in this paper. The notebooks, naturally, are vastly greater in size than the poems.

The fear of being left permanently in a mental state where art means nothing.

You ripen despite history, indifferent to it. The cursed fig tree, the cruelty of the Gospels. My boring Protestant guilt about naps.

Writing letters as a way of getting ready, calisthenics, or more accurately, foreplay: still the poems must be dragged reluctantly out of silence. Char says "to be there when the bread comes fresh from the oven."

The question of what is classic is not to be solved metrically.

Remy de Gourmont says that "All birth pangs are painful, especially those of intelligence. Nevertheless the creative gives transports of enthusiasm and divine inebriations."

To pass your time in the highest appreciable form for saying anything, over that of music, paint, architecture, film—but also the most corroded since the medium is so basic, open to all the corruption of humanness but also more directly attuned to human possibilities.

The poem that began to come—that you weren't ready for, that you didn't listen to, that you rendered dishonestly—probably won't repeat itself.

Carolers with cold hymnals, words of glass and snow.

He has a lead, a trite clue which he follows out of curiosity, a chore that becomes sacred.

The depth of Rilke—"Consider, the Hero continues, even his fall was a pretext for further existence."

Purl sweet, dulcet sounded milk of names. Shawnee. Arapaho.

Li Po a ruthless drunk, brown teeth and saggy eyelids, his western laughter a Dog Star not to steer by but to glitter distant as a god.

To scorn intervals.

The voice must become prodigal, mangled, intolerable.

Lorca—"I am neither all poet, all man or all leaf, but only the pulse of a wound that probes to the opposite side."

I am no more than an apprentice but at last I have accepted it.

To catch the moment when the thorn enters the skin.

The economy of a rock, holding water beyond its use.

The arrogance of the solitary waits upon the sublime—she must be stalked with cunning.

He wants to build but has not time to lay the individual brick—to cover oneself with the skins of animals, guises, in order to leap, fly, not walk.

Josephson says that Rimbaud is avoided because he made the writing of poetry too dangerous.

The lesson of imprecision: the poet has to be a butcher, a hunter, a soldier, a baker, a candlestick maker—in other words an artisan of dough and wax, death and frosting.

He thinks that his concessions like the Eucharist are rites of passage.

A poet becomes attached to the romantic in himself because it flatters his possibilities, all that is distant in him, sloth.

The rhythms of "natural speech" must be tightly controlled or avoided altogether—they lull rather than interest unless compressed into something accelerated, unnatural.

Still marrow from ancient bones—Sappho, Villon, Rabelais.

Who said "Such a price/ the Gods exact for song:/ to become what we sing."?

He wishes to write a poem as immediately fascinating as a dirty picture.

A poet's predictable interest in fairy tales, disasters, storms, the aristocracy, hawks. Let down thy hair, Rapunzel. Dreams of impossible women.

To wait all day upon it then, very late, to have a door open for you that you did not think existed: all fears gone, sweetness, nonchalance—to expand

and draw the whole rotten earth in and mingle with its rottenness and sweetness.

One must write as if things had to be said all over again—though poetry is noncumulative it takes craw or perhaps stupidity to try to write after an evening reading Shakespeare. The great ones create a temporary silence around their work which stuns nearly all of us, excluding doctoral candidates.

You push yourself to the edge until you become the edge and teeter on yourself—but there is no edge, only new modes of consciousness swimming into one another.

These motions are not convinced of themselves. To translate plain into plain, devoid of gaggery.

I can never become an active poet in the sense that I would be willing to become an apologist for a school or group.

The "sublime" and discouragement: you cannot hope, unless you are one of the isolate giants which you are not, to write a sublime poem. But you don't write poems in competition with any other poet—your energies are directed at a final harmony, the balance of imaginative richness and pure form.

Your work will never appear miraculous to you because it has cost you so much effort and pain. The senses that you hammer at nightly are incapable of surprise—the monstrous perception is usual.

When you were still "political" you often despised poetry as a game—now your elaborate sense of play has made you a word addict and bored with the hemorrhage of news.

I heard that Roethke died last week. Along with Lowell he was considered to be the best of the "middle-generation"—the colonizers rather than explorers. Consequently too much of their work is domestic and housebroken to be great. Both of them mildly insane with alcohol problems—cause, symptom, neither? Usually rather read Goll. Polite quarrels between schools here while fine truly new work appears in Spain, South America and Germany. A time of inhalation.

It is possible to tread water until you are unable to do anything else.

A poetry diseased with streetlights, a fine layer of lint and odor of carbon. Unpleasant marriages, smell of the classroom and household gods. No sun, mad dogs or death.

You must often hate poetry in order to write good poems.

Remember: vividness, lucidity, momentum. A poem should not resemble "poetry" too closely. The first impulse on reading a true poem is almost awkward. Lines should not be anticipated nor should a line be diffuse unless it conceals a jolt. Some sort of unexampled tension, not necessarily to be resolved, is characteristic of good poems. And not merely a tension purely of language but in the objects and their emotional equivalents. If a single line is to serve as a fulcrum it must be doubly sharp, hard and lucid. The whole point about a short lyric is to make the moment durable.

1965

Bending the Bow,
by Robert Duncan

Robert Duncan must certainly be our most difficult active poet. *Bending the Bow* is for the strenuous, the hyperactive reader of poetry; to read Duncan with any immediate grace would require Norman O. Brown's knowledge of the arcane mixed with Ezra Pound's grasp of poetics. Though Duncan avows himself a purely derivative poet, his capacities are monstrous and have taken a singular direction: in Duncan the range of affection is great and nothing is barred entrance into the "field" of composition. The structure of *Bending the Bow* is the "grand collage." It is for this reason that his poetry has been called cluttered and self-defeating, even swollen and diversive by his admirers.

These qualifications are only relevant if we are unable to transcend our purely linear sense of what a poem should be. In the "Passages," a sequence that makes up the bulk of *Bending the Bow*, there is a total lack of the usual sociological and geometric hints, the "top to bottom" sensation that usually leads us through the most wantonly modernist poem. Rather, the impression is like a block of weaving, if that is possible. In Duncan the poem is not the paradigm but the source, the competitor and not the imitator, of nature.

Form in the "Passages" is a four-dimensional process, constantly active, never passive, moving through time with the poet. The poems are music-based rather than ideational, the rhythms concentrated in time, avoiding any strict sense of measure. Duncan's poems may be gnomic and expansive, simultaneously aerial and kinetic, though never, as in the work of so many contemporary poets, solely concerned with the fact of a process whose only virtue is to describe itself accurately. Instead of concluding in the orthodox sense, the poems unfold in gradations or seem to reach toward the end of a natural arc.

Another more obvious stumbling point for the reader is Duncan's aggressive syncretism: he is personal rather than confessional and writes within a continuity of tradition. It simply helps to be familiar with Dante, Blake, mythography, medieval history, H. D., William Carlos Williams, Pound, Stein, Zukofsky, Olson, Creeley, and Levertov.

The difficulties in Duncan are mitigated somewhat by his fine introduction. He explains: "The poem is not a stream of consciousness, but an area of composition in which I work with whatever comes into it . . . the poet works with a sense of parts fitting in relation to a design that is larger than the poem. The commune of Poetry becomes so real that he sounds each particle in relation to parts of a great story that he knows will never be completed. A word has the weight of an actual stone in his hand. The tone of a vowel has the color of a wing." The largesse exists for the capable reader— we have the salve, too, of the lyric. Here are the last two stanzas of "My Mother Would be a Falconress":

> My mother would be a falconress,
> and even now, years after this,
> when the wounds I left her had surely heald,
> and the woman is dead,
> her fierce eyes closed, and if her heart
> were broken, it is stilld.
>
> I would be a falcon and go free.
> I tread her wrist and wear the hood,
> talking to myself, and would draw blood.

But to emphasize Duncan's lyric poems is to avoid our responsibility. We have done the same in the past by reading Blake's *Songs of Innocence and Experience* to the exclusion of the *Prophetic Books*. The finest of Duncan's "Passages," numbers 24 to 30, give a sense of war and bleakness that is at the same time physiological and metaphysical. They are neither doctrinaire nor programmatic; we have simply not had their equal as poems in the past several years, not, anyway, since Theodore Roethke's *Far Field* or Robert Lowell's *Life Studies* or Charles Olson's *Maximus Poems*.

I have not done much here but anticipate objections to a splendid book. I don't feel it necessary to inherit all the literary prejudices of a previous generation, whatever the convictions. The failure of readers of poetry to come to terms with Duncan's art is shameful and lazy; as Duncan has said in "Roots and Branches":

> Foremost we admire the outlaw
> who has the strength of his own lawfulness.

1968

A Chat with a Novelist

When I turned up Deep Creek Road the sheep bordered the cattle guard and their "ba ba ba bahhs" seemed to reflect the question: why would anyone live here? But I drove on through the Engleman spruce and withered sedge for a few miles, then turned when I saw BUSHWACK PALACE branded into a rail fence with McGUANE, PROP. below it. I drove another mile through a pasture of sudan grass, noticing the flattened rattlers with their clouds of flies on the road, a few conical piles of bear doodoo with even more flies and prairie falcons hovering in abstract gyres above the trail. Why not live here? I queried myself. When I drew up to the ranch which closely resembled the movie set from *Shane* Mr. McGuane's huge dog jumped bristling onto the car hood but her master's voice called and we walked through the darkened house to a yet darker study. I noticed Mr. McGuane looked a trifle old for his age which hasn't been determined though I would guess between the mid-twenties and mid-thirties. Like the redoubtable Pynchon he makes an unfortunate fetish out of privacy. *Pourquoi?* Who knows. Perhaps no one cares but that's not what we're talking about, is it? There was a two-gallon swiveled decanter of cheapish gin and some ice on his bare desk. Mrs. McGuane, née Portia Crockett, brought in a pewter platter of braised leeks and sweetbreads which we nibbled at with a chilled off-year Château Margaux. Mr. McGuane glowered as if this intrusion for the sake of contemporary letters was unwelcome. He put on Linda Rondstadt and Dolly Parton albums and sang along rather loudly with them, not well I might add. My questions punctuated this noise with some difficulty.

Interviewer:
Is it true what you said about Bob?

McGuane:
Nope.

Int:
You seem to key off the Midwest in your work. You were born and raised there but you commute between Montana and Key West without a nod to Michigan and its rich literary milieu. Why?

McGuane:
I have a genetic horror of the Midwest, a dark image of the past where Mortimer Snerd screwed three thousand times a day to build that heartland race.

Int:
Oh.

McGuane:
Yet I miss those piney woods, those beaver ponds and rivers, the feebs and dolts who run the bait shops and gas stations, the arc welders in the legislature, the ham with chicken gravy that poisoned me in Germfask when I fished the Driggs.

Int:
You're not denying your roots?

McGuane:
Cut that shit out.

Int:
A-OK. What do you think of the Drug Generation?

McGuane:
The Driggs is a fine river for brook trout.

Int:
Must I always be a wanderer between past and pillar, the virgin and the garrison, the noose and the cocktail lounge?

McGuane:
That's your bizness.

Int:
Who do you think is really good right now?

McGuane:
Grass. Hawkes. Landolfi. Cela.

Int:
Do you care to elaborate?

McGuane:
Nope.

Int:
Were it possible, how would you derive the novels you would like to write?

McGuane:
Cervantes, De Rojas, Rabelais, Swift, Fielding. Machado de Assis, Melville. Gogol, Joyce, Flann O'Brien. Ilf and Petrov, Peacock, Dickens, Kafka, Chesterton, Byron of the letters.

Int:
Do you think Nabokov excessively conumdramatic?

McGuane:
Is that like hydramatic?

Int:
You jest, mega-fop!

[*A two-day interruption was made here to attend a Crow Indian powwow. The interviewer became very ill from semipoisonous tequila which he mistook for white table wine. The Custer Battlefield of Thomas Berger fame was visited. How life imitates art!*]

Int:
Officially Montana is your residence, is it not?

McGuane:
Yes, the bleak cordillera of the Absaroka consoles me.

Int:
Why don't you live on one of America's marvel coasts?

McGuane:
I'm glad you asked. I've been to those places. And the Left there to which I belong was developing an attitude toward the people of the interior and the unfashionably pigmented poor that is best described as racist. For example,

the Left implicitly considers any white born in the South to be congenitally evil.

Int:
What about the whole "novel scene" now?

McGuane:
Only that the serial preoccupations of fiction could be replaced by the looped, the circuited and the "Johnny Carson Show." Even something so ductile as an eclaire has an inner dynamism not inferior to a hard-on or a terrified Norway rat.

Int:
I think most of our readers are unfamiliar with your interest in pastry.

McGuane:
It ends with eclaires and their analogue reality (or not).

Int:
I wonder how many of our readers realize that your aunt was the celebrated Irish novelist Flann O'Brien?

McGuane:
Very few.

Int:
What other things come to mind that our readers probably don't realize?

McGuane:
What is the name of your magazine?

Int:
Sumac, which unfortunately some think is French for stomach.

McGuane:
Well, one of the things that *Stomach* readers doubtless fail to realize is that D. H. Lawrence was Norman Douglas's wife. It was the first society function hazarded by the widely resented "surfboard aristocracy" of Tasmania, also I might add their first transvestite wedding.

Int:
Oh. One critic describes your fictions as being "laced with canals of meaning and symbolism."

McGuane:
Yes, yes . . .

Int:
Is that true?

McGuane:
O yes, yes, yes . . . Why gee yes.

Int:
What do you think of, I think it was either Granville Hicks's or George Steiner's contention, that fiction should be spelled "fickshun?"

McGuane:
No.

Int:
What of your fabled love of animals?

McGuane:
I would handily commit 3300 acts of artistic capitulation to keep my dog in Purina.

Int:
Why have you never mentioned the Budweiser Clydesdales in your work?

McGuane:
O god, hasn't that been done to death?

Int:
May I ask for the first sentence of your new novel?

McGuane:
Of course. "Upstairs, Mona bayed for dong."

Int:
MMMMmmm. How ironical. Yesterday in the local tackle shop I was told you had invented a new fly for trout.

McGuane:
Yes, I call it the Republican Indispensible. You tie it up out of pig bristles and carp feathers.

Int:
Have you ever caught Gila trout in New Mexico?

McGuane:
No.

Int:
Arizona?

McGuane:
O, not at all.

Int:
Are you offended by calling a large trout "Larry Lunker" as do many of our sporting writers?

McGuane:
Au contraire. The term frequently hangs on my lower lip like a figment of dawn.

Int:
Are you stoned?

McGuane:
No, intermittently never.

Int:
What constitutes a horse's ass in our literature?

McGuane:
A difficult question! I'd say 1. parsimony 2. surefire Babbitry 3. snorkeling 4. New York 5. San Francisco 6. Irving Berlin 7. this is your life not theirs 8. pick up sticks 9. Mary Jane and Sniffles 10. U.S.A. Meatland Parcels 11. a million baby kisses 12. a bad cold 13. corrasable bond.

[*Mr. McGuane ran out in the rain to install a new starter solenoid in his Porsche 911 T. We then left immediately for the Blackfeet Reservation in Browning, Montana to see the birthplace of James Welch. We were there for three days. Mr. McGuane unfortunately mistook tequila for a widely known ginger ale, hence spent much time yodeling in the thundermug as the Irish would put it.*]

Int:
I'm interested in what you think of Barton Midwood's contention that the modern novelist has lost his audience. They've all gone to the beach.

McGuane:
Hopelessly true. We're lucky if they've gone no farther than the beach. If they were at the beach a year ago when Midwood made the statement they are surely in Tibet by now.

Int:
What is the last book you didn't write?

McGuane:
The Possums of Everest.

Int:
I understand you were working on a contemporary western but have abandoned it?

McGuane:
Yes, the book was centered in Big Pie Country or Big Fly Country, whatever you will. The title was *Ghost Riff-Raff in the Sky.*

Int:
Why did you give up the title *Wandell's Opprobrium?*

McGuane:
It would have sent everybody to a Tibetan beach.

Int:
Don't you think the title should have been *Walkie Talkie?*

McGuane:
Not at all.

Int:
Your politics, rather the lack of them, is a point of interest to some critics. Do you have a comment?

McGuane:
I suppose I am a bit left of Left. America has become a dildo that has turned berserkly on its owner.

Int:
Do you feel lionized?

McGuane:
I feel vermiculized.

Int:
Do you have any deeply felt interest in poetry?

McGuane:
O, a great deal. So much in fact that I find myself overwhelmed. I would like to add this: for decades the Pruniers' restaurants have had the reputation of being the best seafood restaurants in the world.

Int:
What of your college years?

McGuane:
I graduated from Black Pumpkin in 1956. Since then, I might add, our Pumpkin group has dominated American letters.

Int:
What about the underground?

McGuane:
What about the underground?

Int:
I mean, what about the Underground?

McGuane:
Oh. The Underground has become the overground, in essence a parable of the Gay Caballero.

Int:
Is that in the same genre as the Spanish Cavalier?

McGuane:
No. Only that every hamster is a hostage to fortune.

Int:
Have we touched on organic gardening?

McGuane:
We had one of those things out at the end of the lawn. A lot of work. Then a certain horse named Rex got loose in the night and ate the whole plot to ground level. Sad to say but the most organic thing in the world is pus. I read it yesterday.

Int:
Are any of your friends living in domes?

McGuane:
Yes. I have a close friend who has built a $100,000 home that looks precisely like a Spalding Dot.

Int:
The golf ball, I presume?

McGuane:
Yes. From time to time he and his family can be seen scuttling in and out one of its pores. It's a noble way of life. Also, they have a duck inside with them.

Int:
Where has everyone gone?

McGuane:
Bolinas.

Int:
All of them?

McGuane:
All of them.

Int:
For the striped bass?

McGuane:
For the patchouli.

Int:
Why did you call your dog Biff?

McGuane:
Sprat.

Int:
Dink?

McGuane:
Frab . . . [snit]

> [*The interview terminated here. An inevitable tedium seized us. Mr. Mc-Guane attempted to sing from Jarry's* Ubu Roi *accompanying a Merle Haggard record. Then he read to me from some aerosol cans he gathered in the bathroom: "Never spray toward face or open flame, avoid inhaling. If rash develops discontinue use. Contains riboflavin" etc. . . .]*

1971

The Nick Adams Stories,
by Ernest Hemingway

It was certain that he was playing to a much larger crowd than his immediate critical audience or the academic community. It was hard to forgive him this and it would muddle the issue (his true stature) for years afterward, even in 1972. "My God," one would have thought, had one been old enough to think in those days, "Hemingway carries on as if he were Lord Byron, Natty Bumppo and Humphrey Bogart all in one suit of clothes." Even some of his friends who were distinctly small-canvas or pointillist types felt called upon to parody and attack this monster—the most intelligent among us tend to be fans of some sort but we don't really want our writers to act like sports stars or screen heroes, don't want the sacred line between poet and hero to be confused. And the mood after the war, public and private, was for a separate peace: up through the Eisenhower senescence and the McCarthy rampages there was the feeling in the vaporous literary establishment that Hemingway was somehow "out of order," or more plainly, an anachronism. Now all the residual intemperance on both sides is passing and a clearer view is possible. (There is a fine recent statement in the *New American Review* by Reynolds Price called "For Ernest Hemingway." This essay is also included in Price's new book, *Things Themselves*, published by Atheneum.) It seems we will have to forgive Hemingway his fabled idiosyncrasies in favor of his good works, which in the gospel sense are obviously living after him, just as he would have forgiven, or at least not noticed, us for doing nothing much at all.

It is pleasant to see all the Nick Adams stories under one cover, and that is justification enough for Scribners reprinting them. Before, of course, one had to sort through several volumes to find all of them and the chronology was a trifle confusing. Now we have the additional delight of eight fragments and stories hitherto unpublished. Of the latter I liked "The Last Good Country" the best; it runs about fifty pages and serves as a beginning, evidently, of an unfinished novel. In "The Last Good Country," Nick is escaping from two game wardens after killing a deer out of season and selling trout to a hotel. Nick takes his sister with him and though much is left undeveloped the main thread is sort of "if Huck Finn had a sister." It shows an enormously tender, almost maudlin, side of Hemingway's character. I'm sure when Leslie Fiedler gets hold of it, and perhaps justly, some mildly incestuous aspects of the story will be drawn to the surface with a fury. But it is most of all a summer idyll, the writing very relaxed and beautiful, and obviously a first draft with the guard left down.

There is a not very delicate question here, in the eight additions, of whether unrefined or unfinished work should be allowed to emerge. After reading *Islands in the Stream* and *African Journal* serialized in *Sports Illustrated* one would have to opt for a yes. None of the fragments are without interest, and "Wedding Day" and "On Writing" are fascinating sketches. One could have wished that Phillip Young's preface to the volume had been longer and more detailed. Young's prose has all the subtlety of a valve grinder but he perceives some of the joy in Hemingway that was so disastrously missing in the Carlos Baker biography.

After a decade without reading these stories one is struck first by the incorruptible purity of the style, the splendor and clarity of the language as language. We must remember that Hemingway after all was a pointy-headed intellectual and artist and his avowed intent was to write like Cézanne painted. The stories have all the Apollonian precision that his gaudy life apparently lacked; but again it is easy to fall into the perverse monism of the book reviewer or professor. Mistakes have been made trying to teach Philosophy 101 out of the stories, or errantly gathering, as so many young men have done, a life-style from them. Wisdom in a novelist or poet is so often an elaborate hype that is only self-applicable. As an instance one turns to Faulkner again and again to be enriched, to get pleasure pure and simple, not to find principles of conduct though they might be individually perceived. The Nick Adams stories are a young man's stories written by a young man and enjoyed mostly by other young men. The faultlessness of their pursuits is an embarrassment to older, wiser souls who miss the full panoply of contemporary attitudes and beliefs that helped them accommodate themselves to the miseries of the twentieth century. At least half the stories wear their durability as art very openly and easily. And "The Big Two-Hearted River" would be near the summit in any literature.

Surely Hemingway's presence has its irritations and all that he did, wisely and unwisely, between novels continues to live after him. Last October in a bar at the Hotel Europa in Leningrad I had a long, semi-drunken conversation with an East German cello player where it was revealed that I liked to fly-fish and hunt for grouse. The cello player said, "Oh, like Hemingway."

1972

Afterimages: Zen Poems by Shinkichi Takahashi

Properly, we shd. read for power. Man reading shd. be man intensely alive.
The book shd. be a ball of light in one's hands.
                                    —EZRA POUND, *Guide to Kulchur*

Takahashi is a Zennist as purely as San Juan de la Cruz and Saint Teresa are Christian (Dante and Milton remain students of bliss with feet surely stuck in the often muddy field of dogma). Shinkichi Takahashi is a poet, truly a foreign poet, so foreign that our taxonomy exhausts itself until we remember that an encounter with a true poet usually has this quality of foreignness. You need know nothing of Zen to become immersed in his work. You will inevitably know something of Zen when you emerge, but that is not my purpose here. I will try to keep my Western feet out of my mouth by leaving Zen to those who are masters, and opt for a manic attempt to get an American poetry audience to buy and read this book.

The sixties and early seventies have been predominantly an "internationalist" phase in American poetry. The energies behind this phase are ubiquitous and it has slowly gathered a great deal of energy since Kenneth Rexroth said it was happening in a rather cranky New Directions essay back in 1956. He was on the money, it seems, a precursor whose renditions from the Japanese and Chinese never got the interest they deserved in the midst of the new and vibrant introductions to European, Russian, Latin American poetry appearing everywhere. Jerome Rothenberg and others even attempted to introduce us to the poetry of those Native Americans, the Indians.

But work from the East appeared more slowly, despite Whaley, Pound, Blyth, Rexroth, and dozens of others. And after an early interest in a rather Zennist sort of "image" Pound went awry in Confucianism, which is grand for a good society but a less meaty source for poetry. As a poet I would frankly not trade a single *wanka* from Dogen for the sum of Confucius. And if good government interests you more than the Diamond Sutra, take a civil-service exam. But I wander. In my own muddled head the East entered slowly through the proselytizers everyone knows about—Suzuki, Watts etc.—but more dominantly by way of poets like Clayton Eshleman and Cid Corman, and most powerfully of all through Gary Snyder. Snyder is a marvelous poet to read, a very disturbing poet to be around, and a Zen Buddhist. Now Lucien Stryk must be added to this list. He translated *Afterimages* with Takashi Ikemoto, and has published a number of books dealing with Zen in addition to his own poetry. We understand how desperately feeble and parochial our poetry is when Shinkichi Takahashi reaches seventy-two before all but a very few of us know he exists.

Oddly, Takahashi is perilously available. He is not one of those poets of whom we lamely say that "he cannot be quoted." In my notes I find twenty-two poems I want to quote in whole or part. *Afterimages* owns a "thingness," an omniscience about the realities that seems to typify genius of the first order. If one image is worth many volumes as Pound infers, what may a thousand images be worth? Takahashi, of course, would say they are worth nothing. But that is an Olympian view that we need not concern ourselves with. He is there. We are here. Knut Hamsun was within this mode when he told an interviewer he wrote because it "didn't matter." So were Li Po and Tu Fu when they stood on a bridge together one evening composing poems on leaves and throwing them into the river.

But this thingness—when Takahashi writes of a crow, it is an actual crow, not as so often in our poetry, a convenient fulcrum on which to dangle an idea or our neuroses:

CROW

The crow, spreading wide wings,
Flapped lazily off.

239

Soon her young will be doing the same,
Firm wings rustling.

It's hard to tell the male
Crow from the female,
But their love, their mating
Must be fresh as their flight.

Asleep in a night train,
I felt my hat fly off.
The crow was lost in mist,
The engine ploughed into the sea.

This quality of "thingness" is allowed to reach monstrous levels of consciousness in "Destruction":

DESTRUCTION

The universe is forever falling apart—
No need to push the button,
It collapses at a finger's touch:
Why, it barely hangs on the tail of a sparrow's eye.

The universe is so much eye secretion,
Hordes leap from the tips
Of your nostril hairs. Lift your right hand:
It's in your palm. There's room enough
On the sparrow's eyelash for the whole.

A paltry thing, the universe:
Here is all strength, here the greatest strength.
You and the sparrow are one
And, should he wish, he can crush you.
The universe trembles before him.

It is difficult to characterize metaphor except with metaphor. *Afterimages* is
like seeing a long, beautifully filmed movie on a hundred mammals we
didn't know existed. And after the movie many of the animals decide to step
from the screen and live with you. They don't ask. You simply have to
make room. This quality of freedom of imagination is so prepossessing that

other aspects are easily forgotten. But we stumble over all of the greasy dogma we attach to "freedom" while we don't over a sparrow. Or the magpie in "Magpie":

MAGPIE

I start across the bridge.
Coming toward me from the other side,
A woman, drenched and perhaps
Having failed to purchase apples, mutters—
"Sardines, sardines." Below, listening,
A magpie bobs mournfully up and down.

It is a long black bridge,
So long that to cross it is unthinkable.
My white breath dies, rises and dies.
Life: dust on a bridge rail.
Wars, revolutions: bubbles on a stream.

Late in the frosty night, alone,
I cross an endless bridge.

Quite naturally, nearly all poetry is elaborate harness that never smelled a real horse. How refreshing to find a book full of wild horses. The harness that contains their energies is a nearly invisible tracery, a spirit harness. Perhaps it is even a mistake to mention Zen, which is only a word people seem to trip over; rather they trip over false conceptions of Zen. They think of monks sitting around in a full lotus eating rice. This is like trying to visualize an entire, unknown body from a single hair. As an instance, Takahashi's poems can contain anger and profound sexuality.

THE PEACH

A little girl under a peach tree,
Whose blossoms fall into the entrails
Of the earth.

There you stand, but a mountain may be there
Instead; it is not unlikely that the earth
May be yourself.

You step against a plate of iron and half
Your face is turned to iron. I will smash
Flesh and bone

And suck the cracked peach. She went up the mountain
To hide her breasts in the snowy ravine.
Women's legs

Are more or less alike. The leaves of the peach tree
Stretch across the sea to the end of
The continent.

The sea was at the little girl's beck and call.
I will cross the sea like a hairy
Caterpillar

And catch the odour of your body.

There is a lovely humor in Takahashi that catches us unaware. At one moment we may be dwelling on a poem in which the poet wishes to give up his life for an ill wife, and at the next moment encounter a poem such as "Fish."

FISH

I hold a newspaper, reading.
Suddenly my hands become cow ears,
Then turn into Pusan, the South Korean port.

Lying on a mat
Spread on the bankside stones,
I fell asleep.
But a willow leaf, breeze-stirred,
Brushed my ear.
I remained just as I was,
Near the murmurous water.

When young there was a girl
Who became a fish for me.
Whenever I wanted fish
Broiled in salt, I'd summon her.
She'd get down on her stomach

To be sun-cooked on the stones.
And she was always ready!

Alas, she no longer comes to me.
An old benighted drake,
I hobble homeward.
But look, my drake feet become horse hoofs!
Now they drop off
And, stretching marvelously,
Become the tracks of the Tokaido Railway Line.

Nothing is denied entrance into these poems: department stores, the atomic bomb, rats, clouds, Mars, stewardesses, helicopters, penguins, the Thames, trucks, strawberries, rain, dogs. All things are in their minutely suggestive proportion and given an energy we aren't familiar with, lost as most of us are in the romantic lie of the world as a confused extension of our personalities. The poet's stance is nimble and totally devoid of any of the usual crappy whining and self-pity the world habitually isolates as items in the poet's persona. Think how wonderful it would be if, when poets "mooned" over things, the verb would describe the dropping of the trousers rather than the usual Ichabod Crane trip.

Lucien Stryk and Takashi Ikemoto, the joint translators, present useful, occasionally brilliant, introductions. The introductions are extremely helpful, gates through which one enters the house of the book. Ikemoto, a profound Zennist himself, quotes Takahashi—"In short, confidence and action is all. One would present a sorry sight if one kept loitering, fascinated, within the fold of literature. True poetry is born out of the very despair that the word is useless and poetry is to be abandoned." Stryk offers a marvelous Rilke quote that is peculiarly Zennist:

> We play with obscure forces, which we cannot lay hold of, by the names we give them, as children play with fire, and it seems for a moment as if all the energy had lain unused in things until we came to apply it to our transitory life and its needs. But repeatedly . . . these forces shake off their names and rise . . . against their little lords, no, not even *against*—they simply rise, and civilizations fall from the shoulders of the earth . . . .

Perhaps it is our syncretist impulse, that Stryk notes in Rilke, that attracts us so strongly to Takahashi. He was an early Dadaist and that sneaks in.

Some of the poems remind you of the lucidity of Rimbaud's *Illuminations*—all primary colors mixed with nouns, verbs and vision. There are no hedges or temples, grottoes, shrines. At times the impassivity disturbs us until we see the energy just barely contained by the skin of the poem. *Afterimages* has all the dangers owned by a considerable poetry when it implies a Code of Behavior. We shy away. Then return discomfited, with the simple eagerness we owned before we became so smart. We visit places in Takahashi that we once may have visited hastily in a dream, or in a moment too startling to record the perception. We had no equipment to catch it. The book engages and subsumes us. We become that perfectly vulnerable reader that any poet wishes for his work.

Part of the power must come from the fact that the poet has ten thousand centers as a Zennist, thus is virtually centerless. He is not defending a core known as Man Making Literature. All of this in a poet who thinks himself no better or worse than a quail.

QUAILS

It is the grass that moves, not the quails.
Weary of embraces, she thought of
Committing her body to the flame.

When I shut my eyes, I hear far and wide
The air of the Ice Age stirring.
When I open them, a rocket passes over a meteor

A quail's egg is complete in itself,
Leaving not room enough for a dagger's point.
All the phenomena in the universe: myself.

Quails are supported by the universe
(I wonder if that means subsisting by God).
A quail has seized God by the neck

With its black bill, because there is no
God greater than a quail.
(Peter, Christ, Judas: a quail.)

A quail's egg: idle philosophy in solution.
(There is no wife better than a quail.)
I dropped a quail's egg into a cup for buckwheat noodles,

And made havoc of the Democratic Constitution.
Split chopsticks stuck in the back, a quail husband
Will deliver dishes on a bicycle, anywhere.

The light yellow legs go up the hill of Golgotha.
Those quails who stood on the rock, became the rock!
The nightfall is quiet, but inside the congealed exuviae

Numberless insects zigzag, on parade.

1972

The Dreadful Lemon Sky, by John D. MacDonald

The new John D. MacDonald, *The Dreadful Lemon Sky*, is the sixteenth in the Travis McGee series, the color in the title reflecting yet another shade in MacDonald's spectrum of what in an old-fashioned sense must be called "evil." It is not so thrashingly acerbic and bawdy as some of the other McGees but easily compensates by moving even farther toward the autumnal coolness of Chandler, Hammett and Cain.

This is not to say that *The Dreadful Lemon Sky* will disappoint MacDonald addicts. The earlier *Dress Her in Indigo* (1969) might easily be thought of as the pinnacle of brazen seaminess, and later on we noticed a chill of deliberation in *A Tan and Sandy Silence* (1972) and *The Scarlet Ruse* (1973). The colors have become a trifle less gaudy, but the punch is more lethal. There is much less of the "we" against the "they," and the recognizable demarcations between criminal and citizen have tended to blur into "all of us."

But then MacDonald could never be confused with the escapism that dominates the suspense field. You would have to be batty or ignorant or a masochist to read a MacDonald novel for pure amusement. The core of *The Dreadful Lemon Sky* deals with the Florida narcotics trade—quite real by virtue of the juicy opportunities along the extensive coastline. But the non-dopers among us are not let off the hook, covered as we all are by the corruption of business power, pointlessly stupid narcotics laws, and human greed right down to the bacon-and-eggs peddler in the corner diner. As an aside, it would be easy to mention this writer's vast readership if I were not so mindful of just how wrong fifty million or so Americans can be on a bleak November day; MacDonald is across-the-board democratic and if you're not covered in this book you will be in others.

I have often questioned the attraction of this writer, since I'm not much taken by others in the field, or by any lightweight books for that matter. I meet all sorts of poets and novelists who have the MacDonald vice, even those who, like myself, have no tolerance for mysteries. No one makes extravagant critical claims, but they all readily admit that MacDonald is a very good writer, not just a good "mystery writer." He far surpasses the critical conventions of the suspense category. (One is reminded of the nervousness attached to thinking of Peter Matthiessen, Ed Hoagland or Annie Dillard as "nature" writers.)

The other, perhaps more obvious, attraction is that MacDonald is a prodigy with sixty novels and five hundred short stories written since he gave up a business career twenty-five years ago. I remember as a young writer being disgusted when I discovered that Simenon wrote many of his wonderful novels in eleven days or less. Of course, any moron with the energy can write a novel in a hurry, but there are so many examples of good work being done at breakneck speed—Hemingway drafted *The Sun Also Rises* in six weeks and *To Have and Have Not* in less; Faulkner wrote *As I Lay Dying* in ten days; Durrell wrote *Balthazar* in less than three weeks; and Miller's *Aller Retour New York* was a letter to Alfred Perles of a few days' composition.

So perhaps more purely literary writers admire MacDonald's fertility, his ease of producing at great speed works within a specific genre that don't at all seem limited to that genre. In the overwhelmingly autobiographical phrase of a literary writer, something Gottfried Benn said comes to mind: "We are papering our walls with our own skin and we can't last." A gifted literary writer like Joseph Heller may spend a much-bandied twelve years on a novel, and one may wish secretly that he would move to Walla Walla and do a quickie.

It is interesting to note the way certain characteristics of the hero in the Travis McGee series facilitate plot. McGee has all the grief of a moralist. He simply can't stand the way things in our republic have gone from awful to worse, but he hesitates to preach about it. His morals, in short, are not "situational." He does not seduce women. He is kindly, he listens, he responds to their problems with great openness and with little concern for their faults. If he ends up with a page or two lay it is usually because it is good for everyone involved. This openness, as opposed to the closed shop of the usual existential hero, gets McGee into a stupefying array of ugly situations. His sidekick at the Bahia Mar Marina, where he lives on a houseboat won in a poker game, is Meyer, a freelance economist. MacDonald used Meyer to reveal all sorts of fantastic and arcane information about the greasy venality of certain business types. Sometimes one suspects that Meyer is MacDonald himself.

Often when McGee cleans up a particularly hideous mess it remains a mess: In *Dress Her in Indigo* the nice rich girl turned hippie is returned to her hypocrite father as a lesbian heroin addict. In *The Dreadful Lemon Sky* some fine people get their heads blown off. It is a "winner take nothing" world, where blood flows with the smell of "sheared copper" and where you will likely as not finish dead whether you are good or bad or indifferent.

McGee is not an anti-hero type, nor is he allowed any of the macho, fascist qualities that a Spillane and others of that silly ilk offer their heroes. MacDonald's world is a real world: the new Florida, where condominiums put up yesterday are somehow seedy today, where the operators and lawyers live in a cold porcine splendor that an honest sybarite like Balzac or even MacDonald recognizes as nickel-dime formica. It is a visceral commonplace world full of blasts of oxygen, crazy discourses on fishing, alcohol, marijuana, denatured sexuality, the burned-out uniformity of the young at play, the exacerbated efforts of the old to retire with grace like plucked turkeys in the subtropical sun.

The palpability of MacDonald's world is just as convincing in the non-McGee novels, the forty-four outside the series. Two of my favorites are *A Flash of Green* (1962) and *Clemmie* (1958). *A Flash of Green* seems to me the first and best of all novels with an ecological base. It concerns the raw, nerve-exposing effort of a group of people to save some fine tidal lands and flats from the developers. Curious to his genre, MacDonald has a pointillist reverence for the world outside: weather, the ocean, fauna; mammals own their proper share of it. Attention is paid to the way people eat, drink, take showers, sleep. For some strange reason people scarcely ever eat in American novels.

Clemmie is a desperate, harrowing novel about a man inadvertently driven to his limits by his wife taking a vacation, and how he out of loneliness falls in love with a younger woman. It is a desolately uncomfortable novel of passion. Like *The Dreadful Lemon Sky*, both books are without that convenient sacrificial goat, the Italians and their club of ruffians, on whom we easily lay our guilt. Everyone can see himself in *The Dreadful Lemon Sky*. The vision is immediate, painful, recognizable, with just the right load of pleasure to keep you going, like waking on a beautiful summer morning with a terrible hangover and thinking while shaving that at least you are alive.

1975

The Snow Walker,
by Farley Mowat

Depending on one's immediate mood a lot can be found wrong in the writing of Farley Mowat: all sorts of laughable excesses from sloppy style, overweening sentimentality, a kind of *con brio* enthusiasm for windmill tilting, to the sort of verbal keening one associates with a traditional Boston Irish wake, with the whiskey flowing so freely one forgets just who is dead and why.

This is not so much a disclaimer as an announcement of fact, and in Mowat's very particular case the fact doesn't matter. Of Farley Mowat's nineteen or so books I've read twelve, and after a few weeks mulling over the latest it seems to me that *The Snow Walker* is his best. The precious sniping of the "literateur" is simply not relevant here.

The Snow Walker is a book of tales about the Eskimo, stories ranging from the ancient to the overwhelmingly modern. It is passionate, harsh, with a mythic density that puts a great strain on the reader. In fact, the reader will assuredly come up feeling more than vaguely unclean. History is forgetful but ultimately unforgiving, and in *The Snow Walker* Mowat draws us into the beauty and anguish of an extirpated culture; perhaps more than culture, a microcosmic civilization. The beauty of the tales purge, exhaust, draw us out of our skin, but the pain involved is so deep that we feel the nondirectional remorse that characterizes modern man on those rare occasions when he has the wit and humility to turn around and look at his spoor.

In the reading of this book we should first of all forget all the Brotherhood of Man nonsense. We have nothing in common with the Eskimo and they nothing with us other than our accidental simultaneity on earth. It is not profitable to look for similarities, to make a stew of us all to get us off the hook in the usual ritual of breast-beating. Honesty counsels while breast-beating is masturbatory. The simple fact is the Canadian government has no better track record with the Eskimo than we with the American Indian in our mutual courses of empire. Despite all the understandable *cha-cha* of the Bicentennial Year it is healthier to admit we got off the boat and murdered a civilization, as did the Canadians. So many absurd efforts are made to avoid this truth—currently the Army wants Wounded Knee rewritten as a battle rather than a massacre. Maybe this presages "The Battle of My Lai." Certain children will never appreciate these niceties because they are dead. They were dead when we gave the Mandan blankets infected with smallpox as surely as they were dead when the Canadian government conducted some of its scandalous social experiments with the Eskimo. "Ah, Cedric, let's move the buggers to another island this year and see if they can't hustle up something more for the fur trade."

Before we came along the Eskimo were a strange lot. It was not so much that they were alone but that no one had ever joined them in the most hostile environment on earth, so they had no concept of what "alone" was. And no one is sure how many centuries they managed to endure in the tightest survival units imaginable, but "survival" is a euphemism within the framework of the Eskimo's closeness to the earth. The land and sea and the Eskimo owned each other with a degree of intimacy we cannot conceive, a fabled relationship with a visceral quality that is Siamese. One of the grandest things about the ocean is that it can kill you. And as Mowat tells his tales, the immediacy of death assumes a grace totally unknown to us.

The main character of *The Snow Walker* is the cold and the snow. The "snow walker" itself is death. We have an old man telling Mowat a tale going back so far that it recedes into the bottom layer of a glacier—how men with metal helmets with horns on them and wearing breastplates came in a long boat one year. They had blond beards, sang songs, and taught the Eskimo how to build the crossbow. There are tales of starvation, cannibalism out of love, the giving of one body to another with the poignancy of the Eucharist. There are tales so simple and strong that you read them backwards to make sure you haven't been tricked into feeling a story in your stomach for a change. There is a tale of a man and an arctic fox in a suicide pact. There is a tale about a woman named Soosie that exceeds any story I've ever read, save in Kafka, for convincing bureaucratic horror. There is a tale that is a *Romeo and Juliet* for grown-ups—romanticism loses its perversity and becomes convincing. In *The Snow Walker* Mowat is presenting the essence of his thirty-year obsession with the Arctic and its people.

Meanwhile back at the ranch, in the United States in 1976, it is a curious habit of ours to wait for the future when it has happened already, like some genetically foreordained intrusion we would rather not notice. We don't have to live in Buck Rogers bubbles. We already live in them, only they are squares. The true native populations of earth recede into the mist of history. They were engaged in their environment rather than shielded from it. As the Eskimo died as a viable culture an atomic submarine passed under them without their knowledge. Reading about the Eskimo has become a science fiction about the past. Nothing useful in the utilitarian sense can be learned from them, unless you choose to look at them as Buddhists of the snows, who knew how to live. Their life so perfectly marries dream and nightmare that we retreat from their nakedness back within the safety of a book.

1976

The Snow Leopard,
by Peter Matthiessen

It is a curious thing to advertise for an audience for so private, so idiosyncratic a journey. Not that *The Snow Leopard* was written in scorn of an audience, but one feels sure it is the same book Matthiessen would have written had its later publishing been impossible. *The Snow Leopard* is a heraldic book, full of ghosts and demons and largely unfamiliar mythologies; a well-veiled, lowercase Buddhist text set in the virtual top of the world, the Himalayas. It is a book totally devoid of comforting banalities—no kitchens, lingerie, politics, newspapers or clocks other than the timeless clock of the seasons (it's not very helpful to ascribe dates to 10,000 successive Octobers). Like all truly good books it is about death, and the imminence of death is fresh and lively, if you will, because we are drawn hypnotically along into a landscape where neither the beasts nor men are familiar.

On the surface the book is structured simply on the diary of a trek into the Tibetan Plateau of Nepal. In the autumn of 1973 Peter Matthiessen accompanied the zoologist George Schaller (author of the esteemed *Mountain Gorilla* and *The Serengeti Lion*) on a journey to the Crystal Mountain, "walking west under Annapurna and north along the Kali Gandaki River, then west and north again, around the Dhaulagiri peaks and across the Kanjiroba, two hundred and fifty miles or more to the Land of Dolpo, on the Tibetan Plateau." At Crystal Mountain Schaller and Matthiessen hoped to study the bharal, the Himalayan wild blue sheep, protected there from slaughter by the grace of the local Lama. The main complication (an understatement) of the trip was that Schaller needed to study the sheep in their November rutting season when they were most active and accessible, so the hike of over thirty days accompanied by a half-dozen Sherpas and bearers was made in the onset of the mountain winter, with some of the passes to be crossed exceeding in height anything to be found in our lower forty-eight states.

On this particular level the whole trip appears utterly foolhardy. An appendicitis attack or even a minor stumble would very likely be fatal. These are not necessarily major considerations for a scientist like Schaller, but Matthiessen voices them along with his desire to see a snow leopard, a nearly mythological beast, the least accessible of the great cats, perhaps the least accessible mammal on earth. In fact the book could be easily read on the level of a natural history thriller, the manner in which *The New Yorker* excerpted the text, rather understandably in lieu of the difficulty of the core of the book. And the book succeeds admirably as a fabled nineteenth-century action-adventure yarn: vast gorges, impassable rivers, wolves racing across glaciers, crazed village mastiffs, precipitous cliffs with half-foot-wide trails, the hint of the yeti, or Abominable Snowman, blizzards, snow blindness, thievery, harrowing cold and exhaustion. But then that is only partially what the book is about, and the reviewer finds himself as a decidedly minor-league John Huston, wondering how to suggest that this beloved *Moby Dick* is so very much more than a whaling romance.

Peter Matthiessen must be our most eccentric major writer. The fact that he is not readily identified as a major writer is only due to a critical lapse, what with former and potential critics giving themselves over to quasi-ecstasy cults, sexual confession, and the sandlot politics of *The New York Review of Books* (above the quarters of which float the anglicized ghosts of Ché and Fanon). Literature has oddly become the least fuzzy of contemporary arenas, but the bleachers are largely empty. In New York City last April I overheard a fat wag in a chichi *boîte* say that contemporary literature had surpassed homosexuality as a victimless crime.

Matthiessen's eccentricities are not those of language but of thought. His style is nonexotic and owns a studied Brahmin grace and wit, though the wit is rather more discomfiting than funny. He writes cleanly and beautifully with musical density, a nordic resonance coming out of surprising economy. But he is the odd creature who makes us understand how despite the obvious and perhaps over-discussed talents of Bellow, Mailer, Updike, Pynchon et al., they are the philosophically mundane products of university-based thought in the forties and fifties. This is much less a denigration than an observation about a lack of variety.

Matthiessen is a Zen Buddhist, in a manner more consequential to his work than Bellow's Jewishness, or the neo–Barthian (Karl, not John) Protestantism of Updike, the frazzled *existenz* of Mailer. This morning in a small tourist cabin in Montana looking out over the cordillera of the Absarokas with only *The Snow Leopard* on hand I rehearsed my favorites among Matthiesen's other books: *Wildlife in America, The Cloud Forest, The Wind Birds, The Tree Where Man Was Born*, and the novels, *At Play in the Fields of the Lord* and *Far Tortuga*. It has never been fashionable critically in our time to be concerned with the natural world outside of man's presence (witness the long search for serious readers by McPhee, Hoagland and Abbey who have generally succeeded with their least efforts). Oddly, in none of the above Matthiessen books is "Zen" even mentioned, though it certainly could be sensed by anyone familiar with this particular form of Buddhism. But it is nonobtrusive, and the writing, characterized by Olympian austerity as it is, avoids the personal. You are left with the notion of how deeply and to what a vast extent Matthiessen's work surpasses the genre he is identified with, but the man himself remains a puzzle until *The Snow Leopard*.

Running concurrent to the outward journey in *The Snow Leopard* is an equally torturous inward journey, and the two are balanced to the extent that neither overwhelms the other. Matthiessen for the first time becomes utterly candid about his life, though without the strenuous psychological hygienics of the confessional. He describes early experiments with hallucinogens (mostly lysergic acid) which were attempts at a shortcut to the visionary; his apprenticeship in Zen under Eido Roshi and Maezumi Roshi; and most poignantly, the death from cancer of his wife Deborah some six months before the trip.

There is something in the ineffable nature of Zen that nonetheless makes men try to write about it. It is most commonly misunderstood as another glyph for survival available to modern man, a device of comprehension. Beyond the level of flirtation it is not particularly popular because it is so totally nonsupportive. There is nowhere to turn in the unfolding of one's true nature except to the Roshi who only redirects the pain of discovery. To the student, Zen is the ocean and he is the fish; properly understood, it is consciousness itself, unmediated by opinions, hope, or gods, with few and naked precepts. Usually "dogma" is of value only to the convert or adept, i.e., it is a philosophical shorthand for the experiential. In *The Snow Leopard* Matthiessen makes the best run I've ever read at explicating Buddhist and Tantric terminology and hagiography. It is his curious novelistic talent to clarify and dismiss the aura of the secretive and arcane. The burden of the Zen man is ultimate *claritas*, and the occultist urge for the misnomer of mystery is only another excuse for the unlived life. In Zen you give a cup of tea to your demons and disarm them, whether they own interior schizoid colors or the very real apparel of a Himalayan gorge. The life to be lived is in the unintervened moment, where rock, bird, man and beast may be perceived as they are, in league with the universe, captives of time.

Beyond my own clumsily and tentatively stated framework Matthiessen has written a magnificent book: open, vulnerable with his own frailties; thick and lush, a kind of lunar paradigm and map of the sacred for any man's journey, where the snow leopard itself sits grail-like at the edge of consciousness, an infinitely stubborn koan in beast's clothing. Toward the end of the book when Matthiessen's Sherpa guide and mentor, perhaps ally, named Tutken disappears, we return again to the vertigo of the modern. But there is a sense, however slight and fleeting, that the book has transcended the usual limits of language and has given us a glimpse of a world that is not less "there" for the fact that we will never see it.

1978

Fording and Dread

It's always awkward to identify a pattern in life when the language does not seem to reflect the thousand-faceted character of the experience itself. That's why we have novelists, in fact. There's something almost eery, tremendously uncomfortable about the will to change, because we're never quite sure what precipitated it, let alone what might become of us in the process. As an instance I have spent four months, most of it in a cabin alone, trying to understand the nature of the character I have invented. Other than a pile of notes, I have written nothing. It is clear that certain therapeutic notions are inimical to art, but then one reaches a point, a transitional mode between past and future, where art becomes at least temporarily unimportant. Also, it has become apparent that perhaps the character I'm inventing is the one I wish to become. I'm not sure.

I admit I saw the whole process coming over a year ago. I wanted to live but as equally wanted the life I was living to stop. It was as if the force that drove me through forty-four years, five novels, six books of poems, had itself run out of fuel, lost energy and interest. The "inactivity" of summer reflected this refusal to use the same system, the same mnemonic devices to be productive. I wanted something new and stalked new ways, which though they haven't worked, have at least showed some new possibilities. Needless to say none of this was structured as geometrically as I am outlining here.

But where am I now, September 5, 1982? Even the tiredest soul can wail for freedom. Today is cold and rainy and I don't particularly long for a clear sunlit silence because that will come in a few days. The other thing is another matter. I want freedom from dread, alcohol, gluttony, habits of all sorts: "set" ways of thinking, set ways of travel, money anxiety, sexual anxiety, over-sleeping, poor physical condition, questionable marriage, not freedom from marriage but the bad aspects of marriage. That's for starters.

Of course I wouldn't know this if I hadn't already made certain inroads, but the inroads must explode because I want it faster. It must happen before my heart breaks, to be frank. I don't know right now how to make it happen faster. This might sound desperate because it is. Of course I know that desperation is the wrong spirit unless tightly controlled.

I recently came upon a book by a sixteenth-century Japanese swordsman, Musashi, where he speaks of fording, of the opportune time to make a critical move—the metaphor of crossing water at the right time and place. I used to enjoy reading about how the pioneers and settlers managed to cross these enormous rivers. Musashi on the surface is involved with warrior strategy, adding "You must research this well."

How does one regenerate? Especially when one's soul or spirit, mind if you wish, is full of snares, knots, goblins, the backward march of the dead, the bridges that end halfway and still hang in the air, those who do not love you, those who irreparably harmed you, intentionally or not, and even those you hurt badly and who live on encapsulated in your regret. The past never seems to lose its energy, reduced as it is to the essence of all we have met.

But this isn't particularly helpful. Where is the best place in the river to get across? Who have been your guides, dead and living, and are they true or false? This stumped me to the extent that I stopped making these notes for two days and read the galleys of the new James Hillman book. According to Hillman our main guide is the story we have already collected and written for ourselves. We may stop and look the story over in a period of unrest but we stick to it out of convenience. When depressed we might hammer at our psyches as if they were tract houses, but we tend to fall back into the same tale. The cave might be genuinely ugly but it is a familiar ugliness from which to peek out at the world, wrapping ourselves in the detritus of dreams, memories, actualities.

Last night something odd happened. I walked out of the cabin after ten to go have my customary drinks. I had turned off the generator and was looking skyward to check for northern lights when I heard a howl from an area down and across the river in a delta; a real scalp-tingler, long, full and wavering, the pulse accelerating. My dog flattened to the ground in immediate submission. We headed for the bright lights of town. Just now it occurred to me I should have howled back. It is warm after a hard breeze and a wind from the south has strewn rose petals and yellow birch leaves on the grass with an early autumn lushness of color. Flies are active and I hear bats and mice scratching above the ceiling. My present alarm is because I have entered the autumn of my life. What is the fright, as if I had heard Eros in an androgynous contralto reminding me of all that I have forgotten or never knew? Why have I been up here alone for so long? It is certainly unexampled in my life which is typified by a remote sluggishness, alternating with periods of frenzied work every two years. Maybe I am looking for the other beneath the fiction I have created that is my life. Hillman asks, "What have we done with the twin that was given us when we were given our soul?" What is the topography of dread? Why are alcohol and drugs in any quantity brakes for the soul? What is beyond dread? These months have been a refusal to reenter the same cycle. One is reminded of those wells in the Southwest that have lowered the aquifer to such an extent that new immense pumps have been installed. There is a sense of a different reality, a chance to overhaul perceptions. It is a gamble. Walking backwards down the steps to the river at night. To tap arrogant Neuman, what is the origin and history of your own consciousness? Unloose the door from its jambs, as if one lay in a mold and let the sediment of one's life calcify around body, brain and soul, frozen, unmoving.

The particulars and specifics are disarming. Much of life is not disappointing, much of life is really nothing at all, just sort of big open spaces in one's history, a simulacrum of the sparsely inhabited places on maps. There is a deep silliness in psychologisms which treat one as an improperly maintained garden. But there's no point in making light of fads and systems when I've had a go at many and come up short. I've managed a recent humor about success which I treated badly with the attitude of my father which involved deep pessimism, the maudlin, a sense of "this too is martyrdom." This promoted an urge to squander a lot in a daffy retreat back toward the beleaguered, anonymous writer. It's probably a little too late to be anonymous. Being recognizable is certainly the most disabling accoutrement of success but I'm now sure it doesn't have to be. This Japanese cabin in the U.P. where the world is neither known or understood helps a great deal. The concern here is for survival à la Van Gogh's potato eaters.

I was just thinking of the therapeutic process and the fly-fishing method called dredging where you repeatedly cast a deep sinking line in a river, lake, or channel where there are none of the obvious hints of prey you find in other sorts of fishing. A novelist and poet creates realities that he doesn't fully comprehend. It was years before I recognized my *Letters to Yesenin* was a victorious suicide note. There is a banality in the antithetical thinking that says one doesn't deserve to be quite happy quite often. Leopards don't sing arias except their own and toads are poor dancers. The limitless ambition of the young writer, whose vast, starry, nineteen-year-old nights must come down to the middle-aged man in the northern night listening for more howls, trying to learn what he is with neither comparison nor self-laceration, treasuring that autumnal sensuality of one who has given his life's blood to train his soul, brain and senses to the utmost.

It is a testament to captiousness to see how blundering and simpleminded the fiction I created as my own story is, compared to the fiction I give to others. I remember what Rilke said: "Every angel is terrible/still though, alas, I invoke thee/almost deadly birds of the soul." The angel in this case is the anima, the mirror of the figure we wish to stay in the state of becoming. Dread and all her improbabilities are an inevitability we must make our lover. It is singularly stupid not to make yourself ready for anything that could happen. In my own memory, time has never stopped.

1982

Passacaglia on Getting Lost

The most immediate sensation when totally and unfathomably lost is that you might die. I live in a world where I still very much regret the deaths of Romeo and Juliet; even the fate of Petrouchka moistens my single eye— the blind left eye weeps only underwater or when I'm asleep and the dreams are harrowing. The first time I got lost in the winter I think I was about fourteen. I worked my way inside an enormous hollow white-pine stump, the remnant of an 1897 forest fire in an area of northern Michigan. It was quite comfortable in there and it saddened me to start the stump on fire in order to be found.

It is particularly stupid to get lost in the winter because, barring a blizzard, you can retrace your steps. But I hate this in life the same as I do in poems and novels. It is a little painful to keep saying hello. The baked bean and onion sandwich was partially frozen in my coat pocket. The sun was covered with a dense cloud mass. The fire burned orange and balsamic, pitchy, melting the snow in a circle around the stump. I was a little goofy from hypothermia and thought of Cyd Charisse, and what all three of the McGuire sisters would look like bare naked. To retrace your steps; it is not in my nature to want to repeat a single day of my life. Maybe a portion of a day that involved lovemaking or a meal—a sauté of truffles and foie gras at Faugeron's in Paris ruined by jet lag, or a girl that disappeared into heaven in a Chevrolet after a single, brief encounter. I would repeat an hour with the cotton, lilac skirt; the white sleeveless blouse, the grass stain on her elbow. I could breathe through the back of her knee.

I am not going to talk about the well-equipped Republican clones you see marching like Hitler Youth up and down the spine of the Rockies or in any of the national parks, national forests, wilderness areas in America. On the tops of mountains I've seen their cocaine wrappers and fluorescent shoe-strings. At five thousand feet in the Smokies there were tiny red piss-ants crowding around a discarded Dalkon shield.

Hikers, like Midwestern drivers, are bent on telling you how "far" they've hiked. "I did twenty-three miles carrying fifty-one pounds." I usually advise more lateral or circular movement. A trail, other than an animal trail, is an insult to the perceptions. It is the hike as an extension of the encounter group. Over in the Rainy River area a big Cree once portaged eighteen miles carrying 500 pounds in a single day. His sister carried 320.

There is clearly not enough wilderness left for the rising number of people who say they desire it. It's not wilderness anyway if it only exists by our permission and stewardship. The famous Thoreau quote says "wildness," not "wilderness." We have become Europe and each, with a sense of privacy and tact, must secure his or her own wildness.

It strikes me that Peter Matthiessen has the best public understanding of the natural world; I say "public" because there might be someone out there who can still walk on water. It is the generalists who have the grace that translates; the specialist, like those tiny novels that emerge from the academy, want to be correct above all else. The specialist is part of a doubtless useful collective enterprise. We are fortunate to have generalists who make leaps for those of us who are too clumsy or lazy, or who have adjusted to the fact that we can't do everything: Hoagland, Abbey, Nabhan, Lopez, Schulteis, Peacock and his grizzlies, among others, but these come to mind.

Getting lost is to sense the "animus" of nature. James Hillman said that animals we see in dreams are often "soul doctors." When you first sense you are lost there is a goofy, tingling sensation. The mouth tends to dry up, the flesh becomes spongy. This can occur when you disbelieve your compass. Made in Germany, indeed! Post-Nazi terrorists dooming the poet to a night in the woods. But then the compass was only wrong on one occasion—a cheapish Taiwanese compass.

When we are lost we lose our peripheries. Our thoughts zoom outward and infect the landscape. Years later you can revisit an area and find these thoughts still diseasing the same landscape. It requires a particular kind of behavior to heal the location.

Gullies, hummocks in swamps, swales in the middle of large fields, the small alluvial fan created by feeder creeks, undercut riverbanks, miniature springs, dense thickets on the tops of hills: like Bachelard's attics, seashells, drawers, cellars, these places are a balm to me. Magic (as opposed to the hocus-pocus of miracles) is equated to the quality of attentiveness. Perhaps magic *is* the quality of attentiveness, the ultimate attentiveness. D. H. Lawrence said that the only aristocracy is that of consciousness. Certain locations seem to demand consciousness. Once I sat still so long I was lucky enough to have a warbler sit on my elbow. Certain of the dead also made brief visits.

Perhaps getting lost temporarily destroys the acquisitive sense. We tend to look at earth as an elaborate system out of which we may draw useful information. We "profit" from nature—that is the taught system. The natural world exists so that we may draw conclusions about it. This is the kind of soul-destroying bullshit that drove young people to lysergic acid in the sixties.

One night last summer I was lucky enough to see "time" herself—the moon shooting across the sky, the constellations adjusting wobbily, the sun rising and setting in seconds. I jumped in the river at daylight to come to my senses. Checked a calendar to make sure. No one really wants to be Hölderlin out in the garden with a foot of snow gathered on top of his head.

I t is interesting to see the Nature Establishment and the Nature Anti-Establishment suffocating in the same avalanche of tedium and bitterness. There is insufficient street experience to see how bad the bad guys are. They forget it was greed that discovered the country, greed that propelled the westward movement, greed that shipped the blacks, greed that murdered the Indians, greed that daily shits on the heads of those who love nature. Why are we shit upon, they wonder.

I prefer places valued by no one else. The Upper Peninsula has many of these places that lack the drama and differentiation favored by the garden-variety nature buff. I have a personal stump back in a forest clearing. Someone, probably a deer hunter, has left a beer bottle beside the stump. I leave the beer bottle there to conceal the value of the stump.

It took me twenty years to see a timber wolf in the wild. I could have foreshortened this time period by going to Isle Royale or Canada but I wanted to see the wolf as part of a day rather than as a novelty. We startled each other. From this single incident I dreamt I found the wolf with her back broken on a logging road. I knelt down and she went inside me, becoming part of my body and skeleton.

The shock of being lost as a metaphor is the discovery that you've never been "found" in any meaningful sense. When you're lost you know who you are. You're the only one out there. One day I was dressed in camouflage and stalking a small group of sandhill cranes which were feeding on frogs in the pine barrens not far from my cabin. I got within a few yards of them after an hour of crawling. I said "good morning," a phrase they were unfamiliar with; in fact, they were enraged and threatening. I made a little coyote yodel and they flapped skyward, the wind of their immense wings whooshing around my head. I ordered this camouflage outfit from Texas, not a bad place if you ignore the inhabitants and their peculiar urge to mythologize themselves against the evidence. One of the great empty and lovely drives left in the U.S. is from El Paso to San Antonio. Someday I will move to Nebraska for the same reason.

Of course getting lost is not ordinarily a threatening occasion. Two snowmobilers died a few years ago not all that far from my cabin but it was poignantly unnecessary. They could have piled deadfall wood around their machines and dropped matches into the remnants of the gas in the tanks, creating an enormous pyre for the search planes. Euphemisms for getting lost range from "I got a little turned around for a few hours" to "I wasn't lost, I just couldn't find my car until morning." The enemies are the occasional snowflakes in July, the cold and rain, the blackflies and mosquitoes, drinking swamp or creek water when a spring can always be found. Of course the greatest enemy is panic. The greatest panic I've ever felt was at an Umbanda rite in Brazil when I sensed that the others present weren't actually people. I became ill when a man leapfrogged through a garden on his back, and an old woman rubbed her left eyeball against my own and told me pointedly about my life in northern Michigan.

An old Chippewa I know carries a folded-up garbage bag in his pocket. He claims it is his portable home, keeping him warm and dry if he gets lost or tired. He finds coyote dens by scent, and whittles the heads of canes into renditions of his "dream birds." His favorite drink is a double martini. He asked me to check for a phone number of a "love" he had lost in 1931. He was somewhat disturbed, he told me, when it occurred to him that people didn't know that every single tree was different from every other tree. He is making me a cane to repel bears and to attract wolves and women. I will hang this cane on the cabin wall, being genetically too Calvinist to have any interest in sorcery.

It seems I will never be reviewed by Edmund Wilson or Randall Jarrell or Kenneth Burke, something I aspired to at nineteen in the jungle of Grove Street. For years I've wanted to take a walk with E. M. Cioran. I've rid myself of the usual fantasies about money, actresses, models, food, fishing, hunting, travel, by enacting them, though the money evaporated at startling speed through what accountants refer to as "spending habits." Cioran's mind is unique, the modernist temperament at an antipode not reached by novelists. I would get us mildly lost on the walk, which might amuse him. The name of Wittgenstein will not be mentioned. I want to ask Cioran to what degree the perception of reality is consensual. The answer will help me account for all of my bad reviews! Many of us apparently live in different worlds. Do we see the same sky as Crazy Horse? Think of Anne Frank's comprehension of the closet.

I know a pyramidal hill at least fifteen miles from the nearest dwelling. On this hill three small river systems have their beginnings, each of them a hundred or so miles long. I'm not giving out any directions to this place. The first two times I tried to go there I got turned around, succeeding on the third trip. My yellow Labrador was frightened on this hill, which in turn served to disturb me. The dog, however, is frightened of bears, coyotes, thunder, northern lights, the moon. I only stayed a few minutes.

Rilke said something on the order of "With all of its eyes the creature world beholds the open . . . " (Everyone should buy the astonishing new translation of *Sonnets to Orpheus* by Stephen Mitchell.) Unfavorable comparisons to animals are contraindicated. I confess I've talked at length to ravens, porcupines, crows, coyotes, infant porpoises, and particularly beautiful heads of garlic, but then others talk back at the television. It is natural for a child to imagine what a bird sees. "How do we know but that every bird that cuts the airy way is an immense world of delight closed to our senses five?" We don't. We should encourage ourselves to be a whale, a woman, a plant or planet, a lake, the night sky. There was a Cheyenne warrior named One Who Sees As A Bird: the tops of trees are ovoids bending away from the wind.

I'm a poor naturalist. A bird evokes the other times I've seen the bird, a delicious continuity, not a wish to run to my collection of bird books. I'm not against the idea of my work being forgotten if I can be an old geezer in a cabin smelling of wood smoke, kerosene, a bordeaux stain on my T-shirt, cooking a not-so-simple *salmi* of woodcock. It has only lately occurred to me that many of my concerns are anachronistic. Walking in the forest at night can be a cocaine substitute in addition to simply walking in the forest at night. Kokopele owned the best of all spirits for an artist. He led Picasso to do a gavotte at the age of eighty. He made Henry Miller a ping-pong champion.

Last August when I was turned around in a swamp I sat on a hummock and had a vision of death as a suck-hole in the universe, an interior plug, out of which we all go with a gurgle. I gurgled in the swamp. Frogs and birds answered. This is the sensuality of death, not the less beautiful for being terminal.

1986

Revenge

Everyone wants revenge, but scarcely anyone does anything about it. This is probably a good thing; in fact, this "good thing" is thought of as the social contract, wherein there is an implicit agreement by all to behave themselves, and incidents of misbehavior are to be dealt with by specifically designated authorities.

Unfortunately, nearly all of life is lived between the lines. An ungovernable passion in us that is capped by the sheer tonnage of law will squeeze out somewhere. On a certain, albeit low, level many of us regard the idea of capital punishment with mixed pleasure, but pleasure nevertheless. Some of us actually cheer outside the prison walls. In terms of gross receipts, Clint Eastwood has made a lot of people feel good. True, the mass has always loved the easy or childish stroke; only a nation in the most otiose moral stupor would turn out in droves for the profound silliness of *Rambo*. It's the kind of thinking that makes South Africa not all that bad but Nicaragua truly evil.

But before I get too high-minded, I should add that I'd like to see Stallone-Rambo sneak into Lebanon and deal with those crazed shitsuckers who beat, then shot, the young Navy man, Stethem, to death on the civilian American Airlines flight last June. The word civilian is important here. When an acquaintance of mine had his head, arms and legs chopped off as the result of a dope deal gone awry, I was upset—but then, business is business, as we are so fond of saying. It was the equivalent of war, and he was a soldier. Stethem, however, was flying home with a planeload of tourists when he was jumped on the face so relentlessly that his mom couldn't recognize him. More recently, a group of terrorists shanghaied a Mediterranean cruise ship, shot an old Jewish tourist named Klinghoffer and pitched him overboard in his wheelchair. The readily imagined visual is not pretty—the body would float for a while, but the chair would sink immediately. If I were to stop writing at this moment, walk into the bathroom and connect myself to a digital blood-pressure machine, the results would not be pleasant.

Why all this brooding and seething on both a personal and a national level? Despite the mood swings of a nation in disarray, probably no one is going to bring a living POW back from the jungles. And to get out of the level of comic-book mythology, it is doubtful that any recourse can be had in Stethem's death, nor any offered by our government, which is so lame and ineffectual in such matters. The fact that the Egyptian plane carrying Klinghoffer's murderers was escorted to Italy, only to have the ringleader set free, illustrates our bungling. It is obvious that we should be commissioning all the hot items to the Israelis on a piecework basis. Teddy Roosevelt launched a number of warships to secure the freedom of a single, solitary American citizen named Perdicaris, captured by a Moroccan sultan. "We want Perdicaris alive or Raisuli dead," said Teddy. But then, this is no longer a rough-riding world, and if you can't hear a computer whirring in the background or don't watch the news, you are blessedly infantile.

Revenge, frankly, can't be understood on a political level. The news of the most striking horror conceivable can enter Washington at midnight and be extruded the next morning in the studied inanities of a press conference. Revenge is human. Moving back in time, literally as far from a press conference as one can travel, after Bighorn, some Cheyenne squaws drove awls into Custer's very dead ears so he might be more attentive in the afterlife. Custer had been warned before his folly. This is getting closer. Our hearts are territorial, and the things closest to our hearts—our love for another, the deepest of friendships, our sense of our own dignity and even our sense of justice—are so hopelessly fragile that some of us strike out wildly in defense.

But Americans have never made an art of revenge as have the Sicilians, Corsicans or Mexicans. We shuffle and blunder, wanting to be largehearted in victory. We want to be simpleminded frontiersmen who get the job done.

The first revenge story we are likely to hear concerns the fabled dick in a jar. Apocryphal or not, this story is ubiquitous. I recently heard it in bars and service stations in Montana, Wyoming, Nebraska, Iowa and Wisconsin. I first heard it in Reed City, Michigan, probably in 1948 or 1949. A group of boys from ten to twelve would hang around a gas station on their

Schwinn balloon-tire bikes, listening to advice from a not-very-bright World War II veteran. Coca-Cola was a nickel a bottle, and there was the chance we would see Rochester from the Jack Benny radio show pass through town on his way to Idlewild, a black resort, in his huge limousine. Anyway, the pump jockey might show us his "kraut booty," as he called it, including a bayonet with dried blood on it, the blood of an American boy. Mingled with the usual stories of Nazi girls' fucking for chocolate bars was a horrifying tale.

"This buddy of mine over in Luther a few years ago was screwing this rich doctor's wife. She was a spitfire, and no man could handle this crazy bitch. The doctor found out about his wife's cheating. The doctor was sad, because there is no medicine to control a woman hungry for dick. The doctor started drinking and became mad as hell. He tracked his wife and my buddy to their love nest, a deer camp over near Leroy, south of Rose Lake. The doctor peeked in the cabin window and saw that the two lovers were all fucked out and asleep. He snuck in and chloroformed the both of them. He took a surgery knife and lopped off my buddy's cock and balls, then sewed up the hole in his crotch. He put the cock and balls in a jar of vinegar so they could be preserved, like pork tongues or dill pickles. He left the jar on the night table and went on home. So hours later, my buddy and the woman wake up feeling like they been operated on, but a woman, as you might know, has nothing to cut off. She sees the jar and the jig is up."

"Did the guy die?" we asked.

" 'Course not. My buddy had to move to Detroit, because everybody knew. The nuts and bolts of the story is, he is now a girl. He sits down to pee and has taken up religion, because the simple fact is, the boy will never fuck again."

"What happened to the jar?" someone asked inappropriately.

"Got me by the balls. Might still be there in the cabin."

This fruitcake, peculiarly American tale served to make me forever wary of doctors' wives. The most beautiful of them may as well be wearing a fright wig and an Elmer Fudd mask. Perhaps in the safety of a submarine. . . .

Of course, our banal story of rube or bumpkin revenge is a mere skeleton of classic revenge. Much of our mental makeup is a stream of rehearsals of threats, real or imagined, an inventory of resentments that we moderate or else become psychotic. Classical revenge demands a purity of hatred against a backdrop of a specific code of honor usually found only in cultures that have not lost their traditional underpinnings—Sicilians, Corsicans, Mexicans again come to mind. In the United States, such notions are usually limited to rural areas of the South and West and to cities with large ethnic populations. In Detroit a few years back, there was a shoot-out between a group of Albanian cousins and brothers over a question of honor that left the police and the criminal element gasping. With the exception of the Belushi brothers, Albanians win the inscrutability contest over the Chinese.

Revenge doesn't thrive on situational ethics. You can scarcely kill your wife for unfaithfulness if you belong to a swap club. Moral waffling doesn't lend itself to the kind of sharply delineated code of ethics that is the breeding ground of righteous anger. Any wrong committed against you where your first impulse is to call the police or a lawyer is not fit material for revenge. The anger has to be a blow to the solar plexus or the groin: one has to stew, brood, agonize. As Faulkner might have it, the grief must grieve on universal bones.

Perhaps there is something identifiable in our history that makes us clumsy at our revenge in comparison with the Latins. The Romance languages suppurate with blood and intrigue, from the peasantry to the highest Church levels, while English (as spoken in America) has given the world explicit notions of the frontier, the gunfight and the quick-draw artist. Anyone in southern Europe knows it's smarter to shoot your enemy, good or bad, in the back. If you are right, why endanger yourself? The following little story from France is a wonderful example. (This and the other anecdotes are true, with situations and locations changed for obvious reasons— the legal profession has so trivialized human concourse that it can best be understood as a nationwide smear of Krazy Glue preventing freedom of movement. Much of future revenge will center on the legal profession.)

An old man in France told me this one evening over a goblet of calvados. "During the occupation of France, there was a reasonably successful farmer near a small village in Normandy. This farmer did his best to ignore the Germans, had a wife and two teenaged daughters and a son away at war. The farmer raised pigs and fed them primarily on beets and beet greens. Scarcely anyone knew that he and his family provided a safe house for members of the Resistance and for Jews trying to escape from the country. There was an envious couple in town and, as an aside, the husband had been thrashed by the farmer for trying to molest one of his daughters when she was a child. The couple, Vichy types, caught wind of the farmer's Resistance activities and reported them to the Germans. The Germans raided the farm and found two Jewish children, whom they summarily bayoneted. The farmer and his wife were forced to watch while their pigs were killed, their daughters raped and strangled. The Germans then held a barbecue.

"When the son returned from the war, he heard the story but was wise enough to delay his revenge, allowing the couple to think they had gotten away with their betrayal. In 1947, the son and two of his friends bound and kidnapped the couple. They took them to an abandoned quarry where a large cave had been partially filled with a ton or so of beets and a dozen pigs. The son and his friends returned in a few weeks with a dozen villagers. They all toasted the well-gnawed bones of the couple and had a fine pig roast there in the quarry. I cherish the moment the pigs finished the beets and began chewing on those swine. May they be eaten in hell forever."

This is a wonderful piece of classic revenge for not altogether obvious reasons: The son waited in order to give the couple a sense of prosperous grace—revenge, as they say in Palermo, is a dish best served cold—and, more important, the punishment precisely suited the complexion of the crime. There on the dark floor caked with pig shit, you can feel the first bite. Bullets would have been peaceful and unearned bee stings in such a case.

Of course, revenge is frequently captious and childish. A man shoots a recalcitrant cigarette machine. A drunk with a cleft palate was teased and mimicked by snowmobilers in a bar I occasionally visit. He demolished a dozen of their machines with his three-quarter-ton pickup. A friend in San Francisco was justifiably enraged by his landlord. He bored a hole in the roof and gave the landlord's apartment a several-thousand-gallon hosing that, unfortunately, streamed through the floor into his own apartment.

And at a certain point, there is a baffling stupidity to anger. Years ago, when I learned that my sister's first husband had slugged her, I made inquiries to find out how I could get him murdered; but I was on a Guggenheim grant and could scarcely handle the seven-grand fee. I settled for a phone threat. Years before that, I set out to murder the drunken driver who had killed my father and sister; but he, too, had been killed in the accident.

271

I suspect that affairs of the blood and those of love bring us closest to the flash point.

Another acquaintance is a commercial fisherman from Seattle: "I came home from two months at sea. It was barely after dawn when I got to the house. I was too young to know that it's only good etiquette to warn your wife that you're coming home. I took off my boots and tiptoed up the stairs, horny as could be.

"Well, she wasn't alone, and you know who was with her? My best friend! Well, I slipped my .38 out of the dresser drawer and looked down at them through the sights, wondering which one to kill first. I heard my three-year-old daughter cough in the next room. My wife looked beautiful, and I thought of all the good times I had had with my friend Bob. I knew this kind of thing could happen with friends on both sides of the fence, though I didn't know why. Just proximity, I guess. So I was standing there and I suddenly pressed down on his neck with my free hand until his eyes were popping. I jammed the .38 in his mouth up to the cylinder and cocked the pistol. My wife woke up, but she knew enough not to say anything. She was rigid as ice. I lifted the barrel up hard against his palate and ripped the pistol out, with his teeth coming out with the sight. I can say he will never forget me. I walked out of the room, kissed my daughter good-bye, and now I'm here in Corpus Christi."

There are certain people whom one does not advise to seek professional help, a marriage counselor or a minister. They are neither better nor worse than the rest of us, but they are there. To say that such people have atavistic notions of justice is mostly to provide fodder for the modern-living pages of newspapers, where not much can be lost because there was never much at stake. I tried to persuade this man to go back to Seattle and make amends with his wife, and all he did was break into tears and walk out of the bar— and this was ten years after the event.

Naturally, the origin of the taboo of adultery is that the social contract in small communities demands it in the name of order. Modern urban life weakens the taboo a great deal, but many men and women remain distinctly unmodern. I remember telling a feminist that a traveler in the eighteenth century had noted that an Indian tribe in the upper Midwest punished a squaw for adultery by letting everyone ceremonially fuck her in public. If she lived through it, fine. Before the feminist could go for my throat, I added that the guilty man was executed immediately.

The nastiest piece of instant revenge I've ever heard about was told to me by an old Sicilian living in New York. "Back in the early sixties," he said, "there was this old *capo* out in Brooklyn who was semi-retired. He owned a little restaurant and loved to cook. He was a very rich man, but he would put on an apron and cook me his favorite dish, a *cacciatore* made with pheasant and sausage and the ripest of fresh tomatoes. Without the ripe tomatoes, you have nothing, you understand? His youngest son was a bum, almost a hippie. He wanted the old man to get into the heroin business and the old man refused. So the bum makes a deal by getting two hundred grand from this lawyer, saying his dad, the *capo*, will back up the deal. So the son fucks up the deal because he's got no muscle, and the lawyer is out the money, which anyway came from a crooked public-construction deal. The lawyer forces the son to take him to see the father. Right in the father's own house, at the kitchen table, the lawyer loses his temper because the old man won't back his son. The lawyer called the *capo* a flea-bitten old dago, a greasy wop. The old man pretends to be sad and depressed. He shuffles around behind the lawyer's hard-backed chair, grabs him by the hair and snaps his head back, stunning him. He bites out the lawyer's goddamned Adam's apple! Chews it right out! He spits the Adam's apple in his son's face and tells him he'll do the same to him if he brings any more lawyers into the home. The lawyer bleeds to death and the *capo* tells the son to clean up the mess; he told me this story while we were eating dinner. I wanted to ask him if he brushed his teeth afterward, but he's a dignified old man."

This would have made an additional, effective scene in *The Godfather*— but then, true violence is rarely done well by Hollywood, where the texture of the scenes is too stagy and neurotic, lacking the immediacy of a neighborhood bar fight, with the screaming and the spilled blood smelling like sheared copper.

In fact, show business, publishing, the media and the arts in general offer nothing in terms of revenge. The ethics are frankly too blurred for a solid push-off. Years ago, Steve McQueen was visiting the ranch of Tom McGuane and noticed a sign in the kitchen reading, GETTING EVEN IS THE BEST REVENGE. McQueen, a man of sharp edges, thought the sign went a bit far. Once, in a state of pointless rage about Hollywood, I asked the director Bob Rafelson how he could possibly get fired, sue the studio, then go back to work for the same studio while the suit was pending. This man is not known for his wisdom, but he cautioned me that things in the movies moved too quickly to hold a grudge. Hollywood is not Latin America, where you might sit for three years eating mangoes and drinking rum until you decide to shoot the man who called your sister a whore.

People at large don't realize that publishing and the reviewing media are a microcosm of the movies, the boxing world, ward politics, a Serengeti water hole and South African racial postures and, as such, don't merit the ivy-laden respect they manufactured in the past. The most wildly unjustified bad review is simply a bad review, akin to someone's saying your child is ugly. Sometimes your child *is* ugly; but then, what a job is this, sitting there telling people their children are ugly, especially when the viewpoint is last week's Gotham attitude. In any event, duels are no longer fought over such things.

But this is not to say that classic revenge can't occur in business, just that it's less than likely in the media and in show business, where, as Aristophanes would have it, "whirl is king." I can readily imagine the intrigue involved in a corporation like General Motors, where there are several thousand young, hyperintelligent M.B.A.s who all want to be the C.E.O. In first-class compartments, you see these people speaking to one another in short, clipped barks, manicured like bench-bred dogs. But business revenge lacks resonance without some added quality. An American saw dictates, "Don't go into business with your best friend." The following, told to me by a retired sheriff in South Dakota, is a ghastly example.

"Two boys grew up on farms in eastern Nebraska just after World War II. They wanted to be cowboys, so they left school at sixteen and went to Montana, getting jobs on an enormous ranch near White Sulphur Springs. One, named Dave, was smaller, craftier and more imaginative. The other, named Ted, was slower but of normal intelligence, ruminative, a reader of Western novels and a first-rate steer wrestler.

"By their mid-twenties, they made the down payment on a small cattle-hauling business and stockyard by virtue of Ted's rodeo winnings and savings. Dave had spent his money on ladies and flashy pickup trucks, but he was the brains behind the newly acquired business. Ted stayed away from the paperwork, having full trust in Dave because they had been partners since they were kids. As the business prospered, they married cousins and added a farm-equipment dealership and a grain elevator to their holdings. Ted acted as foreman and troubleshooter, while Dave stuck to the office, taking up golf and buying a Cessna. They pretty much stopped seeing each other socially, what with Ted's refusal to learn correct grammar or join service organizations.

"Things came to a head when Ted broke his ankle on a cattle chute. During his short convalescence, he talked it all over with his wife, and they decided to try to sell their half of the business to Dave and find a ranch to buy. They were sick of the vagaries of modern life, and Ted wanted to get back to the life he'd come West for.

"The upshot was that a meeting was arranged, and when Ted arrived, Dave had two local lawyers and an accountant with him. Everyone seemed a tad embarrassed to explain to Ted that he owned nothing on paper and had no legal demand for any monies from the corporation. But in consideration of his hard work, they had decided to give him a check for fifty grand, which would fulfill any claims he might have against Dave. Ted wasn't such a fool that he couldn't immediately figure that the fifty grand was about five percent of what the company was worth. He tried to look at Dave, who naturally averted his eyes. Then Ted picked up the check, tore it in half and walked out.

"Well, everyone in the area knew what had happened, but there were enough new and prosperous people moving in that Dave didn't lack for buddies. Ted moved north with his family and became top hand, then foreman on a big ranch owned by a rich dude from Chicago.

"Then one day, about a year later, Ted calmly walks into a Rotary meeting where Dave was speaking and slaps the shit out of him in front of everyone. This beating took place once a year for seven years, including once on December 30th, and on the following January third, when Dave got out of the hospital. So last year, Dave sells out and moves to La Jolla, California. Dave couldn't stand the behind-the-back laughter and the simple fact that every tavern in town had a calendar pool with a lot of money on his next beating. The upshot is that I got a call from a detective in La Jolla. Seems that Dave was sitting on the beach with a flashy girlfriend. Down the beach comes a cowboy who beats the shit out of him, right in front of all these fancy people. The detective was trying to figure out what was happening, because when they let Ted out of jail in the morning—Dave wouldn't press charges—all Ted would say was that the price of beef had dropped from seventy to fifty-one in the past ten years. So I told the detective the story. He said to tell Ted to stay out of La Jolla. I said he would tell Ted himself when he came out there next year but that I'd be real careful if I was him."

There's a purity here, but perhaps it's a bit too relentless. Maybe not. I know that Dave upped his offer over the years from the original fifty grand, but to no avail. I have no idea whether or not Dave's attitude is that of a smart guy or a penitent or if he's considering a move to London, Deauville or Tibet. The squeamish sensation can come from the question, At what point does the transgressor become the victim? The back wall is that a modestly intelligent man, if sufficiently cautious, can destroy anyone he wishes.

And then there are stories that are pointlessly foul: "This farmer's wife was going to divorce him because he was all the time beating the hell out of her. Once, at a church picnic, he shoved her face down into a hot bowl of scalloped potatoes and a couple of us brethren couldn't stand it and kicked the shit out of him. Well, this farmer knew if she divorced him he'd have to sell the farm to pay the divorce settlement, so he goes up to Minneapolis and hires this ex-con. He probably got the idea on TV, but he tells the ex-con he'll pay him five grand to rape and rough up the wife. The farmer gives the ex-con a date to do the job while the farmer is supposed to be in Grand Forks."

"The ex-con is suspicious, even though he has been given half the money up front. So when he comes to town, he leaves a note under his pillow in his motel, knowing if things go well, he'll be back in an hour. He goes out to the homestead and rapes the poor lady. While he's in the saddle, the farmer—who was supposed to be away—shoots him through the window three times with a 30.06. Naturally the slugs went through both bodies.

"So the farmer drives off to the sheriff's office and collapses on the desk with the rape story. The bastard is still weeping when the deputy shows up with a note from the only motel in town and the farmer goes ape shit. It was real sad we couldn't have hung him right there."

This is a transparently disgusting piece of low life. As a tonic, I offer a story told to me by a French count about his own father, an eccentric gentleman, now dead: "I think I told you that my father was an ace in both wars, in addition to being an inventor and a *bon vivant*. As a young pilot during World War I, he was flying out of the Dordogne. The situation was indescribably tense, and between missions he played with his two friends, Joseph, a crow he had owned for years, and Simon, a kit fox. He even took those two for plane rides. Everyone in the barracks loved these animals, except for an officer who was my father's immediate superior. This officer was a nasty character who hated my father because he was a count and because he was very successful with the girls in the neighboring town. One day while my father was on a mission, this officer returned to his room to discover that the crow and the fox had tipped a good bottle of wine off his desk and had eaten some smoked sausages and bread. The animals had also shit on the floor. The officer flew into a rage and strangled both animals, hanging them from the doorknob to my father's room.

"When my father returned from his mission, he pretended to be only mildly upset, though he was grief-stricken. He buried the animals together and mourned them in private. Even after the war, he visited the grave of his beloved friends, Simon and Joseph. Anyway, all the pilots in the barracks— including the guilty officer—kept waiting for my father to do or say something, but after a month or so, they were lulled into thinking the incident was over.

"One evening, my father shared a bottle of good brandy with the officer, and they decided to go to town and visit some girls. On the way back, when the officer was feeling drunk and well-fucked, my father threw him off a high bridge down into the river and the rocks far below. The body was found the next afternoon, and it was assumed that the officer had fallen over the rail while drunk. Everyone knew what must have happened, but no one said a word."

This story has a lovely purity to it, despite the question of whether or not the death was merited, or if any death is ever truly merited. I recently heard a hick radio preacher say that AIDS was "God's judgment on the homos," as if God were the drum major in the band composed of Reagan, Falwell, the Pentagon and the U.S. Congress. "'Vengeance is mine . . .' saith the Lord," or someone said that He said it. It's hard to put the money on a bet you're not going to collect until dead.

Years ago, I wrote a novella, *Revenge*, in a collection called *Legends of the Fall*. The story concerns the nearly implausible anguish between two friends, an American fighter pilot and a Mexican *barone*, caused by an act of betrayal. The relatively innocent woman over whom they are fighting dies. I don't think good novels are written for dogmatic reasons, to offer principles of right conduct, and I certainly didn't figure out the soul of revenge other than that, like many other forms of human behavior, it destroys innocent and guilty alike. As Gandhi said after Hiroshima, "The Japanese have lost their bodies, now we will see if the Americans have lost their souls." This is the kind of question Melville filed under "the whiteness of the whale."

On the way back from Montana last summer, I stopped at Fort Robinson, Nebraska. The site of the murder of Crazy Horse was closed due to "budget restrictions." I felt a surge of anger akin to a lump of hot coal under the breastbone. The scene of one of the most momentous events in the soul history of the nation was closed while gaggles of tourists wheezed through the cavalry-horse barns. I would gladly have given up my own life to see a few thousand mounted Sioux come over the hill and torch the whole place. You can get consciousness and a conscience free by reading history. It awakens a desire in you, thought by many childish, to see parity on earth with no hope of heaven.

And if in weak moments you hope for heaven, you want to see the bittersweet surrealism of Crazy Horse riding double with Anne Frank on Ruffian, riding through the cosmos from the Southern Cross to Arcturus, from Betelgeuse to the morning star.

1986

Night Walking

It is an oddly Protestant notion that life is a form of punishment to be endured to reach a greater end. Even when this idea isn't allowed to be overwhelming, it's still hiding behind the curtains like a headless leper ready to reach out and grab you in case you're feeling a little too good.

Life is a vale of woe, they used to say, during my childhood in Michigan. The illustrated Bible was full of pictures of bleeding folks, vipers biting kids, sorrowful ladies, old guys sleeping on beds of rags, rocks and ashes. If we survived the Nazis and Japs, that wouldn't prevent God, in all his justified anger, from snuffing out the sun, moon and stars. At the end of the road was probably the Lake of Fire, but before that could be reached, there was a lot of hard work and grinding poverty to go through. My own distinct case history reached its theological nadir when I was blinded in one eye at age seven by a little girl wielding a broken bottle. We had our clothes off in a heavily wooded vacant lot on an exploratory venture.

A severe childhood injury is not a bad preparation for life in this portion of the twentieth century. It makes you empathetic and wary, and you lack the built-in compass your friends seem to have: fence posts and trees contort into question marks, and at any moment you might fall through the earth where the crust is thin. Much later, certain news photos would have a natural resonance: the girl's mouth torn open in a simian howl at Kent State, and the Oriental tyke trotting nudely down the road after a napalm bath. Happier images are arrayed above my desk: a crow wing and a heron wing, an antisuicide button, a dried grizzly turd, a small toy pig, a Haitian baby shoe found on the beach in Florida after the boatload of blacks had been carted off to jail, having missed the Statue of Liberty by a thousand miles.

The northern Midwest night I grew up in was the only immediately available mystery, other than the bombazine Saturday matinees featuring the likes of Roy Rogers and the Sons of the Pioneers. There was a whole theater full of village and farm kids trying to figure out what tumbleweed was, only to be released back out into a black sky and immense snowbanks. Years later, while hitchhiking to California, I was in a car accident and finally saw tumbleweed an inch from my nose and heard again the warbling of the Pioneers.

But summer nights, winter nights and walking. My father, who owned the unlikely name of Winfield Sprague Harrison, built a cabin on a lake with the help of his brothers for the grand sum of a thousand dollars in 1946. My uncles had just returned from full-term service in World War II and were particularly kind to me as one of the fellow injured. I took walks with them and was referred to as Little Beaver, after the Red Ryder comic strip. Then, while my uncles busied themselves fishing or getting drunk, I began to walk during the day and evening alone. I discovered that twilight was a fine time to walk, and night herself was even more wonderful. I walked along creeks and a river and around the lake, with the voices of bass fishermen carrying to the shore. Once, through a cabin window, I saw a nude girl dancing with a Dalmatian dog in the light of an oil lamp; another time I saw a very old couple in utter hysterics listening to "Fibber McGee and Molly" on a battery-operated radio. The old man slid off his chair, kicking his feet with laughter. The old woman helped him back up on the couch, and they began pelting each other with popcorn. There was no electric power in the area, so night was truly dark.

I envied Jesus' ability to walk on water, imagining how I would look down through the surface of the lake as if it were glass, observing the secret lives of fishes and turtles and the fabled and elusive water bird, the loon, which could swim faster underwater, it was said, than the penguin or dolphin, a Jap torpedo or a German submarine.

I had a particular spot favored for a big moon—a grove of white birches where deer wandered and where, if you stupidly missed the point, you could read a newspaper in the shimmering light. Blue herons lived near the grove, and they often fished in the shallows on bright nights. There was a Chippewa Indian burial mound, and a girl I knew said if you put your ear to the ground, you could hear dead warriors talking with their wives and children. Frankly, I never dared put my ear to the ground. Terror at night, though, was a splendid antidote to the lassitude of hot August afternoons for a boy freelancing with a hoe and earning a dime an hour.

Often I spent weeks on the farm of my Swedish-immigrant grandparents, especially when my mother was having yet another baby. I walked down long rows of corn twice my height, through wheat fields, often ending up near a pond where the white bones of slaughtered cattle and pigs were dumped and mammoth water snakes glided across the sheen of algae on the water. If there was rain or a thunderstorm, I sat in the Model A or under an upended pig-scalding pot on sawhorses, listening to what my brother said was Chinese music. In the barn I sat on a milk stool and listened to the cattle and draft horses eating in the dark, or up in the mow I could lie back in the hay with all the barn cats, uncatchable in the daylight, surrounding me at night like true friends.

It is amusing to think that the God I thought had ruptured my eyeball and propelled me into the dark is now, evidently, a mascot of the Republican party. Times change.

I remember slipping out of the farmhouse and walking three miles across the fields to a small village by a lake, where there was a roller-skating rink, roofed but with sides open to the night air. Girls in dresses as brief as bathing suits would float around and around to improbably beautiful organ music. When the girls stopped for a rest, they would chatter and brush back their damp hair. Standing by the railing, I thought they all looked and smelled very good. I would move as close as courage allowed, exposing the uninjured side of my face and hoping to be noticed. I was always bumping into things, what with missing the whole left side of the world.

My father, as the county agricultural agent, helped run the annual fair. It was basically an exposition and competition of farm animals and produce, with the highlights being a horse pulling contest and a 4-H amateur talent show. Along with the last day of school, after which my failings would no longer be noticed for three months, the fair was the main event of the year. I never managed my behavior very well, then or now. One evening I ate cotton candy, hot dogs, french fries, drank a half dozen pops at a nickel a bottle and smoked a filched cigar. For some reason I became ill and walked off into the dark beyond the parked cars and stock trucks, up a long slope and through a field of oats to an elm tree, where I lay down and puked my heart out. When I recovered and looked back down the hill at the fair, it was a wildly colored and beautiful jewel: the gold, vertical bracelet of the ferris wheel, the smell of the cattle and horse barns, the merry-go-round music, the racked machinery of the tilt-a-whirl, and from a stage in front of the bleachers, a blond girl I favored sang "Candy Kisses," followed by a man playing "The Old Rugged Cross" on a musical handsaw.

We are more equal at night. At nineteen, in New York City and San Francisco, I admired Ginsberg's "Howl" and wanted to be among the "best minds of my generation destroyed by madness, starving hysterical naked/ dragging themselves through the negro streets at dawn looking for an angry fix." I wasn't quite sure how to go about it, but I tried, crisscrossing both cities, discovering garlic and Benzedrine, playing the music I loved in my head—Charlie Parker, Stravinsky, Thelonious Monk, George Shearing, Telemann, Sonny Rollins. Later there were night walks in Paris and London, Costa Rica and Ecuador, where I flushed a tree full of vultures on a cliff far above the Pacific swells; Moscow and Leningrad, where I walked the Neva embankment, thinking about my distant cousin, the poet Sergei Yesenin; the beach north of Mombasa, where tiny, finger-size poisonous snakes tried to get in my pant cuffs; Rio, where you can store minuscule bikinis in your cheeks like a Buddha squirrel. Foreign oceans have the aura of countries that cartographers have forgotten to put on maps.

At present I have tried to stop everything, pure and simple, stuffing time and memory into a custom-blown fishbowl from Belgium, but without success. At my cabin, miles from the nearest neighbor in the Upper Peninsula of Michigan, I walk at night when the moon isn't shrouded by the fog or the cold rain that dominates the area—weather that seems to suit my temperament. I hear coyotes, whippoorwills and loons, bears wallowing off through swamps, and once I heard and saw a timber wolf. If you are bored, strained, lacerated, enervated by the way we live now, I suggest a night walk as far as you can get from a trace of civilization. This form of walking is a dance, and the ghost that follows you, your moon-cast shadow, is your true, androgynous parent, bearing within its distinct outline the child who has always directed your every move.

1987

From the *Dalva* Notebooks, 1985–87

The thirteen-year-old girl walks out into the damp moonlight. It's after midnight and I'm trying to imagine the freshness of her emotions.

Only when I'm fatigued do I worry about being vindicated.

I explained to Ms. ——— that life was a vastly mysterious process to which our culture inures us so we won't become useless citizens.

I'm inventing a country song, "Gettin' Too Old to Run Away." In the middle of these sloppy ironies I remembered the tremendous silence of the midday eclipse last summer. Nature was confused & the birds roosted early. I was full of uncontrollable anger because I had to leave for L.A. in a few days for a screenplay conference. No one liked my idea of the life of Edward Curtis except me.

In a dream a ranch foreman named Samuel Creekmouth appeared to me and told me how to behave. I became irritable but in the morning had a lush & jubilant vision of what the novel was to be.

On the walk there were two small beaver, a huge black snake, a great blue heron feathering into a southwest wind, sand dunes caving into a furious sea on a rare hot day in late April.

Hard to keep the usual interior balance when the dream life is kicking the shit out of you during, as usual, the waxing moon. In the same place I saw an actual wolf last year, I found a female wolf in a dream, her back broken.

I went to her, knelt down and gathered her up, and she disappeared into me. This experience was frightening.

That peculiar but very beautiful girl I saw in a dress shop in Key West ten years ago reappeared. She told me you can't give up Eros. Then, as with most of my dream women, she turned into a bird (this time a mourning dove), and flew away.

Awoke in the middle of the night and wrote down that it is important not to accept life as a brutal approximation. This was followed by a day of feeling quite hopelessly incapable of writing my "vision" of the novel which I haven't begun to compose.

In New York City staying with my agent Bob Dattila over by the river on East 72nd. We are trying to make business deals on the phone, and play gin rummy though we can't quite remember the rules of the game. Bob asked me what was even deeper than the bedrock in the huge excavation next door. I told him watery grottos full of blind, albino dolphins. Then in the night, in a dream, I climbed out of the excavation in the form of a monster: my eyes were lakes, my hair trees, my cheek was a meadow across which a river ran like a rippling scar. In the morning it was a comfort to walk the dog up to Ray's for a breakfast slice of pizza. Since I have three at home it is a considerable solace to have a dog friend in NYC, and when I come to town Bob's dog knows she can count on me for a slice of pizza. In short, we make each other happy.

What I don't want for myself is called a "long ending" with the vital signs not altogether there. This thought occurred to me after reading a biography by John Dos Passos.

Upset that this novel is going to make me too "irrational" to earn a living. In my background it is inconceivable for a man not to offer the full support for his family. A half-dozen years ago I made a great deal of money but didn't have the character appropriate to holding on to any of it. This must take training. Now the accretion of beloved objects & images in my life and dreams has become more totemistic & shamanistic: grizzly-bear turd & tooth, coyote skull, crow and heron wings, a pine cone from the forest where García Lorca was executed. Probably nothing to worry about as it began when I was half-blinded as a child, and for comfort wandered around the forest and lake and you don't find any trinkets there.

Always surprised on these days when the mind makes her shotgun, meta-phoric leaps for reasons I've never been able to trace. Remembered that Wang Wei said a thousand years ago, "Who knows what causes the opening and closing of the door?"

Alliance: Nebraska reminds me of what America was supposed to look like before it became something else. Along Rte. 20 the almost unpardonable beauty of desolation. I could live along a creek in the Sandhills. I've established no strengths outside the field of the imagination, which is a fancy way of saying I'm hungover from an American Legion barn dance a wait-ress invited me to. She disappeared with a cowpoke who could wrestle a truck. Woke at first light laughing. Stepped on a steak bone.

Re: the banality of behavioral and emotional weather reports. My life is still killing me but I am offering less cooperation. I want to know what you do, rather than what you quit doing.

Up at my cabin more attacks of irrationality. Been here too long in solitude. Blurred peripheries so I "am" the bitch coyote that killed the rabbit in the yard. My longest & strongest literary relationship is with McGuane—twenty years of letters and we don't even see each other once a year.

Rode an enormous crow, flying down to the Manistee River to drink from a sandbar. Used a martingale. Easier to stay on than a horse and a better view! James Hillman says that dream animals are soul doctors. Bet I'm the only one around here who reads Cioran & Kierkegaard after working his bird dogs.

Disturbed that I am creating this heroine because I'm lonely and wish to have someone I can utterly love. Relieved of sanity fears by reading Angus Fletcher on the subject of the borders of consciousness.

There are many hidden, unnumbered floors in the apartment buildings in NYC, or so I have thought.

My coffin was made of glass and she ran out of the woods and shattered it! She is E. Hopper's girl at the window.

This must be a novel written from the cushion—silence, out of water, the first light, twilight, the night sky, the farthest point in the forest, from the bottom of a lake, the bottom of the river, northern lights, from the clouds and loam, also the city past midnight, Los Angeles at dawn when the ocean seems less tired having slept in private, from the undisturbed prairie, from attics and root cellars, the girl hiding in the thicket for no reason, the boy looking in the wrong direction for the rising moon.

At the cabin the fog is so dense you can hear it. A rabbit near woodpile, fly sound, crackle of fire in the hush. Can't drink much or my heroine escapes, evades me. The voice just beyond hearing.

Hot tip from Taisen Deshimaru on the writing of this book. "You must concentrate upon and consecrate yourself wholly to each day, as though a fire were raging in your hair." Reminded me again of the injurious aspects of protestantism for an artist—one's life as inevitable, or predestined, causing a looseness in the joints, the vast difference between Calvin (and John Bunyan). You must transfer these banal energies toward self-improvement to your work.

The post-modern novel suffocates from ethical mandarinism. It is almost totally white middle class, a product of writer's schools, the National Endowment, foundations, academia. The fact that this doesn't matter one little bit is interesting. Who could possibly give a fuck during this diaspora. The literary world is one of those unintentionally comic movies they used to make about voodoo and zombies.

Who said, "You can't do something you don't know if you keep doing what you do know"? Drinking prevents vertigo and that's why I can't get her voice if I drink. A trip to NYC restored my vertigo. If you enter a bookstore or a publisher's office your life again becomes incomprehensible. Fear refreshes. Luckily you can head immediately for a good restaurant.

Back home the troubling dream image of myself emerging like the "Thing" from a block of ice full of sticks and leaves.

In another dream she ran backward nakedly into history which was an improbable maze. Another night an unpleasant visit with Herman Melville who didn't look well.

Went up to my winter retreat at a hotel in Escanaba to edit *Paris Review* interview. Can't get beyond first page by the second day because I'm not currently interested in anything I've ever said, what with a hot eyeball from being two-thirds done. Zero degrees and a five-hour walk in the woods be-cause I got lost, followed by rigatoni & Italian sausage, and two bottles of red wine. Next day I walked miles out onto the frozen harbor ice—a mar-velous polar landscape of glittering sun & ice as far as you can see. Fisher-men have driven their pickup trucks out on the ice and are pulling nets where the ice was divided by a fuel oil tanker. They are Chippewas and offer me a partially frozen beer that thunks in the bottle.

A strange March walk: broke, can't write, sick from new blood-pressure medicine, out in an area of juniper, dunes, pine culverts out of the wind. Thoughts about the degree to which I'm a slave or lowly employee of the system I've created: cigarettes smoke me, food eats me, alcohol drinks me, house swallows me, car drives me, etc.

"She" comes and goes. I had to talk to Hollywood today (to say why I was fired from the last project) and she fled top speed. An utterly enervating & fatal game of pursuit.

It seems that severe emotional problems, neuroses, are born, thrive, mul-tiply in areas where language never enters. The writer thinks that if he can solve these problems his quality of language will vastly improve. This is the fallacy of writing as therapy. Dostoyevski maintained that to be acutely conscious is to be diseased. One could imagine a novel that murders the writer. You don't want to discover a secret your persona can't bear up un-der. But then you can't rid yourself of the hubris of wanting to create a hero or heroine of consciousness.

Completely flipped from nervous exhaustion on page 430. Take my wife and daughter to Key West, a place I had feared returning to after so much "disorder and early sorrow" from a dozen previous trips. Turned out pleas-antly. Good chats with Brinnin, mostly on how to determine pathology when everything is pathological. Studied the giant ocean river, the Gulf Stream, where Duane committed suicide on his buckskin horse. We forget we have blood in us until it starts coming out.

All your aggression is directed toward discovering new perceptions, and consequently against yourself when you fail to come up with anything new. But then I "made her up" knowing very well we will abandon each other.

Bernard Fontana warned me about getting the "Indian disease." It takes a great deal of discipline not to shatter into fragments. The wonders of negative capability & allowing her to decide what she's going to do next. What Fontana meant is the intense anxiety I felt at the Umbanda session seventy miles outside of Rio de Janeiro when the ladies went into their whirling trance to heal the black drummer who was a drunk. If you've seen and lived the supposed best the white world has to offer it's "harmless" to check out the rest of the world. We are all in the Blue Angel in that respect. The actual world is Dietrich's thighs.

Startled to read in Jung that violently colorful dreams & physic events occur to people in psychic flux who need more consciousness.

At the cabin just saw a chipmunk leap off the picnic table & tear the throat out of a mouse, lapping vigorously at the blood. I am chock-full of conclusions. Must write Quammen to find out what's going on here. Lopez told me the only way to feed ravens is to gather road kills, a rather smelly business. Peacock has studied bears so long he has become one, not entirely a happy situation. Dalva is probably my twin sister who was taken away at birth.

Nearly finished. It's like going outside to estimate the storm damage. Want to avoid stepping into a thousand-story elevator shaft. As a ninth grader I was very upset to discover that Ross Lockridge committed suicide when he finished *Raintree County*.

My friend ——— thought that all of his concessions, like the Eucharist, were rites of passage. He forgot how easy it is to earn the contempt of your fellow writers.

Was amused to realize that the mess I am always trying to extricate myself from is actually my life. The other night I played ranchero music & thought how different the music is in areas of fruit, hot peppers, garlic, hot sun, giant moths, & butterflies. An old woman in Brazil had a worn photo of a group of men ice fishing in Minnesota which she thought was amusing. We drank rum and I tried to explain away the lugubrious masochism of life in the upper Midwest.

For almost ten minutes I looked forward to the second volume when Northridge's voice will become mangled & intolerable, a prairie Lear.

Finishing any large piece of work makes one dense and irascible. I cooked the fucking brook trout too long! I demand more of myself and life than it is suited to offer. I look for the wrong form the reward is to come in—thus it is a full year before I realize how good a certain meal was: during bird season we stopped by a river, started our portable grill and watched four English setters and a Lab swim lazily in an eddy in the October sunlight. We grilled woodcock and grouse over split maple, had a clumsy salad, bread, and a magnum of wine, napped on the grass surrounded by wet dogs.

Nearly done at the cabin, a specific giddiness. Last night wild pale-green northern lights above scudding thunderheads. On the way home from the tavern I saw a very large bear on the two-track to the cabin, thus hesitated to take a midnight stroll, possibly disturbing both of us. He was not my friend, but a great bear, a Beowulf, trundling across the path & swiveling for a look at me, his head higher than mine was in the car.

Hard to develop the silence and humility necessary for creating good art if you are always yelling "look at me" like a three-year-old who has just shit in the sandbox.

Postscript. Finished the novel in July and have since driven 27,000 miles to get over it. Perhaps it is easier to write a novel than survive it. Driving is a modest solution as the ego dissipates in the immensity of the landscape, slips out into the road behind you. Watched an Indian, Jonathan Windyboy, dance seven hours in a row in New Mexico. That might work but as a poet I work within the skeleton of a myth for which there is no public celebration. Publication parties aren't quite the same thing. I can imagine the kiva late at night under a summery full moon; the announcer asks the drum group from the Standing Rock Sioux to play a round from the Grass Dance for Jim's beloved Dalva! But perhaps our rituals as singers are as old as theirs. Cadged my epigraph from Loren Eiseley's tombstone: "We loved the earth but could not stay."

1988

Everyday Life:
The Question of Zen

I often think that because I am quite remote up here in northern Michigan from others who practice, and am intensely stubborn, I learn so slowly that I will be dead before I understand very much.

But "Who dies?" is a koan I posed for myself several years ago. To know the self, of course, is hopefully to forget the self. The especially banal wine of illusion is to hold on tightly to all the resonances of what we see in the mirror, inside and out. In our practice the self is not pushed away, it drifts away. When you are a poet there is a residual fear that if you lose the self you will lose your art. Gradually, however, (for me it took fifteen years!) you discover that what you thought was the self had little to do with your own true nature. Or your art, for that matter.

When I learned this I began to understand that the period of *zazen* that lays the foundation of the day is meant to grow until it swallows both the day and night. Time viewed as periods of practice and nonpractice is as fanciful a duality as the notion that Zen is Oriental. The kapok in the *zafu* beneath your ass is without nationality. The Bodhidharma and Dogen saw each other across an ocean river that is without sex, color, time or form. What is between Arcturus and Aldebaran?

I was wondering the other day about this body that wakes up to a cold rain from an instructive dream, takes its coffee out to the granary to sit on a red cushion. The body sees the totems of consolation hanging around the room: animal skins, a heron wing, malformed antlers, crow and peregrine feathers, a Sioux-painted coyote skull, a grizzly turd, a sea-lion's caudal bone, a wild-turkey foot, favored stones, a brass Bureau of Indian Affairs body tag from Wyoming Territory, a bear claw, a prehistoric grizzly tooth. These are familiar, beloved objects of earth, but the day is not familiar because it is a new one. The bird that passes across the window is a reminder of the shortness of life, but it is mostly a bird flying past the window.

"The days are stacked against what we think we are," I wrote in a poem. The point here, albeit blunt, is that when you forget what you are, you truly "see" the day. The man who howls in anger on the phone, because he has been crossed, an hour later is a comic figure dog-paddling in a sump of pride. He isn't conscious enough at the moment to realize that there is evil afloat in the land, within and without. This condition can be called "self-sunken." A little later, when he takes a walk on the shores of the lake, he does himself a favor by becoming nothing. He forgets being "right" or "wrong" which enables him to watch time herself flickering across the water. This is a delightful illusion.

The hardest thing for me to accept was that my life was what it was every day. This seemed to negate notions of grandeur necessary for an interest in survival. The turnaround came when an interviewer asked me about the discipline that I use to be productive. It occurred to me at that moment that discipline was what you are every day, how conscious you are willing to be. In the *Tao te Ching* (in the splendid new Stephen Mitchell translation) it says "Act without doing; work without effort." So you write to express your true nature, part of which is an aesthetic sense that reflects the intricacies of life rather than the short-circuits devised by the ego. Assuming the technique of the art has been learned, it can then arrive out of silence rather than by the self-administered cattle prod to the temples that is post-modernism.

After this body eats a tad too much for lunch it returns to the granary, stokes the fire, and takes a nap with its beloved dog who, at eleven, is in the winter of her life. A distinct lump of sorrow forms which, on being observed, reminds the body of the Protestant hymn, "Fly, Fly Away," and we are returned to the fragility of birds. The sense of transience is then embraced. When the dead sister reappears in dreams she is always a bird.

On waking with a start, because it is the dog's nature to bark on occasion at nothing in particular, the work is resumed. There has been an exhausting effort in recent years through the form of poetry and novels to understand native cultures. The study of native cultures tends to lead you far afield from all you have learned, including much that you have perceived and assumed was reality. At first this is disconcerting, but there are many benefits to letting the world fall apart. I find that I have to spend a great deal of time alone in the natural world to be of use to anyone else. Above my desk there is a wonderfully comic reproduction of Hokusai's blind men leading each other across a stream.

Whatever I have learned I owe largely to others. It was back in 1967 that I met Peter Matthiessen and Deborah Love, then Gary Snyder, though in both cases I had read the work. But in these formative stages of practice the *sangha* is especially important. George Quasha introduced me to the work of Trungpa—*Cutting through Spiritual Materialism* is an improbably vital book. Shortly thereafter I met Bob Watkins, a true Zen man, who had studied with Suzuki Roshi and Kobun Chino Sensei. The work of Lucien Stryk has been critical to me though I have never met him. Then, through Dan Gerber, I met Kobun himself, who has revived me a number of times. Through all of this I had the steadying companionship of Dan Gerber who is presently my teacher. Without this succession (or modest lineage!) I'd be dead as a doornail since I have been a man, at times, of intemperate habits. I'm still amazed how the world, with my cooperation, can knock me off Achala's log back into the fire. There is something here of the child who, upon waking, thinks he can fly, even though he failed badly the day before.

There is an urge to keep everything secret. But this is what Protestants call the sin of pride, also greed. They have another notion relevant here, that of the "stumbling block" wherein the mature in the faith behave in such a way as to impede the neophyte. There is, sadly, a lot of this among Buddhists, the spiritual materialism that infers that I have lived in this town a long time and you are only a newcomer. This is like shouting at a child that he is only three years old. It is also the kind of terrifying bullshit that has permanently enfeebled Christianity. Disregarding an afterlife, he who would be first will be last.

We should sit after the fashion of Dogen or Suzuki Roshi: as a river within its banks, the night sky in the heavens, the earth turning easily with her burden. We must practice like John Muir's bears: "Bears are made of the same dust as we and breathe the same winds and drink the same waters, his life not long, not short, knows no beginning, no ending, to him life unstinted, unplanned, is above the accident of time, and his years, markless, boundless, equal eternity."

This is all peculiar but quite unremarkable. It is night now and the snow is falling. I go outside and my warm slippers melt a track for a few moments. To the east there is a break in the clouds and I feel attended to by the stars and the blackness above the clouds, the endless blessed night that cushions us.

1990

Poetry as Survival

There have been quite enough exquisite apologias for poetry written over the centuries, from Aristotle to Catullus and Vergil, Wang Wei, Dante, Shakespeare and Dryden, down to Whitman, Yeats, Pound and García Lorca. But then, unlike the sciences, such knowledge is not easily transmittable or cumulative, and an art so seemingly fragile to the masses has its value in continual question by even apparently educated men.

Frankly, this is not my fault, and I have long since given up concerning myself with the matter. As a poet I am the bird, not the ornithologist, and I am not going to spend my increasingly precious days stuffing leaks in an educational system as perverse and sodden as the mercantile society for which it supplies faithful and ignorant fodder. If you wished to draw attention to poetry in a country where anything not at least peripherally attached to greed is considered nonsense, you would have to immolate a volunteer poet in a 751 BMW. In a Giorgio Armani suit. Wearing a gold Rolex. With the first infant porpoise to wear eye shadow on his lap. That sort of thing.

In other words, if you have to ask what poetry is good for, it's never going to be any good for you. Poetry came into being before the first club was swapped for an attractive antler, and about the same time Orc traded a lady a wild melon for raising her otter-skin skirt. Poetry, like the grizzly bear, is good for its own magnificent selfness and is not a utilitarian cog to improve someone's life-style. Poetry may very well help you get behind. Your legs might grow downward into the ground in certain locations. You will also turn inside out without warning.

The most ubiquitous misunderstanding of poetry is that it is heightened and energized daily speech. Martin Heidegger said, "Poetry proper is never merely a higher mode of everyday language. It is rather the reverse: everyday language is a forgotten and therefore used-up poem, from which there hardly resounds a call any longer." Poetry at its best is the language your soul would speak if you could teach your soul to speak. Poets are folks who know they are going to die someday and feel called upon to make up songs about this death and the indefinite reprieve they are traveling through. Rarely a philosopher, the poet hopes to celebrate life on life's terms, even though he works within the skeleton of a myth to which there is no longer a public celebration. As Gerald Vizenor (the astounding Native American author of *Griever: An American Monkey King in China*) would have it, "He holds cold reason on a lunge line while he imagines the world."

Of course, such temperaments are capable of grand absurdities, and the presumption of the comic is a more graceful *modus operandi* than a longish face, or waving your heart around by its bloody strings; like the ministry, poetry is thought to be a calling, but unlike specifically religious vocations, poetry can't cut off the horse's legs to get him into a stall. In order for Shakespeare to create the character of Hamlet he must also be capable of creating Falstaff, and *A Midsummer Night's Dream*.

But to return to earth: Americans seem to wish to live within situation comedies and unquestionably elect their officials on this basis. Yet there is a wild spiritual longing in the landscape that surfaces in dozens of odd forms: Jimmy Swaggart, est, channeling and other New Age nostrums, body-Nazi fitness mystics, drug obsessives, music goofies, even the nether forms of the ecological movement where Smokey the Bear seems to want to mate Saint Teresa.

You particularly notice this on long first-class, expense-account flights when your seatmate invariably asks, "What do you do?" When you say "Poet" you get either a quiet ride or the sort of weirdly fascinating conversation I imagine you might receive if you admitted you were a psychiatrist. What emerges, à la those fictive Russian train rides of the nineteenth century, is the secret life, the unlived life, the immense weight of longing, the puzzlement of mortality, the concealed idiosyncratic religion everyone carries around like a bulletproof (one hopes) vest. It is important to keep the conversation visceral, so you insist that a poet is only "the pulse of a wound that probes to the opposite side" (García Lorca). You tell your seatmate that when he looks in the mirror he might say, "Jeezo-peezo, I'm getting old," while Shakespeare said, "Devouring time, blunt thou thy lion's paws," and the latter scans better. You tell him that when he sees a lovely naked woman on a bed he might say "Wow," while García Lorca said:

> Your belly is a battle of roots,
> your lips a blurred dawn,

under the tepid roses of the bed
the dead moan, waiting their turn.

If my fellow passenger is involved with computers or becomes irritable, I like to use Vizenor to remind him that "we remember dreams, not data, at the wild end." Of course it is important to remain light, loose and friendly through all of this. The average highly placed executive is more macho than a Mexican assassin, what with the executive's insistence on playing hardball around the clock. In return for my modest *bon mots* I receive insider stock tips, although I am too mistrustful to indulge myself in these.

Who shall revoke jubilance?" Rilke asked, rather innocently, to which we could answer, "Everyone and everything." Joseph Campbell pointed out that in mythological terms the "rejection of the call" walls the Hero up in boredom and dread. A poet is supposed to be a hero of consciousness, and the most destructive force in his or her life is liable to be the unwritten poem. There is a touch of the schizoid to the practice of any art, and the poet becomes an outsider to maintain the integrity of what he writes. During not infrequent depressions (an occupational hazard) I wonder how black and Native American poets survive at all, for they are enveloped in a double schizoid bind, the Indians perhaps more than the blacks because they are our most thoroughly ignored minority.

Perhaps I've rejected too loudly certain utilitarian aspects of poetry, if only because we are capable of turning everything—from a simple rock to a guitar to violent death—into a nostrum, another of those self-help missions we use to hammer ourselves as if we were tract houses. D.H. Lawrence insisted that the only aristocracy was consciousness, if we consider all the other limitations within and without our lives. If this notion is valid, and I suspect it is, then poetry could be the primary aid if you wish to be more conscious, a somewhat singular ambition when you take a sideward glance at popular culture.

The flip side comes from that grandiose, rather romantic philosopher Friedrich Nietzsche, who once said, "I'd rather be a satyr than a saint," when he, in fact, was a tertiary-syphilitic hunchback. But he also said,

"Stare into the abyss long enough, and it will stare back into thee." It has become apparent to many that the ultimate disease, the abyss of postmodernism in art and literature, is subjectivity, and that the disease is both sociopathic and terminal. In other words, if the poet or aficionado of consciousness does not own a coequal passion for life herself, the social contract, he better be wary about the abyss he chooses. The obvious traps are the two halves of the brain in incestuous embrace, neurotic noodling, and ordinary spiritual adventurism of the most claustrophobic sort.

I remember that in my weakest moments I have regretted the problems I've caused my family and myself for refusing to be a poet-teacher: the shuddering economic elevator of the self-employed to whom the words *boom* and *bust* are euphemisms; the writer as farm laborer, block layer, journalist, novelist, screenwriter, but still thinking of himself as a poet. At times when I actually needed a battery of psychiatrists the alternatives were fishing, bird hunting, and drinking. I suspect this intimacy with the natural world has been a substitute for religion, or a religion of another sort. I remember as a young bohemian discovering garlic in New York City in 1957 when a Barnard girl made me listen to Richard Tucker sing something from Jewish liturgy. I was swept away by beauty, also jealousy, as the music was so powerful and unlike the sodden Protestant hymns of my youth. I felt the same thing years later in St. Basil's Cathedral in Leningrad, where I was told that in the Russian Orthodox Church one does not talk to God, one sings.

I am reaching toward something here by a circuitous route. At the very least the life I have chosen, although it always lacked a safety net, made up for the lack with pure oxygen. I remember a single year when I went to Europe, the Soviet Union, Africa and South America. I kept recalling Allen Ginsberg's line about "the incredible music of the streets." Cultures less economically sophisticated than our own began to fascinate me. Gabriel García Márquez's "magical realism" doesn't seem unrealistic in South America, but you don't have to go that far to discover a different way of looking at things.

Up until half a dozen years ago I had collected a large library on the Native American, but was unremarkably short on firsthand knowledge—unremarkably and typically, as it is far easier to read about a people than to encounter them. I had been to the Blackfeet Reservation in Browning, Montana, on a prolonged drunk with Tom McGuane; we were actually kicked out of a local bar, and that takes some doing in Browning. I had also attended the Crow Fair, a massive gathering and celebration in Crow Agency, Montana, with five to seven thousand Native Americans in attendance. This was more than a decade ago, and there were only a few whites present. I watched the dancing for two days and nights, sleeping sporadically on the Custer Battlefield. It was a *spellbinding* experience, one of the few of my life, and there was a deep sense of melancholy that there was nothing in my life that owned this cultural validity except, in a minimal sense, my poetry. Thousands of people in traditional costumes dancing together! What the hell's going on here? My bubble of reality had temporarily burst; it was as if I were stoked on peyote on the planet Jupiter.

The power of the experience passed, although it nagged until a few years ago when I worked on an abortive film project about Edward Curtis, the photographer of Indians. There was research money so I left my books at home and wandered around Indian reservations for several months. I was a quiet observer, quite shy in fact, because I didn't want to be confused with the anthropologists and spiritual shoppers who drive these people crazy.

On the Navajo reservation up Canyon de Chelly, on the branch called Canyon del Muerto, two very disturbing things happened. A man, ragged and plainly insane, rushed out of a thicket, skipping across the shallow river, and began beating our truck with a club. His head appeared to turn nearly all the way around in the manner of an owl's head. Our Navajo guide, who was Christian, yelled, "Get out of here, you demon, in the name of Jesus," explaining as the lunatic fled back into the thicket that what he yelled was the only thing that "worked." A little later I spent hours helping get a truck loaded with crab apples unstuck from the river. There was a young Navajo man, his wife, and two children, and the children were terribly frightened of me. I found this embarrassing and sorrowful as I worked away half under the truck, glancing up at the Anasazi petroglyphs. If you're from northern Michigan you know how to get a pickup unstuck. I tried everything to charm the children, and the parents attempted to help, but I was plainly a "demon" to them. Later I was told that the terror might have come from my blind left eye, which is foggy and wobbles around with a life of its own.

What actually began that day was an obsession, fueled less by guilt than by a curiosity that was imperceptibly connected to my poetry. Charles Olson said that a poet "must not traffick in any but his own sign," but I thought these people might clarify why I had spent over forty years wandering around in the natural world. I hoped the two cultures had more to offer each other than their respective demons.

This little essay, in fact, was occasioned by absolute exhaustion after a book tour, a retreat to my cabin in Michigan's Upper Peninsula, and the reading of the novel *Love Medicine* by the Native American Louise Erdrich, and then *A Yellow Raft in Blue Water* by her husband, Michael Dorris, somehow equal and absolutely first-rate books that restored my equilibrium and energies and an intense and nagging curiosity. Then I reread *Survival This Way*, a series of interviews with American Indian poets by Joseph Bruchac, published by the University of Arizona Press (whose Sun Tracks series seems to lead in the publishing of American Indian writers); *Songs from This Earth on Turtle's Back*, an anthology edited by Bruchac and published by Greenfield Review Press; and the new and comprehensive *Harper's Anthology of 20th Century Native American Poetry* edited by Duane Niatum.

After I had read through a sequence of fine prefaces and introductions (especially that by Brian Swann in the Niatum volume), there seemed to me to be a vacuum or missing chord. Over the years I had read the work of James Welch, Simon Ortiz, Leslie Marmon Silko, and Scott Momaday, whose wonderful novel *House Made of Dawn* was a ground breaker for other Native American writers. These four poets are known, but not widely, and certainly not in proportion to their talents. Of late, Louise Erdrich has achieved a measure of fame but there ought to be room for more than one, not to speak of a dozen other specific talents in the anthologies. Why are these poets so rarely reviewed or represented in "white anthologies"? I mulled over this problem for a couple of months as if it were a raw and abrasive Zen koan. Then, on a recent driving trip through Nebraska, the Dakotas, and eastern Montana, I revisited the site of the murder of Crazy Horse and the small church graveyard that overlooks the site of the Wounded Knee massacre, and a possible answer occurred to me.

First you must try to imagine a map of the United States covered with white linen as if it were a recently (true, in the sweep of history) murdered corpse. Carefully note where the blood is soaking through, from right to left, beginning with the splotches on the black slave ports of the East and South. Make a point of ignoring Civil War battle sites, as they constitute something we did to ourselves out of a mixture of necessity and vainglory.

You will now notice that the rest of our linen map is riddled with the blood of over two hundred Native American civilizations we virtually destroyed, from Massachusetts to California. This is an unpleasant map and is not readily available for purchase or publication, especially not in history books or in what is blithely referred to as the "American conscience." Our nation has a soul history, not as immediately verifiable as the artifacts of the Smithsonian, whose presence we sense in public affairs right down to the former president's use of the word "preservation," or his cinema-tainted reference to oil-rich Indians. In any event, schoolchildren who we think need a comprehension of apartheid could be given the gist of this social disease by field trips to Indian reservations in big yellow buses.

A logical assumption, then, is that Native American writers are largely ignored by readers because they represent a ghost that is too utterly painful to be encountered. Actual readers of literature are people of conscience (I am discarding the sort of literacy that never gets beyond the Sports and Modern Living pages and is ignorant of the locations of Nicaragua and Iran), but conscience can be delayed by malice, stereotypes, a natural aversion to the unpleasant. I'm old enough to remember when Langston Hughes and Richard Wright were considered the only black writers of interest. Publishers come largely from the East and anything between our two dream coasts tends to be considered an oblique imposition. There is also the notion that the predominantly white literary establishment idealizes a misty, ruined past when life held unity and grace. The late (and great) Richard Hugo pointed out that for Native American poets the past isn't misty, that the civilization that was destroyed was a living memory for their grandparents, and thus the Indian poet is a living paradigm of the modern condition.

Oddly, when you study the anthologies, or separate volumes by individual poets, you find very little romantic preciousness and almost no self-pity (certainly the most destructive emotion). And there are none of the set pieces of current "white anthologies": the workshop musings, campus melancholy, the old-style New Yorker poem in which the city poet sees his first seagull of summer, then nuzzles the wainscot of a clapboard cottage and reflects on the delicacy of Aunt Claudia's doilies; none of the Guggenheim or National Endowment year poems about fountains in Italy, the flowers of Provence, English weather, the buttocks of bullfighters in Madrid. There is a natural and understandable sorrow over losing a vast cathedral and being given an outhouse in return. Even the renowned Indian killer General Philip Sheridan admitted that "an Indian reservation is usually a worthless piece of land surrounded by swindlers." Quite naturally, Native Americans don't agree with Robert Frost's drivel about the land being ours "before we were the land's."

I suspect I am attracted to these Native American poets because there is a specific immediacy, urgency, a grittiness to the work. Of the thirty-six poets in the *Harper's Anthology*, fifteen are women; such a proportion is unthinkable in current, broadly based anthologies. The women are, if anything, more stridently energetic, natural and instinctive feminists, and I was reminded of the Sioux woman who drove an awl in dead Custer's ear in hopes that he would hear warnings better in the afterlife. Another oddity is that some of the best poets are also equally fine novelists: Momaday, Welch, Silko, Erdrich, and Vizenor. This is less frequently true among white poets.

An additional urgency is found in mixed-blood poets such as Erdrich, Vizenor, or Linda Hogan, an extraordinary Chickasaw writer:

> Girl, I say,
> it is dangerous to be a woman of two countries
> You've got your hands in the dark
> of two empty pockets.

Louise Erdrich's poem "A Love Medicine," a miniature tale of doom, almost an English ballad, will bring you near to weeping or you are not human. It begins with a novelist's sense of detail, almost as if she were fitting a noose around your neck. You can find out how it ends by buying the book (in *Jacklight*, published by Henry Holt, or in the *Harper's Anthology*).

> Still it is raining lightly
> in Wahpeton. The pickup trucks
> sizzle beneath the blue neon
> bug traps of the dairy bar.

> Theresa goes out in green halter and chains
> that glitter at her throat.
> This dragonfly, my sister,
> she belongs more than I
> to this night of rising water.

When the poetry is political it assumes a quiet hardness, all the more effective because of the simplicity and control. James Welch, the Blackfoot author of the striking novel *Fools Crow*, writes in "The Man from Washington":

> The end came easy for most of us.
> Packed away in our crude beginnings
> in some far corner of a flat world,
> we didn't expect much more
> than firewood and buffalo robes
> to keep us warm. The man came down
> a slouching dwarf with rainwater eyes,
> and spoke to us. He promised
> that life would go on as usual,
> that treaties would be signed, and everyone—
> man, woman, and child—would be inoculated
> against a world in which we had no part,
> a world of money, promise and disease.

I am drawn to the way Ray A. Young Bear and Lance Henson treat nature, as if they, in fact, were part of the natural world rather than observers shouting the presumptive "I" of post-modernism. Young Bear writes in long, powerful forms difficult to quote. In "north" Lance Henson finishes with:

> in the house my daughter
> has disappeared into dream
>
> her small trembling hands
> flower into a cold wind that smells
> of the moon.

It is equally true of the work of Duane Niatum, Peter Blue Cloud, and Joseph Bruchac, in whose work nature is treated in terms of familiarity, love and a little fear, as if they were speaking in another mode of their parents.

Joy Harjo is an engaging wild woman of a poet. She has seen de Soto

> having a drink on Bourbon Street,
> mad and crazy
> dancing with a woman as gold
> as the river bottom.

Harjo's style is somewhat incantatory; there is an urge to hear her read aloud. Her "Anchorage" is one of the strongest single poems in the *Harper's* volume; it ends:

> And I think of the 6th Avenue jail, of mostly Native
> and Black men, where Henry told about being shot at
> eight times outside a liquor store in L.A., but when
> the car sped away he was surprised he was alive,
> no bullet holes, man, and eight cartridges strewn
> on the sidewalk
>   all around him.
>
> Everyone laughed at the impossibility of it,
> but also the truth. Because who would believe
> the fantastic and terrible story of all of our survival
> those who were never meant
>   to survive.

There is a rich comic spirit, perhaps the quality that whites are most ignorant of in Native Americans. In *Survival This Way* there is a splendid comic poem, too long to quote here, "Hills Brothers Coffee" by Luci Tapehenso. For reasons never clear to me, the very richest core of humor is found in oppressed people, whether blacks, Jews or Native Americans. At the few powwows I've attended, I've noticed the wild, delightful humor of people to whom "dirt poor" would serve as a euphemism.

What I've offered here is a rather slight sampling in an attempt to whet some appetites, not necessarily the best material but certainly representative; this I think typifies a renaissance in Native American literature similar to that of black writers in the sixties.

I have saved the most difficult of Native American poets for last, perhaps out of aversion to entering the often painful labyrinth of his work, which I have followed carefully for over twenty years. Simon Ortiz is an Acoma Pueblo Indian and for some time now I have thought of him as a major poet; this is an unstable category but the range is there, as is the depth, volume, and grace. It is a matter of absolute emotional credibility married to craft. Among others he has written *Going for the Rain, From Sand Creek, Fight Back, A Good Journey*, the latter just recently reissued by the University of

Arizona Press. Ortiz has said that he writes poems because writing is, finally, an "act that defies oppression." In a curious way Ortiz reminds me of that great contemporary Russian, Vosnezensky. It is a peculiarity of genius that no concessions are made, and in Ortiz there is a quiet omniscience expressed only by talents of the first order. I understand he is a modest though difficult man, given to disappearing. I would hope that his selected or collected poems might appear so the work might reach a larger audience, whether we deserve it or not. It is the kind of poetry that reaffirms your decision to stay alive.

Almost as an afterthought, but really a cruel whim, a wish to rub our collective noses into the beauty and horror of the situation, I conclude with the rest of Louise Erdrich's poem "A Love Medicine":

> The Red River swells to take the bridge.
> She laughs and leaves her man in his Dodge.
> He shoves off to search her out.
> He wears a long rut in the fog.
>
> And later, at the crest of the flood,
> when the pilings are jarred from their sockets
> and pitch into the current,
> she steps against the fistwork of a man.
> She goes down in wet grass
> and his boot plants its grin
> among the arches of her face.
>
> Now she feels her way home in the dark.
> The white-violet bulbs of the streetlamps
> are seething with insects,
> and the trees lean down aching and empty.
> The river slaps at the dike works, insistent.
>
> I find her curled up in the roots of a cottonwood.
> I find her stretched out in the park, where all night
> the animals are turning in their cages.
> I find her in a burned-over ditch, in a field
> that is gagging on rain,
> sheets of rain sweep up down
> to the river held tight against the bridge.

We see that now the moon is leavened and the water,
as deep as it will go,
stops rising. Where we wait for the night to take us
the rain ceases. Sister, there is nothing
I would not do.

In a curious way Native American poetry is written in our language but not in our voice. Perhaps it's because the taproot of ritual poetry is closer to the surface, and the traditions of Shaman and Trickster are often right out there in the dark, looking in the window of the poem. This is partially true, but there is an even more dominant factor. Chief Seattle once told us in specific terms how his people were going to haunt us. He also said that the earth does not belong to man, man belongs to the earth. This simple notion offers a schism larger than that between Jew and Muslim, or Christian and Jew. We have always believed we owned the earth and could do what we please, and our current and frontier theocracies never hesitated in their pillage for a moment. In *American Indian Holocaust*, Russell Thornton points out that in 1492 there were at least 5 million Native Americans and in 1890 there were only 250,000, the decline resulting from introduced diseases and sheer firepower. It is indeed ironic that those whom we crushed could help us survive.

1990

Paul Strand

When I look at the photos of Paul Strand, as I have done since the sixties, I am invariably reminded of an old Buddhist adage "ashes don't return to wood," which is to say as an artist one must consume one's "self" entirely in the work. Basil Davidson pointed out of Strand, "The photographs seem to have come into existence without the camera . . ." The photos have been passed on to us as facts of nature, austere and somehow in the arena beyond the artful and humane, informed as they are by an unforgiving sense of authority. We are left wondering how work that so massively bespeaks genius may arrive in so utterly fragile a form.

When I look at Susan Thompson, the wife of a Maine fisherman, she effortlessly transcends my notions of lover, mother, sister, daughter, nor is she the academic abstraction known as the Eternal Feminine. She is Susan Thompson and within the gift Strand has offered to us, she owns something of the Venus of Willendorf, Botticelli's Venus emerging from a shell, and the representations of the Brazilian goddess Imanja. But foremost she is Susan Thompson, and in this portrait a great artist has captured the immutable mystery of human personality. Susan Thompson, whoever she is otherwise, has become immortal, and while looking at her we only remember with specific effort that Paul Strand has created a photo in which he neither dominates or obtrudes, but evokes.

I have often thought that any night I may be lucky enough to have Susan Thompson enter my dream life. Within the crush of our time it is fatuous to think of what we would take along to a desert island, where we are likely to find cigarette butts or theater stubs in the sand and hypodermics on the beach. But if I were condemned to whirl alone to death in a space capsule for an unnameable crime I would take along the photo of Susan Thompson.

I would look at her. I would hear from the unknown peripheries of the photograph a crow calling, a screen door slam, a distant dog's bark. I would look at Susan Thompson and think, what a fabulous memory of earth. What more can any artist give us?

1990

Dream as a Metaphor of Survival

Come to think of it, the world has taken me out of context—physically, mentally, and spiritually. There is a not quite comic schism inherent in the idea that on a daily basis *The New York Times* and "All Things Considered" tell us everything that is happening in the world, but neglect to include how we are to endure this information. If I had not learned to find solace in the most ordinary preoccupations—cooking, the forest and desert—my perceptions and vices by now would have driven me to madness or death. In fact, they very nearly did.

It should be understood at the outset that a poet's work (like that of an analyst) frequently parodies his or her best intentions. The following is decidedly "creationist" rather than informed, bearing up as it does under the burden of a mind that creates its living out of a perceptual overload, rather than a gift for drawing conclusions. As an instance, the memory of a mother's angry slap quite naturally suggests the flour on her hand: *she was making bread and I was eight. I said I didn't eat the seven Heath candy bars in the pantry though the wrappers were under my bed and I didn't break the hen's eggs against the silo. Sent to my room I crawled out the window never to return and found Lila. We lay down on the wood bridge and tried to count fish but they kept moving in the green water. I felt my face where mother slapped me. I sat up and looked at the back of Lila's knee. She said "thirty-three" when I looked up the back of her blue skirt to where her underpants drew up into the crack of her butt. Lila didn't mind my injured eye because her dad had been shot in the war and maybe he had been shot right through the eye, she said. The girl who cut my eye moved away. I got back through the window just before I was called to dinner, a pocket full of violets for my mother who asked me how I picked them in my room.*

In other words, what a mess, but then a dozen years ago I couldn't remember "everything" and all the memory knots were tiny claymores that blew up on contact, or more accurately, on encounter, as the miniature explosions were frequently accidental, causing all sorts of personal havoc.

It only gradually occurred to me that our wounds are far less unique than our cures. There is a specific commonality in the nature of the spectre of anguish that arises and expands within us that makes us seek help, whether from an analyst, guru, roshi, shaman, preacher, even a bartender, those experts at symptomatic relief. In the north country of my youth mental pain was implicitly tautological; omnipresent and unaccounted for, something to be endured with quiet manliness, another hazard to test the mythical fortitude of country folk (Michael Lesy's *Wisconsin Death Trip*).

The bottom line, as they like to say nowadays, is that we no longer feel at home either within, or without, our skins. There are thousands of ways to adorn this fact. It is largely the content of modernist and post-modernist literature and art, not to speak of the relentless fodder of self-help books and columns in newspapers. Rilke, that grand master of dislocation (he moved virtually hundreds of times) said, "Each torpid turn of this world bears such disinherited children / to whom neither what's been, nor what is coming, belongs." Alienation, so ubiquitous as to be banal, fuels our nights and days, our hyperactive adrenals gasping from fatigue. Where, and how, do I belong?

But then there have been quite enough general assessments of this theory and practice of dread. One nearly envies the bliss-ninnies, the New Agers, proclaiming from mountaintops that help is on the way. How can so many ladies have been Pocahontas or Mary Queen of Scots in a previous life? It seems no one was the serf's child who was fed to the lord's hounds on a whim. On a recent bypass through Santa Fe for a bite to eat (broiled chicken with red chile sauce), I saw a huge crystal for sale for ten thousand dollars. In a time and country when absolutely everything is possible for those with sufficient greed and power, this crystal in the shop window was so wildly awful as to be somehow comic and comforting.

What do I mean by dream as a metaphor of survival, even, in fact, the path toward home? I am certainly not qualified to describe the way the unconscious struggles to heal wounds, and such published descriptions strike one as finite indeed, in that they try to render a magnificent fiction (the dream itself) into an immediate, therapeutic solution. (So what, of course, if it helps?) Part of the struggle of the novelist is to convince the reader that the nature of character is deeply idiosyncratic to a point just short of chaos, that the final mystery is the nature of personality.

In my own, not very extraordinary case the biographical details are explicit: there was a severe eye injury causing blindness at age seven (I had been playing "doctor" with an unkind little girl). My instability was further compounded by the deaths of my father and nineteen-year-old sister in an accident when I was twenty-one. These were the two people closest to me, and in the legal entanglements of the aftermath, I was witless enough to look at the accident photos left on an absent lawyer's desk. Both of the death certificates read "macerated skull."

These were the main events along with a number of other violent deaths of friends and relatives including seven suicides. The capstone seems to have been the accidental death of my brother's fourteen-year-old daughter about a dozen years ago. There had been a hundred-day vigil while she was in a coma, and a wintry funeral near Long Island Sound. Much later I dedicated a long poem to her called "The Theory & Practice of Rivers," of which this is a small part:

> Near the estuary north of Guilford
> my brother recites the Episcopalian
> burial service over his dead daughter.
> Gloria, as in *Gloria in excelsis*.
> I cannot bear this passion and courage;
> my eyes turn toward the swamp
> and sea, so blurred they'll never quite
> clear themselves again. The inside of the eye,
> *vitreous humor*, is the same pulp found
> inside the squid. I can see Gloria
> in the snow and in the water. She lives
> in the snow and water and in my eyes.

(Only now do I connect the eye material to my wound at seven.)

There was, quite naturally, a cycle of predictably severe depressions, beginning at age fourteen, then nineteen, twenty-three, twenty-seven, thirty-three, thirty-seven, and forty-three. Curiously, this cycle of lows, along with what dogs, cats, horses I owned at the time, is the way I ascribe "chapters" and carve up my life. It is evident to me now that the first of the depressions was caused when my father had to move our family of seven from a rural, heavily wooded area in northern Michigan south to near East Lansing so we could ultimately attend college. I remember that my first reaction to our new quarters was that there were no trout, the rivers were muddy and the lakes were warm, and the pheasants in the field behind the house were no substitute for the herons, turtles, bobcats, deer, coyotes and loons of my early years. And even more poignant for an utterly self-conscious twelve-year-old, a new community would have to adjust itself to my wounded left eye.

This is only the skeleton of a life, albeit a tad melancholy. I should add, before I reach the heart of the matter, that I attacked this life with a great deal of neurotic arrogance and energy (fifteen books, fifty or so articles, twenty screenplays) though I certainly would not have survived without the help of my beloved wife, my daughters, my remaining family, and a group of faithful friends. And (of course) a psychoanalyst in New York, Lawrence Sullivan, whom I began to visit the year before Gloria's death. Coincidental with her passing was the death of my father-in-law, the diagnosis of my mother's colonic cancer, and I, quite pathetically, fractured my foot while chasing my bird dog. In addition, after ten years of averaging twelve grand a year, I noted amid these disasters that I was making exactly as much that year as the president of General Motors. However, my first success had become quite meaningless within the framework of my life, and I added cocaine to an increasing alcohol problem. My sole survival gesture at the time, other than infrequent visits to Sullivan, was to drive north into the Upper Peninsula of Michigan and buy a remote log cabin on a river. Typical of my behavior, I had not bothered going into the cabin before I wrote the check.

It has dawned on me that we appear to make certain specific decisions on a subconscious level far before we realize them, then simultaneously war against these decisions on a conscious level. This is only to say that pigs love their mud, and unless one is sufficiently desperate one continues to fritter away at the perimeters, recreating the problems of the neglected core on a daily cycle that is shot full of self-drama. As an instance, after five years of visiting Sullivan in New York, I took back to the hotel our extensive correspondence and was appalled to discover that I had created a serial repetition of complaint, a "Volga Boatman" dirge of whining about the same things: drinking, drugs, the loss of my loved ones, life as a continuum of defeat despite my apparent worldly success. Compulsive, ritualistic behavior tends to hold back chaos no matter how self-destructive. At the time I cherished a quote from Yeats, "Those men who in their writings are most wise, own nothing but their blind, stupefied hearts," conveniently neglecting another Yeatsian question, "What portion of the world can the artist have, who has awakened from the common dream, but dissipation and despair?"

Slowly, and mostly in my imagination, I had begun to swim in waters that sensible folks would readily drown in, mostly in the area of consensual reality. The therapy began to take effect and my outward life gradually became more and more absorbed in hunting and fishing, and walks in the undifferentiated wilderness of the U.P. that began as short, lazy jaunts, and which lengthened with the years to ten miles or so. There were quite wonderful comic aspects of a brown, burly man fighting crotch chafe plunging through swamps, thickets, over steep hills, down a gully holding a startled bear. I rewarded these exertions by preparing enormous, complicated dinners. Concurrently my work began to revolve around more "feminine" subjects, the acquiring of new voices, and away from a concern with the "men at loose ends" that tends to characterize the fiction of most male writers.

It was in the arena of mortal play that is the dream that these changes had their source and increased in volume. One's dream life has always struck me as curiously Buddhist as the dream points toward the feeling that "the path is the way," rather than Western geometric constructs vis-à-vis ladders, steps, guideposts, the Ten (not eleven) Commandments. I became absolutely convinced that barring unfortunate circumstances we all are, in totality, what we wish to be, and if something were quite wrong, the "wrongness" came from a radically skewed and wounded core that had to be approached.

I'm a little hesitant to admit that the majority of the striking dreams occurred in the last few days of the waxing moon and at the cabin rather than my home, hesitant as the notion of any relation between dreaming and the moon is too daffy and hopefully accidental. Perhaps I am closer to a dream life in the wilderness. The time span involved is about twelve years in this sampling.

1. There were slides of glass in my spine preventing the free flow of whatever flows up and down the spine. This is too obvious to com-

ment on, other than the way an "Ur" dream may release the possibility of others. I knew nothing of Kundalini yoga at the time.

2. For the first time I saw the faces of my father and sister, not as torn or macerated, but normal, except they had the bodies of mourning doves. They were serene.

3. A comic one but not at the time. An enormous, glistening-faced wild boar appeared at the foot of my bed in the cabin loft and told me in a radio baritone to "change your life." I began doing so by starting the generator and turning on the lights.

4. I went into a room which was full of a dozen rather soiled and sweating women, some lean but most really chunky. My dick was sticking out of my trousers and I was embarrassed. They put me at ease and mentioned with laughter that it was a hard life being immigrants. We wallowed, sucked and screwed for hours and I awoke exhausted and happy. Since I have a fantasy penchant for austere "ice queens" this was a little puzzling. Versions of this dream reappeared and years later it occurred to me that our culture tends to treat older women as immigrants.

5. I was out in a wilderness of extreme cliffs and sharp-edged boulders. I leapt off a cliff with the manuscript of my new novel (*Sundog*) in my arms. I was injured horribly but survived, crawling around to pick up the pages. I looked up at the cliff edge far above me and was rather pleased with myself. I wondered why my dread of publication took itself into the wilderness.

6. At dusk one rainy autumn evening I saw a timber wolf near my cabin after hearing her howl several evenings. A few days later I dreamt I found her out near the road, her back broken by a passing car. I knelt beside her and she flowed into my mouth until I held within myself her entire body. I remember idly thinking in the dream that I had tried so hard to lose weight and now I was pregnant with a female wolf.

7. My father and sister are being driven down the middle of a river in a soundless car by two Native Americans. The four of them are quite

happy. The driver pulls up to the shore and tells me flat out that I was never supposed to be a chief in the first place, but a medicine man. I interpreted this to mean that though I was a miserable failure at life I was doing quite well in my art, and if I pursued my art strongly enough I could heal myself and might help heal others. Soon after I began to write a long poem called "The Theory & Practice of Rivers."

8. A very disturbing dream. I was with two medicine men who were dressed in leather and furs. One was mortally wounded and embraced me, asking me to take his place. Again, I interpreted this as a message to bear down on my art. I've long been a student of Native Americans since my childhood but would not dream of trying to "become" one. As Charles Olson inferred, a poet must not "traffick" in any but his own sign.

9. I was surrounded by a crowd of people who were trying to kill me. My skin began to ache and I crouched there with feathers shooting painfully out of me. I became a bird and flew away. This reminded me of the "ego" as an accretion of defenses that no longer functions. When we are alive, we are always ahead of it.

10. I was staying in New York City with my agent. Both of us were having a difficult time. One afternoon we decided to play gin rummy though we were unsure of the rules. While playing cards we watched the progression of a massive excavation next door. My agent asked what was even farther below the five-story excavation. I told him there were watery grottos full of blind albino dolphins. He is accustomed to such explanations from me. That night I dreamed that we were playing cards and a monster came out of the excavation and broke through the window of the ground-floor apartment. It was towering above us but we continued playing cards because the monster was only me. My eyes were lakes, my hair trees, my cheek was a meadow with a river (I first thought it was a scar) flowing across it. In any event, I had become the landscape I most loved.

11. A more didactic dream, like the wild boar, beginning with a voiceless lecture to the effect that there were three worlds and I only knew

two of them. I remain unsure of this. Then the dream downshifted into a hyper-reality where alternately a cobra and a coyote entered into my chest cavity, taking the place of my spine and skull. In my youth I enjoyed snakes, but then was frightened of them for a long time. After this dream they didn't bother me. I remembered that in my childhood I was somewhat confused over the difference between people and farm and wild animals. Once while we were fishing I asked my father and he said, "People live inside and animals live outside." I accepted this explanation as adequate.

12. A wonderfully obvious dream. I am in New York City in the form of an ordinary red-tailed hawk, the most common hawk in the northern Midwest. I am trapped in a narrow opening between buildings where I have been investigating the evident fact that there are secret, unrecorded floors in New York apartment buildings. I thrashed my wings, tearing feathers and spraining a pinion. Sullivan discovers me and draws me out of the wedge. He holds me as a falconer would smoothing my feathers and allowing me to fly off.

13. I am in a clear glass coffin, dead amid soil, moss, vines and flowers, being looked at by a crowd. A slender, brown youth breaks through the crowd and breaks the coffin open with a club and I jump out. At first I thought the brown youth was me, but on a closer look I saw it was my fifteen-year-old daughter, whose recent problems had brought me quite painfully back to life.

14. I was in L.A. working on a movie project and felt quite literally peeled in body and mind. I dreamt of a crow I had stared at for a long time at my grandfather's farm as a child. The crow grew larger and I noticed that there was belled harness around its neck. I got on and we flew to a sandbar in the Manistee River where we fished and bathed. The crow did not fly me back to L.A., so I had to get on a plane.

15. One night I thought I was awake but wasn't. I heard someone crying and discovered it was a weeping boy lodged behind my organs and against my spine. When I awoke I immediately realized that this weeping boy, retained from post-trauma times, had caused me a lot of problems and I set about getting rid of him.

16. This is a recurrent dream, though only once was Judith there, and only once was the dream resplendent. The hillside continues to reappear. My dead sister Judith was in a gown on a hillside, bare except for a dense thicket which was virtually throbbing with life. She beckoned me to this thicket so I might be restored.

17. A comic, literary incident. I was in an estuarine area near the seashore. A combination crypt, vault, septic tank floated up. I was urged to put all literary jealousies, ambitions, anger in it. I did so and nudged it seaward. Far from shore it stuck itself on a sandbar along with others and I wondered who else had done the same thing.

18. Last winter I suffered a period of extreme exhaustion from writing two novellas, plus six versions of two screenplays, within a year. On April Fool's Day I began a month's car trip with no specific destinations, highlighted by wandering through the canyon country of southern Utah. But when I opened the cabin in early May I was still exhausted in spirit and body. I dreamt several nights in a row that I should walk the "edges," the fertile area in terms of flora and fauna between the darker forest and the open country. There was also the suggestion in the dream that the birds of North America are largely misnamed. I took off on foot, rediscovering again that the surest cure for mental exhaustion is physical exhaustion, though only if you keep it "light." Dream advice must not be taken as another sodden nostrum.

19. I was way back in *terra incognita* with a friend. At the edge of a black-spruce bog in a thicket we found a moss-covered cement slab with iron rings. We were fearful. We questioned, what's under it—hell, a snake pit, the repository of nightmares? My friend indicates it's up to me, I mean the contents. We lift the slab aside. The pit is full of brilliant blue sky.

20. A huge Italian miner from the western Upper Peninsula is sitting at a laden table with his family. He points to a large glass of red wine and pronounces "Anything more than this is an emotional hoax." I found this recent dream quite disturbing as I like a before-dinner whiskey or two, though on occasion it makes me unhappy with its stun-gun effect. Wine, by comparison, is gentle.

21. At home I have insomnia, falling asleep finally an hour before dawn. I am jolted back awake by a dream where I am whirling on the bed, shedding and sloughing layers of skin in a blur. Now I am much smaller and painted half bright yellow, half pitch-black. Out the window above me I can see far into space to thousands of multicolored galaxies far beyond the Milky Way. I feel totally at home in this universe.

The above represents about one-third of what I think of as the key dreams since I first visited Sullivan. They seem curiously simpleminded, like surreal children's stories. But within a socio-historical framework it is the primitive aspects of psychoanalysis that appeal to me. There never was a culture in fifty thousand years that ignored dreams (except our own) or wherein, as Foucault puts it, a healthy mind did not offer wisdom and succor to a weak and sick one.

Of course it is difficult to avoid trying to screw the lid on too tight, to find closure where there are maybe only loose ends. I see the evident attempt of my dream life to relocate me, to protect me from an apparent fragility I tried to overcome with drugs and alcohol, the overdominance in my life of "manly" pursuits. I no longer try to "guts out" anything.

Ultimately, in Zen terms, "to study the self is to forget the self." We wish, ultimately, to understand everything and belong everywhere. I have learned, at least to a modest degree, that I must spend several months a year, mostly alone, in the woods and the desert in order to cope with contemporary life, to function in the place in culture I have chosen. In the woods it is still 1945, and there is the same rain on the roof that soothed my burning eye, the same wind blowing across freshwater. The presence of the coyotes, loons, bear, deer, bobcats, crows, ravens, heron and other birds that helped heal me then, are still with me now.

I locate myself freely when I have the courage to ask myself a koan I devised, "Who dies?" What does this man look like to himself when he is away from the mirror? When I walk several hours the earth becomes sufficient to my imagination, and the lesser self is lost or dissipates in the intricacies, both the beauty and the horror, of the natural world. I continue to dream myself back to what I lost, and continue to lose and regain, to an earth where I am a fellow creature and to a landscape I can call home. When

I return I can offer my family, my writing, my friends, a portion of the gift I've been given by seeking it out, consciously or unconsciously. The mystery is still there.

> *Who is the other,*
> *this secret sharer*
> *who directs the hand*
> *that twists the heart,*
> *the voice calling out to me*
> *between feather and stone*
> *the hour before dawn?*

1991

Bibliography

All of the pieces listed below appeared originally in a slightly different form. I would especially like to thank Ray Cave and Pat Ryan, formerly of *Sports Illustrated*, who supported this weary writer over a number of years. I would also like to thank John Harrison, Rebecca Newth Harrison and Terry McDonell. —J. H.

"*Afterimages: Zen Poems*, by Shinkichi Takahashi." *The American Poetry Review*, 1972.

"Bar Pool." 1973.

"*Bending the Bow*, by Robert Duncan." *The New York Times Book Review*, 1968.

"Bird Hunting." 1985.

"Canada." *Sports Illustrated*, 1974.

"A Chat with a Novelist." *Sumac*, 1971.

"Consciousness Dining." *Smart*, 1989.

"A Day in May." *Esquire*, 1976.

"Don't Fence Me In." *Condé Nast Traveler*, 1989.

"*The Dreadful Lemon Sky*, by John D. MacDonald." *The New York Times Book Review*, 1975.

"Dream as a Metaphor of Survival." *Psychoanalytic Review*, 1991.

"Everyday Life: The Question of Zen." From *Beneath a Single Moon: Buddhism in Contemporary American Poetry*, 1991.

"The Fast." *Smart*, 1990.

"Fording and Dread." *Smoke Signals*, 1984.

"From the *Dalva* Notebooks, 1985–1987." *Antaeus*, 1988.

"Going Places." *Outside*, 1987.

"Guiding Light in the Keys." *Sports Illustrated*, 1973.

"Hunger, Real and Unreal." *Smart*, 1989.

"Ice Fishing, the Moronic Sport." *Sports Illustrated*, 1972.

"The Last Good Country." *Esquire*, 1977.

"Log of the Earthtoy Drifthumper." *Automobile Magazine*, 1986.

"Meals of Peace and Restoration." *Smart*, 1989.

"A Memoir of Horse Pulling." 1973.

"Midrange Road Kill." *Smart*, 1990.

"A Natural History of Some Poems." M.A. thesis, 1965.

"*The Nick Adams Stories*, by Ernest Hemingway." *The Washington Post*, 1972.

"Night Games." *Esquire*, 1976.

"Night Walking." *Rolling Stone*, 1987.

"Okeechobee." *Sports Illustrated*, 1976.

"The Panic Hole." *Smart*, 1990.

"Passacaglia on Getting Lost." *Antaeus*, 1986.

"Paul Strand." From *Paul Strand: Essays on His Life and Work*, 1990.

"Piggies Come to Market." *Smart*, 1990.

"A Plaster Trout in Worm Heaven." *Sports Illustrated*, 1971.

"Poetry as Survival." *Antaeus*, 1990.

"The Preparation of Thomas Hearns." 1980.

"Revenge." *Playboy*, 1986.

"*The Snow Leopard*, by Peter Matthiessen." *The Nation*, 1978.

"*The Snow Walker*, by Farley Mowat." *The New York Times Book Review*, 1976.

"Sporting Food." *Smart*, 1988.

"A Sporting Life." *Playboy*, 1976.

"Then and Now." *Smart*, 1989.

"The Tugboats of Costa Rica." *Smart*, 1989.

"La Vénerie Française." *Sports Illustrated*, 1972.

"The Violators." *Sports Illustrated*, 1971.

"What Have We Done with the Thighs?" *Esquire*, 1991.

INTERIOR ILLUSTRATIONS AND COVER PAINTING,
JUST BEFORE DARK, BY RUSSELL CHATHAM.

BOOK DESIGN BY STACY FELDMANN AND JAMIE POTENBERG.
COMPOSED IN BEMBO BY WILSTED & TAYLOR, OAKLAND.

JIM HARRISON, A POET AND NOVELIST, LIVES WITH HIS FAMILY
ON A FARM IN NORTHERN MICHIGAN.